Don't Touch My Hair

EMMA DABIRI

Don't Touch My Hair

ALLEN LANE
an imprint of
PENGUIN BOOKS

ALLEN LANE

UK | USA | Canada | Ireland | Australia
India | New Zealand | South Africa

Allen Lane is part of the Penguin Random House group of companies
whose addresses can be found at global.penguinrandomhouse.com

First published 2019
001

Copyright © Emma Dabiri, 2019

The moral right of the author has been asserted

Set in 10.2/14.25 pt Sabon LT Pro
Typeset by Jouve (UK), Milton Keynes
Printed and bound in Great Britain by Clays Ltd, Elcograf S.p.A.

A CIP catalogue record for this book is available from the British Library

ISBN: 978-0-241-30834-9

www.greenpenguin.co.uk

MIX
Paper from
responsible sources
FSC® C018179

Penguin Random House is committed to a
sustainable future for our business, our readers
and our planet. This book is made from Forest
Stewardship Council® certified paper.

In honour of all the black brilliance and beauty,
squandered and diminished
yet never extinguished.

Contents

I

It's Only Hair

YOUNG, IRISH AND BLACK

It is not from my mouth
It is not from the mouth of A
Who gave it to B
Who gave it to C
Who gave it to D
Who gave it to E
Who gave it to F
Who gave it to me.

That it be better in my mouth
Than in the mouth of my ancestors.
(West African poem)

The year I turned eight, the consumption of Christ's body and blood became imminent. After months of deliberation, extravagant miniature bridal dresses had been bought; lace, satin and net hung expectantly in wardrobes. The communion money, which could quite reasonably be expected to stretch into the *hundreds* – a veritable fortune in 1980s inner-city Dublin – was the hot promise occupying everyone's thoughts. After months of slaving over the catechism, of hard work and dutiful preparation, my peers were ready to make their first Holy Communion.

No catechism for this badman, though. I had elected not to take the sacrament. Young Emma's contribution, having reached the 'age of reason', was instead the production of a spiffy little anti-slavery pamphlet called 'Break the Chains'. The length of a copy-book, it was based on the story of Olaudah Equiano, the eighteenth-century abolitionist. The conclusion, I remember, attempted to locate the contemporary conditions of Black America in the brutal experiences Africans had endured in that land and sought to suggest solutions. Hence the title. Nice and light. Standard childhood fare.

While I wasn't particularly praised for my efforts, I certainly wasn't forced to join in with the other children either. With hindsight, this is telling, if unsurprising. There was always the insistence that, despite my being born in Ireland and having an Irish mother whose maternal ancestry stretches back into Irish pre-history, I wasn't *really Irish*. I was frequently singled out for special attention. I seemed to be a firm favourite of nuns, particularly those who had been missionaries in Africa. I remember on one occasion being apprehended outside the Bird Flanagan pub in Rialto and presented with a Miraculous Medal by a concerned nun who wished to bestow the grace of the Virgin Mary on my little brown body. It was not the only time I was presented with one of these – I seemed to be quite the miraculous magnet! And I remember visiting a friend's elderly great-aunt – another nun – whose watery eyes refocused then blazed upon sighting me. 'I spent years in Nigeria,' she thundered, before proceeding to pull my lips back over my teeth, because 'Your people have such beautiful teeth.' Given that this rather intimate exchange occurred before even the most basic of introductions, one might think it, at the very least, rude.

So yeah, I had a complicated relationship with the world I lived in. And I think the fact that I embarked on the Equiano project was most likely interpreted as just the sort of weird shit that a 'foreigner', a 'blackie' might do. I mean, 'What d'ye expect from the likes of them, like?'

Thinking about Equiano now, my decision does seem radical. I can't remember precisely what my motivation was, but my childhood was often characterized by unusual choices and interests, informed by a strong sense that my impulse to tell black stories originated from a source that pre-dated my birth: '*It is not from my mouth . . .*'

Though it might sound peculiar and it certainly felt strange to me: I felt intuitively that I had a working relationship with the past and with my forebears. It was as though the past happened to be particularly foregrounded in my present. Of course, I couldn't articulate this, even to myself, and had I been able to, I would most likely have elected not to. As a child, I was considered strange enough. No need for further ammunition. It was only when, years later, I went to university and studied African cultures that I learned about the centrality of ancestral veneration, that ancestral spirits were intentionally invoked. On my paternal side I am Yoruba. The Yoruba are the largest ethnic group in south-western Nigeria and one of the third biggest in Nigeria, Africa's most populous country. Many Yoruba were sold into slavery, particularly during the nineteenth century. As a result of this relatively recent, wide-scale movement, many Yoruba beliefs, practices and customs can be identified to this day throughout the 'New World'. During the 1980s and 1990s a more recent Yoruba diaspora was created, as Nigerians fled their tragically failing economy to migrate to countries such as the US and the UK.

One result of colonialism was a disregard for many Yoruba beliefs; therefore it was only at university that I learned that traditional Yoruba concepts of time were cyclical, and of the belief that the 'past' is not necessarily dispensed with but is in fact in dialogue with the future.

I discovered that Yoruba names such as Babatunde ('Father comes again') and Yetunde ('Mother comes again') are so common because of an indigenous belief in the transmigration of the soul. This invocation of the past, like the Ghanaian philosophical concept of *Sankofa* (which urges us to take from the past to design a better future), does not limit progress or place emphasis on doing things 'the old way'. On the contrary, improvement is the objective. The urge to ensure 'that the mine be better in my mouth / Than in the mouth of my ancestors'. It is believed that our successes are our great-greats' successes too. Finally, I could locate my experiences in a belief system where they made perfect sense.

Received Western wisdom routinely denigrates African history. The attitude was summed up by the esteemed historian Hugh Trevor-Roper in his famous 1963 address at Sussex University, which was broadcast on national television, as well as being published both in a popular periodical and as a book:

> Perhaps, in the future, there will be some African history to teach. But at present there is none, or very little: there is only the history of the Europeans in Africa. The rest is largely darkness, like the history of pre-European, pre-Columbian America. And darkness is not a subject for history.

Assessed through a biased, Eurocentric framework, perhaps this is the case. Yet if we shift the optic, we begin to realize, in the words of Nigerian Nobel Laureate Wole Soyinka, that 'the darkness so readily attributed to the "Dark Continent" may yet prove to be nothing but the willful cataract in the eye of the beholder.'[1]

And in banishing that darkness, I am far more interested in how African peoples understood themselves and their cultures – in examining their methods for telling and documenting their lives – than I am in attempting to situate them through a European lens that proposes universality but is inherently culturally specific.

We should remember that communication and learning in oral society are not limited to the spoken word. Complex non-verbal languages are part of the milieu. Take for example the *bata*, or 'talking drum', as it is translated into English. Echoing the tonal patterns of Yoruba, the *bata* literally speaks. Were the British colonialists, unable to decipher what the drum said, illiterate too? Or is the term one we apply only to 'primitive' peoples?

The Anglo-Ghanaian philosopher Kwame Anthony Appiah describes African hairstyling as a 'subtle interplay of the sociological and the aesthetic'. As a practice, hairstyling has much to offer

and opens up excitingly decolonized possibilities for better understanding the African past in order to shape a better collective future.

In terms of my early attempts at decolonization, the freedom
demonstrated by the Equiano project was sadly not to be repeated.
I think it was permitted on this occasion primarily because it kept
me out of the way. Until the late 1990s, being black and Irish in
Ireland was to have almost unicorn status.

Except everybody loves unicorns.

There has not been a significant black population in Ireland for
very long. When I was growing up there were very few of us indeed.
Many mixed-race people I met, certainly those who were any older
than me, had grown up in institutions. They were often the 'illeg-
itimate' offspring of Irish women and African students. Not to
put too fine a point on it, unmarried mothers were generally, in
Ireland, treated like scum. Add the disgrace of a black child and,
sure, you couldn't really sink much lower. Commenting on the
mixed-race children unfortunate enough to be placed in Ireland's
now-infamous industrial schools, a report submitted to the Irish
Department of Education had this to say in 1966:

> A certain number of coloured children were seen in several
> schools. Their future *especially in the case of girls* presents a
> problem difficult of any satisfactory solution. Their prospects
> of marriage in this country are practically nil and their future
> happiness and welfare can only be assured in a country with a
> fair multi-racial population, since they are not well received by
> either 'black or white'.
>
> The result is that these girls on leaving the schools mostly
> go to large city centres in Great Britain . . . It was quite appar-
> ent that the nuns give special attention to these unfortunate
> children, who are frequently *found hot-tempered and difficult
> to control.* The coloured boys do not present quite the same
> problem. It would seem that they also got special attention and
> that they were popular with the other boys.[2] [my italics]

According to alumnae of these abhorrent facilities, this 'special attention' seems to have extended to racist assaults which served to compound the physical, sexual, emotional and mental abuse many of the children were subject to. During my own schooldays twenty plus years later, attitudes didn't seem to have changed that much. Yet the Ireland emerging on the horizon today seems almost unrecognizable to me. There is now a visible black Irish population and, in terms of social progress, in 2015 we became the first country in the world to legalize same-sex marriage by popular vote; and in 2018, following another referendum, the draconian Eighth Amendment that criminalized abortion was repealed. This seemingly kinder, more diverse Ireland is a far cry from that which defined my miserable years at school, days when the smallest indiscretion – real or, usually, imagined – invoked punishment far disproportionate to the crime. And just like 'our tempers', my hair, too, was 'difficult to control'.

From my earliest memories, my hair was presented as a problem that needed to be managed. The deeply entrenched idea of 'managing' black women's hair operates as a powerful metaphor for societal control over our bodies at both micro and macro levels. Whether it's historic bondage during the trans-Atlantic slave trade, or indeed the attitude of the education system, the thousands of black women held in immigration detention centres today or the disproportionate number of black women in prison (in the US, black women are incarcerated at four times the rate of white women), our bodily autonomy cannot be assumed. Barely a month seems to go by without there being another news report about a black child excluded from school for wearing their hair natural. The 2016 case in Pretoria High School in South Africa was particularly shocking, not only for the violence of the altercation but also because of the geographic location. This didn't happen in Britain or Ireland or America but on the African continent! Protests broke out because little girls wanted to leave their hair alone, yet Pretoria High maintained that natural hair was 'messy'. The administration claimed that by not straightening their hair black female students were not conforming to the rules regarding 'appropriate' presentation, and protests broke out when schoolgirls simply refused to straighten their hair.

Pretoria High School, August 2016. Zulaikha Patel, 13, refused to 'tame' (chemically straighten) her hair and started a silent protest insisting that black girls be allowed to come to school with their natural hair. I would like to point out that Patel's hair is well combed and oiled, certainly not 'messy'. Despite Patel's bravery, the emotional costs of such efforts are high for children. The second picture shows a weeping Patel being comforted by a schoolfriend (who, interestingly, has straightened hair). It reminds me all too keenly of the many incidents in my childhood where I was subjected to the rage of incensed white adults who felt, I assume, that I did not know my place.

As a black child with tightly coiled hair, growing up in an incredibly white, homogeneous, socially conservative Ireland, I certainly wasn't considered pretty, but that started to change in my mid teens. I remember being told that I was 'lucky I was pretty', which meant I could 'almost get away with being black'. However, there remained the unquestioned expectation that certain measures would be taken to keep my affliction at bay. Needless to say, the most offensive manifestations of my threatening blackness had to be rigorously policed.

As I got older, my skin colour could almost correspond to the 'tan' my peers were all obsessed with achieving. I still got the jokes about needing a flash to take a photograph of me, or the classic likening of my complexion to dirt, but it was my hair that remained unforgiveable. Anything that could be done to disguise it, to manipulate and mutilate it, was up for consideration. The concept of leaving it the way it grew from my head was simply inconceivable.

There is long evidence of both weaving attachments as well as the use of wigs throughout Africa. In most black cultures the frequent and radical transformation of hair is typical, and the wearing of artificial hair, including wigs, is not traditionally stigmatized in the same way it is in mainstream – no, let me dispense with polite euphemisms, I mean 'white' – culture.

Considering the great diversity of styles available, it is worth noting that throughout the twentieth century and until recently (with the exception of the Black Power period and immediately afterwards) very few included working with Afro hair texture. Personally, I was trying to get as far away from my own texture as possible. Today, I'm much freer and, now that I've embraced my natural texture, I'm also happy to rock a pink body-wave wig, although I'm more likely not to. There is untold fun to be had experimenting with hair. But when I was in school it was emphatically not about fun. My actions were a bid for assimilation, by way of disguise. My efforts stemmed from a cardinal terror that people would catch sight of my real hair. From weaves, to extensions, Jheri curls, curly perms, straight perms and straighteners, my hair was hidden, misunderstood, damaged, broken and completely unloved. It is hardly surprising. I never saw anybody with hair like mine. Afro hair was – and in many places still is – stigmatized to the point of taboo.

Growing up, I was made to feel terribly conspicuous; always under scrutiny, an object to be examined. When people saw me they did not see me, they saw a symbol, a poorly cobbled together approximation of an African. In the famous train passage in *Black Skin, White Masks*, Frantz Fanon, the renowned Martinican psychiatrist and post-colonial icon, explores the psychological effects of the white gaze upon the black subject: 'Look, a Negro . . . Look at the nigger! . . . Mama, a Negro!'[3]

I vividly remember his analysis of these words soothing like a balm when I first encountered them at nineteen years old. I wasn't mad. I wasn't solely motivated by a 'chip on my shoulder'. Fanon legitimized my experiences and identified their psychological cost. Such validation was met with a sense of relief I still feel all these years later. As an isolated 'mixed-race' or black individual in a pre-dominantly white environment, you become a cipher, a representation of a coming anarchy. The barbarians have breached the gates and you are the manifestation of all the fantasies, fears and desires that have been absorbed by a population fed a steady diet of racist dis-course. You are constantly under surveillance. You become achingly aware of your every gesture; your movements, your very posture, are at all times under analysis. Mundane details, the minutiae of your daily routine, are a performance for public consumption.

While I could not articulate it at the time, I experienced the suffocating weight of such an existence deeply. I felt like some kind of experiment, like a sideshow freak, and I eventually became incredibly paranoid. It got to the point where I was extremely uncomfortable with people even looking at me. My hair, in par-ticular, was a spectacle, the site upon which most of this attention was concentrated.

When we think about what we are taught constitutes beautiful hair, the characteristics of Afro hair are notable only for their absence. Straight, shiny, glossy, smooth, flowing . . . that's cer-tainly not my hair. What's my hair like again? Oh yes, of course. Coarse. Dry. Tough. Hard. Nappy. Frizzy. Wild. The English lan-guage has bequeathed us this list of pejoratives, which are perceived as adequate to describe Afro-textured hair in its entirety. Now don't get me wrong, I know Caucasian hair can be described as greasy, lank or thin, but it is not *routinely* described thus – and can you imagine the horror if I casually referred to a white woman's hair in this way, to her face!

The words we use to describe Afro hair do not relate to its texture and, judged by another's metric, it will always come up lacking. But we do not possess a list of words that reflect the qualities of Afro hair, words that demonstrate its strengths, beauty and versatility.

Even the labels on our bloody natural hair products can't seem to shift out of this mode of thinking. We are assaulted by words like 'defiant', 'wild', 'unruly', 'unmanageable' and 'coarse'. We might manage to squeeze out a 'cool' or a 'funky', but our hair is never just 'normal'. Beauty is, as ever, imagined through the characteristics of a standard not designed to include us. The only way Afro hair can seemingly fulfil the criteria for beauty is if we make it look like European hair – if we make ourselves look like something we are not.

The world around us fuels a powerful narrative about hair and femininity. From fairy tales to advertisements, movies and music videos, our icons tend to be lusciously locked. For girls and women, femininity is intricately bound up in hair. For a long time long, flowing hair remained one of the most powerful markers of being a woman. But that is not how Afro hair grows; generally, it grows up. Of course, femininity – like beauty – remains a culturally specific project, and certainly not one designed with the physicality of black women in mind. Nonetheless, we are expected to conform to these standards, and woe betide us if we cannot.

This pressure to conform to European standards of beauty is far more than the 'grass-is-always-greener' type of vanity it is often dismissed as. In the Pretoria High School incident, these little girls were told they couldn't come to school looking like themselves because they had to look 'neat'. Two weeks later, a US Federal Court ruled that it was legal to fire a female employee for having dreadlocks, deeming them 'unprofessional'. But the terms 'neat' and 'professional' are both highly constructed, and to deem black people's hair as it grows naturally from our heads *neither* neat nor professional is incredibly revealing. The way language operates in the politics of power here is significant. 'Unruly', 'defi-ant', 'unmanageable', 'coarse'. Consider these terms in the context of the regulatory nature of policies around our hair. Language that is now culturally unacceptable – the language of the colony or the plantation, the language once employed to describe black *people* – has not vanished; it has simply shifted to head height.

Hair-straightening for people of African descent emerges from a traumatic historical legacy. Since the advent of the slave trade – the centuries-long trans-Atlantic trade in black flesh – our humanity has not been something straightforwardly assumed. While most of the world's population is melanated (is that a word? It should be!), there are few populations beyond those of African descent (and some Polynesians, Micronesians and Melanesians) who have Afro hair. Our hair is the physical marker that distinguishes us from all other racial groups.

In denying black people their humanity, the hair that grows from their heads was – one might argue, still is – considered more similar to the wool or fur of an animal than to the straight *human* tresses of Europeans. One of the enduring problems of the modern age, the real reason that racism continues to plague us, is that we continue to advance ideas of blackness that were invented during the psychotic period of European global expansion. The 'knowl-edge' produced in that era remains with us to this day, its echoes ricocheting down through the centuries and settling to fix and frame people of African descent as characters not of our own mak-ing. The idea that Africans are culturally inferior to Europeans was widely advanced from the 1700s, but by the nineteenth cen-tury this had evolved into 'scientific racism', which established the idea that empirical scientific evidence could be used to demon-strate that 'Africans' were an entirely distinct species.

An Essay on the Inequality of Human Races, written by Arthur de Gobineau in 1853, famed for his development of the idea of a superior Aryan race, had rejected unity between humans, proclaim-ing, 'According to the natural law already mentioned, the black race, belong[s] as it does to a branch of the human family that is incapable of civilization.⁴ 'Negroes' were granted the privilege of occupying the lowest rung of all the species, closer to apes than to whites. Gobineau's writing inspired many, not least American white supremacists. *Types of Mankind*, a collection of letters and articles by six scholars attempting to explain the most 'cutting edge' scientific knowledge regarding race, written a year later in 1854, stated, 'The differences observed among the races of men are of the same kind and ever greater than those upon which the anthropoid monkeys are considered as distinct species.'⁵ Josiah Nott, one of the contributors to *Types of Mankind* and himself an owner of slaves, conveniently claimed that 'the negro achieves his greatest perfection, physical and moral, and also greatest longevity, in a state of slavery.'⁶ He ignored the sections in Gobineau's writing where the latter spoke disdainfully about white Americans themselves, whom he believed to be an inferior, racially mixed population.

Yet despite the centrality of hair texture as one of the primary features in marking 'blackness', its importance is routinely overlooked. The Harvard sociologist Orlando Patterson explains:

> Hair type rapidly became the real symbolic badge of slavery, although like many powerful symbols, it was disguised – in this case by the linguistic device of using the term 'black' – which nominally threw the emphasis to color. No one who has grown up in a multiracial society, however, is unaware of the fact that hair difference is what carries the real symbolic potency.⁷

Patterson argues that during slavery it was hair texture more than skin colour that distinguished Africans specifically as degenerate. Think about it: an African albino is still read as black due to their hair and features. There are East Asian and South Asians who have darker complexions than some Africans and who are certainly darker-skinned than many African-Americans and African-Caribbeans, yet they are not 'black'.

The nifty little 'hair gauge' opposite resides in a collection at

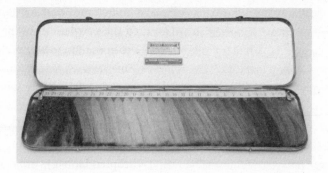

University College London. It was designed by the German scientist
Eugen Fischer in 1905. Fischer used hair texture to determine the
'whiteness' of people of mixed race, the offspring of German or Boer
men and African women in modern-day Namibia. He carried out
experiments on these people before recommending that they should
not be allowed to 'continue to reproduce'. Accordingly, interracial
marriages were banned in all German colonies in 1912. Fischer's
'work' in Africa was hugely influential in German discourse on race
and went on to inform the Nuremberg Laws, the legislative framework for Nazi ideology. Fischer's interest in the 'hereditarily unfit',
as mixed-race people were classified, didn't end in Africa. In fact,
Fischer was just getting started. Between 1937 and 1938 he oversaw
tests on 600 mixed-race children, the product of liaisons between the
French-African soldiers who occupied western areas of Germany
after the First World War and German women. Following this, the
children were forcibly sterilized to prevent the contamination of the
white race 'by Negro blood on the Rhine in the heart of Europe'.

HAIR TEXTURE DISCRIMINATION

My own hair has been disappointing people since my birth. Its
texture didn't correspond to the expectations accorded someone
of my skin colour.

Although I was born in Ireland, a couple of months after that happy event we relocated to Atlanta, Georgia, where my pops was studying at Morehouse College. We lived in the Black Mecca of the South for four years. I was too young to remember a sense of the colourism that is so deeply entrenched there, but my mother tells me people would frequently express sentiments such as 'What a *beautiful* [read 'light-skinned'] child. Let me see her hair.' When they peeked under my bonnet and were confronted with my kinky naps, disappointment and awkwardness would quickly replace their enthusiasm.

Colourism in black communities is a product of slavery and colonialism. Under the laws of slavery black people were considered property and, as such, subject to rape at a systemic level, at the hands of their owners and other whites. One result of this was the rise in mixed-race slaves. Mixed-race blacks were more likely to make up the free coloured populations and, even when enslaved, might receive treatment preferable to that bestowed on their non-mixed brethren. These relative advantages often carried over post-Emancipation, and the elites of Negro Society were often individuals who possessed a significant amount of European, as well as African, ancestry. Georgetown professor Michael Eric Dyson describes colourism as such:

> There is, too, a curious color dynamic that sadly persists in our culture. In fact, New Orleans invented the brown paper bag party – usually at a gathering in a home – where anyone darker than the bag attached to the door was denied entrance. The brown bag criterion survives as a metaphor for how the black cultural elite quite literally establishes caste along color lines within black life. On my many trips to New Orleans . . . I have observed color politics at work among black folk. The cruel color code has to be defeated by our love for one another.[8]

But there exist other important dimensions too. Ayana Byrd and Lori Tharps echo Patterson's observations about hair, explaining that 'essentially the hair acted as the true test of Blackness.'[9] They point out that, historically, the fact remained that, if the hair betrayed the tiniest trace of kinkiness, the person – regardless of their complexion – would be unable to pass as white. Like the paper-bag crew, they describe black churches to which membership was dictated by hair texture. A comb had to pass smoothly through the hair for membership to be awarded, for which purpose one was placed on a string at the entrance to the church. If successful, you may proceed, pass go, collect £200 on your way. If, on the other hand, the comb snagged, you needed to get the hell gone; the good lord Jesus didn't want to see you or your nappy head in this exclusive house of prayer. This is like an early precursor to South Africa's pencil test, where a child's race was determined by whether or not their hair could hold a pencil.

Colourism is undoubtedly about proximity to racial whiteness, but proximity is determined by far more than just complexion. In addition to lighter skin, the texture of one's hair, one's facial structure, the shape of one's nose and lips and even one's body type are assessed in calculating who has, and who is denied, proximity to whiteness. Consider Iman, a dark-skinned Somali model who achieved success in the 1970s, when African features were emphatically not 'in'. In 1976 an *Essence* magazine article by editor-in-chief Marcia Gillespie referred to Iman as 'a white woman dipped in chocolate'. Quite understandably, the model was enraged and retorted: 'I don't look like a white woman. I look Somali.'[10]

And she does indeed. Yet despite Iman's dark complexion, her facial features, in comparison to those associated with West Africans, have a look that is perceived as more comparable with Caucasian features and are therefore understood as superior to the looks of those who remain further from the European standard.

In 'Hair Race-ing: Dominican Beauty Culture and Identity Production' (2000), Ginetta Candelario examines the role of hair texture in racial identity on the Caribbean island. She shares an exchange between herself, a 'white-skinned and straight-haired Dominican', and another 'white-skinned and straight-haired Dominican' woman named Doris. Doris is married to a 'brown-skinned, curly-haired Dominican man' and is describing their children. Doris explains that, in Dominican society (which remains notoriously anti-black, despite the fact that most of the population are to varying degrees of African descent), entry into whiteness and its subsequent 'rewards' are determined by your features and your hair texture far more than by the colour of your skin: 'For Dominicans hair is the principle signifier of race.'

GINETTA: Tell me something. You've just told me that we value hair a lot and colour less, in the sense that if hair is good you are placed in the white category. What happens in the case of someone who is very light but has 'bad hair'?

DORIS: No, that person is on the black side because it's just that the *jabao* in Santa Domingo is white with bad hair, really tight hair. Well, that one *is on the black side*, because I myself say if my daughters had turned out *jabao*, it's better that they would have turned out brown, with their hair like that *trigueno*. Because I didn't want my daughters to come out white with tight hair. No. For me, better *triguena*. They're prettier [*triguenos*]. I've always said that. All three of my children are *triguenos*.[11]

The examples from the Dominican Republic demonstrate the fact that in non-English-speaking countries different terms exist that recognize the role that hair texture and phenotype play in proximity to whiteness. In English terms like 'colourism' place all the emphasis on complexion. The word 'colourism' comes from the US and was coined only as recently as 1983, when Alice Walker used it in *In Search of Our Mother's Gardens*, identifying the phenomenon as an impediment to black progress. The word acknowledges the huge discrimination faced by people with darker skin in black communities but overlooks the other factors of racialization. The use of the word 'colour' also arguably contributes to a false equivalency between complexion and racial categorization. Most 'black' women are brown! Being racialized as black isn't reducible to skin colour.

We have to remind ourselves that 'black' is not merely a descriptive term for skin colour; rather, it is a historically loaded ideology.

Being light-skinned mediates my experience of blackness, placing me highly within a distasteful ranking of value and worth, yet I also have tightly coiled Afro hair, for which my status, alas, tumbles several notches. (Within this perverse hierarchy those with both dark skin and tightly coiled hair would feel the weight of it most fully.) But as a black South African friend told me, when a mixed-race child is born with my hair texture, the consensus is usually, 'Ahhh, what a shame!' Of course, hair is far easier to disguise than one's complexion. But look at the lengths to which many black women go to hide their natural hair and we start to see where some of that motivation might originate. We need to interrogate the fact that, despite one feature being easier to disguise than another, the expectation that we hide our African features still remains.

Hair has the power to confer classification as black or not. Growing up, I knew another girl who had a Nigerian father and an Irish mother. We shared a similarly light complexion – she was perhaps slightly darker than me – but our experiences were very different. Somehow, the fates had bestowed upon her a head of glossy, tumbling black curls by virtue of which she could – and did – pass as Spanish. Now, don't get me wrong, 'Spanish' wasn't a particularly easy path to tread in 1980s Ireland either, but it was a far sight better than 'African'.

African was not the one. My family returned to Ireland around the time Band Aid had a number-one hit with 'Do They Know It's Christmas?' and the nation was united in song. And so we all learned that not everyone was as lucky as us. That, beyond the pale, firmly located in the valley of tears, lurked 'darkest Africa', a world of dread and fear, where the only Christmas bells are the clanging chimes of doom. Or something.

Two themes filled people's imaginations when it came to Africans and black people more generally. The first was crushing poverty, the result of an inherent black backwardness. Hope, it seemed, appeared only through the benevolence of 'white' saviours like Jesus, missionaries or Geldof himself. The second, more gendered, theme hung loosely along the lines of the criminality of the men and the sexual promiscuity of the women. There was a healthy intersection between these themes, so I was fortunate enough to experience the full hand. These were the ideas my presence provoked, marked by stigma and a sense of 'dirtiness' that was only compounded by ideas about sin and cleanliness, a consequence of the toxic Catholicism that still held the country in its grip.

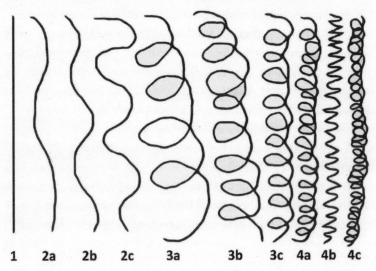

1 2a 2b 2c 3a 3b 3c 4a 4b 4c

Isn't it crazy to think that this is what all the fuss is about? Black hair starts from 3A, although there are plenty of non-black women who have this curly hair texture too. As we work our way to the world of 4s we enter a realm inhabited only by black people and, unsurprisingly, we move further away from what is considered 'good hair'. For the record, I'm around 4b. Shout out to my Nigerian ancestors.

Type-4 Afro hair – the tightly coiled type – is elliptical in shape. This means it is very tightly curled. Asian hair is generally round, while Caucasian hair is round also, or slightly oval, but much more similar in both shape and appearance to Asian hair. Many people who are racialized as black, even some who might have a dark complexion, are in fact of mixed ancestry. Their hair might be a combination of all these types, and this is the reason we see more African-Americans and African-Caribbeans whose hair conforms to the standards of 'good hair' than West Africans.

Generally, in black communities there is an acceptance that loose, curly hair is the ideal, while tightly coiled hair demands serious intervention. The expectation is that you will radically transform it in some way, whereas curls can (these days) require a lot less interference. Tatyana Ali, who played Ashley Banks in *The Fresh Prince of Bel-Air*, has spoken about her personal experiences of the phenomenon of colourism. Although she is not light-skinned her mixed heritage (her father is Indian) has bequeathed her a head of long, thick, silky black hair. Ali explains that, growing up, she was 'singled out' and experienced what was essentially 'light-skin privilege' (you see we need a new term for when these processes relate to hair) because of her 'good hair'. Although her hair texture has undoubtedly been advantageous to her career, by her account, however, she did not like it as a child and desperately wanted the same hair texture as her black mother, cousins and aunts. Similarly, the Bahamian-British journalist Elizabeth Pears has spoken about the way in which her hair informed both other's and her own perception of herself.

Recently, my mother told me a story of myself as a child. When strangers approached me and said things such as: 'Isn't she lovely?' or 'What pretty hair you have!' I would innocently answer: 'I know.' My unassuming arrogance would take people aback, then everyone would laugh at the adorable curly-haired prima donna . . . Many of these compliments came from white women, but the majority came from black women, inside and outside of my own family. I was light-skinned with long thick hair thanks in part to my father's white English heritage. That was all that qualified me to be considered 'beautiful'. It had nothing to do with being funny or smart but plenty to do with physical attributes over which I had no control. [12]

By contrast, my hair was a constant source of deep, deep shame. I became fixated on it, imagining that, if it just looked 'normal', I, too, might be normal. I wept myself to sleep most nights between the ages of eight and ten, desperately imploring the night-time to work its magic and by morning to have transformed my tight, picky coils into the headful of limp, straight hair I rightly deserved. But yeah. That didn't happen. With hindsight, I can say, 'Thank God.'

It may seem unimaginable that an adult would cosset or indeed be abusive to a child depending on the gradation of their shade of brown or their hair texture, but, as many of us know, it happens more often than you might think. I have witnessed it many times, for example when a lighter-skinned sibling is put on a pedestal while the darker-skinned one is ignored or mistreated. And it happens in the public eye too. Consider Blue Ivy, the first-born daughter of Beyoncé and Jay Z. At the time of writing, typing Blue Ivy's name into search engines produced 'Blue Ivy ugly' as a top result. Blue Ivy's biggest crime seems to be that she wasn't born with hair that has the texture of one of her mother's weaves. Blue has the audacity to have tightly coiled hair, hair that is uniquely black. This is the source of most of the abuse; in fact, the public were so incensed by Blue's hair that a petition called 'Comb Her Hair' was launched when she was two years old. Although it was ostensibly concerned with her parents combing Ivy's hair, the evidence of the hatred that over 6,000 signatories felt towards its texture is palpable:

Blue Ivy's hair looks despicable.

Nappy-headed child.

Her hair is out of control.

She's the kinda person to shame black people's name.

Her momma wears weave. Does she perform looking like that or does she have to look her best? Why does Blue not have that choice?

It's not right for a child to have nappy hair.

She needs not to be neglected. Look at that crazy hair.

She ugly, bruh.

You get the picture. It goes on and on. These comments are taken from the petition itself but, four years later, both Instagram and Twitter are awash with the same sentiments and the vitriol shows no sign of abating: 'That's got to be the ugliest fucking child I've ever seen. Admit it, she is ugly.'

When you look at the way Blue Ivy and North West, the daughter of Kanye West and Kim Kardashian, are compared to and pitted against each other, the whole thing becomes even more sinister. Not only is there the fact that the physical appearance of two little girls is being forensically discussed by grown men and women, it is also a clear demonstration of the way in which colourism is about more than complexion alone. Both children are light-skinned. There is little difference between their complexions. However, North is declared infinitely superior, partly because of her ambiguous racial features but mostly because of her hair: a very loose curl that can achieve a long, straight look with ease. The difference in attitude to North is glaring:

OMG I love her hair. She looks pretty.

Say whatever you all want about Kim, but you can't deny North is gonna be one of the prettiest women on the planet when she's older.

Northie is too damn gorgeous.

While people created petitions about Blue Ivy's hair, *Vogue* declared North West 'a natural hair icon' in a 2015 article entitled 'How North West's Curly Styles are Inspiring a Generation of Natural Hair Girls'.

It seems that all people of African descent are subject to scrutiny, fetishization or censure, and sometimes all three, because of our hair. Plenty of people with this looser curl associated with mixed ancestry have experienced the pain of not knowing how to care for it properly, especially those with a white primary caregiver.

All black hair requires knowledge, skills and products which are not always easily accessible. So rather than gorgeous curls, many people with 'good hair' still spent their childhoods with straightened, dried-out or even matted hair. Even if they had known how to keep their hair well maintained and make those curls *pop*, goddammit, the tyranny of straight hair was such that almost everybody felt they needed to achieve it. So ingrained was the culture of hair-straightening that many girls with 'good hair' didn't even realize they had it until they were much older and finally quit relaxing it.

The direction your hair grows in is important. Does it grow *down* rather than *up and out*? The direction hair grows in dictates whether it can conform to beauty standards such as 'shiny' and 'glossy'.

The darker the hair, the more light is reflected; the rounder the hair strands, the less light is reflected – so elliptical hair would be shinier if it weren't for its kinks, which are the cause of its matt appearance. However, if your hair can 'clump', making all the strands fall in the same direction so they reflect light in a uniform way, then it will shine. Hair that doesn't clump directs light in multiple directions and will not appear to shine. That's why, in the chart on p. 18, from 1 through to the 3s, straight, wavy or curly hair that aligns together can look shiny, while type-4 kinky and coily hair looks matt.[13]

The use of relaxer was in many ways a great leveller because you couldn't really see what anyone's real hair texture was, although, of course, the length to which it grew, as well as the degree of white-girl swish one could achieve, were indicators.

The sad spectacle opposite is childhood Emma. Childhood Emma is sporting the type of hairstyle commonly associated with being mixed race and having a primary caregiver who doesn't know how to maintain your hair.

Like so many mixed-race girls, the blogger Nikisha (formerly Urban Bush Babe) knows all about it.

[Her] *one ponytail braid with a scrunchy just killed it for me*!!
The constant teasing and abuse made me want to crawl under

'The ugliest fucking child in the world' sporting the bun-and-scrunchy look. My expression says it all, really.

a rock and disappear. I saw changing my hair as the easiest way of fitting in. So in an attempt to fit in, I turned to relaxers, hot combs, flat irons, curling irons, blow driers, and lots of sheen. Oh Lawd, the sheen put grease stains everywhere, the mats in gym class, headrests . . . You name it, I stained it!

I am often struck by the points of shared experience between black women when it comes to our hair, despite the fact that we might be continents apart. Little Nikisha was in New York, baby Dabiri was in Dublin, but these words could be straight out of my mouth. I tried it all! My mum was sound in that she would let me do anything to my hair and often went to great pains to take me to the UK to get my hair done, even though money was tight. I have a sneaking suspicion that the Jheri curl perm I travelled to Tottenham, north London, for as a twelfth-birthday gift (shout out to my aul wan) puts me in the running as one of the first people staining up the cushions and couches of Ireland with my curl acti-vator* in early 1990s Dublin.

At this time there was no online information available, and cer-tainly there were no suitable hair-care products in Ireland, and, although my mother had a handful of black female friends, black people overall were pretty scant in 1980s and early 1990s Ireland.

The few products I did manage to get my hands on were from my mum's work trips over to the long-gone rag-yards of Liver-pool's docklands. My mum was one of the first people to import second-hand clothes – their status later upgraded to vintage – to Dublin. Unless one of her friends – who were quite emphatically *not* hairdressers – cornrowed my hair or texturized it – it was pretty much left in the aforementioned scrunchie bun. Thinking about it now, all the wahala seems so unnecessary because, if you know how to look after it, my hair is beautiful and capable of so much; but even the black friends my mum had were more used to applying chemicals than caring for hair in its natural state. The freedom I was granted to do anything with my hair extended to the application of any known chemical under the sun.

I remember one particularly traumatic attempt at texturizing. A friend of my mum's left the chemical solution on longer than recommended to take into account my unusually defiant bonce. The immediate result was long, silky waves. I was ecstatic! By the following morning, however, it was coming out in handfuls.

Today, in globally connected, multicultural London, I still see mixed-race children with dried-out, matted hair. I'm not talking about hair that is untidy – I am no stickler for precision myself – I mean hair which, like mine, was clearly never oiled and certainly rarely combed or untangled. A lot of people ask for advice about raising mixed-race kids. One of the most practical answers I can

---

* To maintain the glossy, loose curl one had to apply a greasy curl-activator spray daily, which left a weird, greasy grey residue on my hair as well as a sticky sheen on any surface I leaned against. You had to sleep with a plastic cap over your hair to prevent it drying out.

give is to learn how to oil and comb their damn hair. (Don't forget to cream the skin too. Sheesh!)

In her beautiful, heartfelt essay 'Cassie's Hair', feminist scholar Susan Bordo, who is white, details her immersion into the world of black hairstyling through her adopted daughter, Cassie. While Cassie is in pre-school, a hitherto unknown world opens up for Bordo. For the first time in her life she becomes privy to black mothers' 'bemused disdain for white mothers of black and biracial children who don't know or *learn how* to take care of their children's hair'. Bordo proves a keen scholar, listening attentively as her black female friends include her in their conversations about hair care. She learns that, 'for many black women, anything less than perfectly coiffed hair (which, by default, means not respectable, not cared for, or liable to be seen as "wild") is a big no-no.'[14]* She acknowledges that her own lack of regard for the neatness of her child's hair was, in her own words, a 'privilege of [her] race'.

Black hair intimidates a lot of white people, and this can extend to parents as well. Bordo described one mother who was so stressed out by the very prospect of combing her daughter's hair that she just left it, and, sadly neglected, it tangled into one matted clump and had to be cut off. It's a familiar story: I know a number who suffered a similar fate. Stories such as these galvanize Bordo, who understands: 'That poor child. I never wanted my daughter to be the object of that kind of pity. Or me the object of that kind of scorn.'[15]

There are numerous reasons behind these cultural differences. Firstly, 'shabbiness' in general does not feature within African aesthetics. Historically among the Yoruba, the main method of enhancing natural beauty was cleanliness. Traditionally, one of the worst insults was *obùn*, which means 'filthy'.[16] A great premium was put on hygiene; while the average British person in the

---

* On one level this is what is behind the outrage over Blue Ivy's hair, but in that case it goes far beyond that, with the texture of the hair itself calling the value of the child's very being into question.

nineteenth century might wash their body every few weeks, a traditional Yoruba person would wash at least once a day.

Secondly, the white body is not subject to the same regulatory procedures as the body racialized as black. The carefree insouciance of shabbiness does not invoke the same social costs for a white person: their lack of effort will be afforded a value, perhaps elevated to chic, interpreted as bohemian, even. In contrast, the shabby black person might be read as dishevelled, wild and threatening. With such perception comes the use of regulatory power against the black body, perhaps resulting in arrest, or even death.

So, for me, there were two things going on: my hair was ugly, judged by European beauty standards; but also Nigerian and black diasporic norms were entirely abandoned. While I lived in the US, my hair was styled in a way that is quite typical for a lot of little Nigerian girls. It was worn neatly in a short Afro. This keeps maintenance issues to a minimum. It was only after we moved back to Ireland and my hair grew longer that all normal black hair culture seems to have been dispensed with. If you look at little black American girls' hairstyles, which could also have been easily achieved with my hair, and compare them to how my hair looked, you will see a huge difference.

Yet, beautiful as these hairstyles were, because we now lived in Ireland they would also have been stigmatized. Their intricacy, and the use of brightly coloured barrettes, would have been seen as 'common', outlandish and generally tacky. Even if my mother could have done my hair like this, I doubt she would have. These styles belong to a black aesthetic that is dismissed as 'ghetto', until, of course, it becomes popularized by a white person and is re-imagined as a trend.

The thing is that it's really quite simple: Afro hair just has different requirements from straight hair. Regardless of hair texture, everybody produces a lubricant called sebum. Along with water, this is what keeps hair moisturized. The difference is that the shape of Afro hair prevents the sebum and water travelling all the way down the hair shaft and the hair doesn't absorb it in the same way. This is not a problem per se, it just means that – and I repeat – *Afro hair has different requirements.*

Many white people seem shocked when they discover that I wash my hair only every two weeks or so. But where straight hair is prone to greasiness, mine is prone to dryness, and washing it daily would further strip it of its essential oils and dry it out even further. Afro hair needs products that would make white people's hair greasy and oily but keep ours moisturized. In the same way that I do not expect white people to use the same products as me, or to go two weeks, maybe even three or four weeks, without washing their hair, there is no reason that I would wash mine daily, unless it were borne of some masochistic motivation which I like to think I've now mostly healed from.

By the time I reached my teens, the attention I received developed into something more sinister, acquiring more of a sexualized edge, but when I was younger that had not yet begun in earnest. However, even long before I hit adolescence I felt as though there was some sort of depravity associated with me. There was often explicit judgement of white women with black children, which in turn informed perceptions of me.

Sleeping with a black man remained illicit, and I remember when I was in my later teens a tendency among a couple of my boyfriends towards irrational jealousy over my supposed affections for hypothetical black men, despite the fact that there was (sadly) precious little chance of me ever meeting one in 1990s Dublin.

But even at an earlier age, my hair let me down, assuming something of an embarrassing, sexualized nature. I remember being thirteen or so and sleeping over at a friend's house. (I have a white mum; sleepovers were allowed lol.) I use the term 'friend' loosely because, when I left home and gained more autonomy over the spaces I frequented and the people I chose to surround myself with, I realized that most of these girls were never really my friends. We were just thrown together through the combined misfortune of coincidence and a distinct lack of options on my behalf. (Hiiiiiii, if you're reading, hope yisser grand.)

But to return to the sleepover: making her bed in the morning, my host reached down and plucked something from the pillow. 'Ugh, ugh, ugh! Gross!' she shrieked, ramping up the dramatics to full effect. We were all going: 'OMG! OMG, what? What is it?'

'Eugh! There's pubes in my bed.'

'Ugh, gross.'

'No, hang on, it's just Emma's hair.'

Cue squeals of laughter all around.

I wanted to die!

The sensation was sharpened by the disparity between my own hair and my host's, hair that I secretly coveted. It was dead straight, a luminously shiny black, and hung the whole way down her back; she was complimented on it all the time. Her hair framed almost cartoonishly blue eyes, a particular blue that exists in Ireland. Even when I am abroad, if I see somebody with that eye colour I can immediately identify them as Irish. Of course, only a minority of Irish people possess this uniquely beautiful blue eye colour, but it exists with a frequency one rarely finds elsewhere.

To heighten my sense of unfairness, my own mother has eyes of this colour. In addition to being denied the bright blue eyes that were my birthright, it seemed a peculiarly personal punishment that I had a head of tight, frizzy knots, while every other girl in the feckin' country seemed instead to have long, straight shiny locks which they could toss and flick with the carefree abandon of whiteness.

Growing up, I rarely saw any black women on TV (or anywhere, for that matter), but there were a few exceptions: the popstar Neneh Cherry, and Hilary and Ashley Banks of *The Fresh Prince of Bel-Air* fame. Cherry, in particular, I tried to emulate, but her big black curls, which grew down over her shoulders, as well as Hilary's honey-blonde locks and Ashley's super-sleek jet-black hair, which was damn near waist length, well, actually, it all made me feel worse. All these women had hair which seemed as unachievable for me as the hair of my white

28

counterparts. If anything, seeing black women with 'good hair' made me feel even more inadequate about my own shortcomings.

I now know about the politics of visibility. Think about the fact that on black TV shows today, as back then – from the ethereal Lisa Bonet, to Karyn Parsons, to Ashley Banks, to Tia and Tamera Mowry, to Yara Shahidi – the 'beautiful' members of idealized onscreen black families are played by actresses who in real life have one white or non-black parent. Yet onscreen they are the product of two black parents.*

This reveals a lot about the type of fantasies we ourselves continue to uphold about what constitutes black beauty. The fact that until very recently the only 'black hair' granted onscreen visibility corresponded to European standards of beauty highlights the fact that beauty is the possession only of those with features deemed permissible by a racist criterion.

When Lauryn Hill emerged on to the scene, in *Sister Act II*, it was a revelation. I saw myself reflected more in Lauryn than in women like Neneh Cherry or Karyn Parsons, primarily because Hill and I had the same type of hair but also because I saw for the first time a woman with facial features comparable to my own. And she was being celebrated as beautiful!

IT'S ONLY HAIR

The question 'Is black hair political?' is something of a straw-man argument. Of course it is. It would make more sense to ask how it is that, in this day and age, where a Public Religion Research Institute (PRRI) poll from November 2015 showed that 43 per cent of white Americans believe discrimination against whites has become as large a problem as discrimination against blacks, black people wearing their hair in its natural state is still enshrined in law as permissible grounds to be fired.

* In the case of Yara Shahidi in *Blackish*, her on-screen mom is 'bi-racial'.

And it's a global issue, from South Africa to Brazil, to the UK, to the US and Ireland. Wherever people of African descent exist, we continue to be discriminated against because of our hair.

Magazines have got the woke memo but, as recently as 2007, a *Glamour* magazine editor presented a slideshow on 'Dos and Don'ts of Corporate Fashion' to a New York law firm. A prominent 'Don't' was a picture of a black woman with an Afro; it was accompanied by the editor's exclamation: 'it was "shocking" that some people still think it "appropriate" to wear those hairstyles at the office. "No offence" . . . but those "political" hairstyles really have to go.'[17] It was only as recently as 2014 that the US army permitted black female soldiers to wear protective styles like cornrows and eliminated the use of words such as 'matted' and 'unkempt' in relation to black hair. It is only since January 2017 that locs have been permitted.

British theorist Kobena Mercer points out that haircare remains a universal cultural practice. A person's hair 'is never a straightforward biological fact'. It is 'almost always "worked upon" by human hands'.[18] Hair is a material used to express one-self but also to comment upon, reflect or indeed contest society. While there is of course a degree of universality to this, it is impor-tant to note that, for multiple reasons, hair occupies a position of greater significance in African and African diaspora cultures than in most others. Cultures develop to reflect the interests and the needs of their people. Historian John Thornton notes that, at the most simple and practical level, 'the tightly spiraled hair of Afri-cans makes it possible to design and shape it in many ways impossible for the straighter hair of Europeans.'[19]

Thornton describes black hairstyling as a lively, dynamic, pop-ular art form responding to contemporary life. Traditionally, hairstyling could operate as a means of organizing people into different social categories and contribute to the maintenance of these categories. Hairstyling also functioned symbolically in marking important life stages, as well as signifying the transition from one status to another, such as puberty, initiation into societies and guilds, or marriage. Hairstyles were an integral part of ritual, constituting a visual form of language in oral societies.

Yet one of the legacies of European political, physical and cultural dominion was the stigmatization of Africa and its customs and practices. Within that framework, African hair, too, is degraded. It's a system that operates according to the same logic that places *everything* that is African as inferior to that which is European. It is no coincidence that the students in Pretoria High were also forbidden from speaking their 'backwards' African languages.

Despite all this context, I have lost track of the amount of times I have sent the 'It's Only Hair' brigade into paroxysms of apoplectic rage by having the temerity to talk about the politics of black hair in the media. In one appearance on BBC's *Newsnight* I argued that I really couldn't give a flying fig about whether or not Justin Bieber wore dreadlocks. The point I was making was that it is all about power imbalances and the continued extraction of Africa's physical, material and cultural resources over a 500-year period. This line of reasoning provoked a barrage of online abuse. I learned that I am an ungrateful nigger who should be thankful to whites for liberating me from the darkness of barbarism. Indeed, where was my gratitude for colonialism's gifts of civilization, clothing and technology? This affected outrage is not only wearying, it is wildly inaccurate.

In their groundbreaking book *The Invention of Tradition* (1983), historians Eric Hobsbawm and Terence Ranger detail the way in which European colonialists were essentially blind to many cultural practices they encountered in Africa. Contrary to colonial propaganda, for example, Africa has many long written traditions. In Timbuktu during the city's Golden Age (fifteenth and sixteenth centuries), books were reputed to be the most valued and valuable commodity.[20] However, unless something had a direct parallel in European society, usually it went unseen. As a result, many rich, complex cultural phenomena were merely discarded and dismissed as primitive, and certainly never made it into the annals of history. European culture placed value only on the written word, on art and on monuments that stood the test of time. This, it was believed, is what conferred civilization on a people. Without evidence of these markers,* it was debatable whether or not Africans were even human. The European benchmark of value obscured colonial vision, and the emissaries of European culture remained illiterate in much that existed of value in oral societies, including the intricate language of hairstyling, unable to understand the ephemeral temporality of this art form.

African aesthetics have their own norms, which do not always correspond to European ones. Take the Afro hairstyle, particularly when not worn neatly. Kobena Mercer discusses the inherent irony wherein the Afro is read as traditionally 'African', despite the fact that in West African contexts hair is rarely left unmoulded or unbraided. The Afro is a symbol of diasporic resistance, a rejection of an imposed value system that denigrated us. Sporting an Afro is a defiant up-yours to such a system, but that fact alone does not make it inherently 'African'.

The African-American ethnographer Sylvia Boone writes that, for the Mende people of Sierra Leone, the opposite of well-groomed hair is *yivi-yivi* – untidy, unkempt, messy, without shape. A dirty home is *yivi*, as are dirty political dealings. Hair that looks dirty and untidy is seen by the Mende as evidence of mental-health problems – 'those who buckle under the strains of everyday life, retreating into madness, signal their illness graphically by no longer grooming their hair, thus abandoning the community's standards of behaviour' – or of loose morals.[21] Shane White and Graham White point out that these cultural norms give insight to the 'humiliation slave women may have felt in being prevented from grooming and styling their hair as they wished, as well as indicating the importance they are likely to have attached to whatever hairstyles they

---

* Where the evidence existed it was obscured and credited to fictional, non-black earlier inhabitants of the continent, colonialists being unwilling to believe that Africans could have been responsible.

were able – during the time of their enslavement and after – to achieve'.[22] This is yet another example of the context in which black hair became politicized and where the choice of styles can be read as contestations.

Hair has power in many different ways. To this day, in African and Afro-diasporic cultures people remain hesitant about their hair falling into a stranger's hands. My stepfather was not a great guy and we'll say no more; nonetheless, through him I was exposed to a lot of Guyanese and Trini beliefs (I have a Trini connection via my mother as well, who was born on the island and spent the first fourteen years of her life there until her Irish parents returned to Ireland). Among these I remember strongly the belief that, if somebody had access to your hair – from a comb, for instance – they could do witchcraft or *obeah* on you. These ideas have their antecedents in earlier African cultures, whereby a person's hair was considered so potent that possession of it could confer certain power over said person. Recently, at a hair and material cultures event I attended at Goldsmiths, University of London, I was reminded of this, when the non-black attendees shared cuttings of human hair with little hesitation. I had kept a bag of my relaxed hair that I cut off when I 'big chopped'.* I brought this in to illustrate my presentation but realized that, unlike my peers, there was no way I could pass it around the assembled group of strangers.

Many other taboos that dictate the behaviour and beliefs surrounding hair can be found throughout the hairdressing cultures of Africa. Among the Yoruba, these included the idea that a hairdresser must not eat while working on a client; otherwise, the client will get dandruff. A stylist must not wash their hands immediately prior to or following a session; if they did, the partings would not be well structured: *irun e ko ni didi* (hair that does not part well); the reverse of this – *irun e o ni yin owo* (hair that does

---

* In the natural-hair community, the big chop is the process of cutting off the relaxed or permed ends of one's hair when you are transitioning from chemically processed hair to natural hair.

part well) – is a compliment demonstrating that neat partings were considered a criterion for beautiful hair.

More significantly, as hairdressing moved away from being a practice that was carried out in an exchange economy by an intimate and well-trusted individual to something one paid a stranger to do, a taboo developed that forbade bartering, something that is usually a mainstay of Yoruba culture. Accordingly, a client must not under any circumstances bargain with the hairstylist about the price of the style: *A kii na eleda eni* (One does not bargain for one's destiny).

The explanation for this taboo's potency has to do with the centrality of the *ori* (the head) and, by extension, the hair in Yoruba metaphysics. Like the Mende, in Yoruba society hair that is left uncared for is anathema. In Yoruba, the phrase for 'dreadlocks' in adult hair is *irun were*. This translates as 'insane person's hair-do'. In the Yoruba world, each human being has a personal *ori*. This spiritual head, or *ori inu*, is responsible for an individual's fate, and this is preordained before birth. Because the physical head, or *ori ode*, houses the spiritual head, the maintenance and grooming of hair are seen as acts of spiritual significance.

Yoruba cosmology, which governs all socio-political relations, is organized in three tiers. The pre-eminent is Oludumare, or the Supreme Being. So great is Oludumare that human beings (the third tier) cannot interact with Oludumare directly. Mediating between humanity and Oludumare there exists a pantheon of intermediaries known as the *orisha*. Individual *orisha* have certain abilities and are charged with particular areas of responsibility. One of the most powerful of these *orisha* is the goddess of love and fertility, Oshun, who is associated with the Oshun river and fresh waters more generally. Oshun is understood to be the primary and most skilful hairdresser in Yoruba mythology. A well-known *oriki*, or poem of praise, introduces her thus:

> *Oshun, embodiment of grace and beauty,*
> *The pre-eminent hair plaiter with the coral beaded comb*

Given the importance hair is granted by means of its association with an individual's spiritual well-being, Oshun's relationship to hairdressing is no coincidence. In fact, in Yoruba culture, hair is of such significance that the earth itself is sometimes personified as a woman having her hair combed with farming hoes. Because hair is associated with spiritual well-being, no price is too high to pay for your hair. This was a savvy ruse created by hairstylists to avoid having to argue with clients and ultimately, to make more cash.

Every 2 February on the north-east coast of Brazil, the descendants of millions of enslaved Africans – from the Ga-Adangbe, Yoruba, Igbo, Fon, Ashanti, Ewe, Mandinka – look back out across the sea towards Mbundu and Bakongo and pray to another powerful *orisha*, Yemanja, the 'Queen of the Sea'. As well as connecting the diaspora, water also connects the land of the living to the land of the ancestors. The *orisha* Olokun (who, like a number of *orisha*, transcends gender) is associated with the deep sea, heralding the way for the spirits that are passing into ancestorship.

Both saltwater and freshwater are symbolically powerful in many African traditions. For the Mende of Sierra Leone, the water deity Tingoi is renowned for her beautiful hair. Extra caution will be taken to prevent a little girl with especially long hair from drowning because it is believed that such a girl would be particularly attractive to the water people, who may mistake her for one of their own and desire her to join them.

The Mende have a powerful female-only society known as the Sande; its male counterpart is Poro. These are key institutions within the community, and both require lengthy initiations before entry is granted. According to Mende custom, the water people crown female visitors to their underwater domain with extra-ordinarily beautiful hairstyles. Boone explains that during the extensive Sande initiation ceremonies 'the girls are believed to reside underwater. When they are ready to re-join the community, they rise from the waters, displaying magnificent hairstyles more dazzling than any that could be done by human hands.'[23] Their hair is a beautiful demonstration of an engagement with the divine.

If we seek to decolonize, it is imperative that we explore how African people understood themselves and their own cultures, to gain a clearer understanding that is not warped through the biases of colonial documentation. In her study of the important Yoruba oral tradition *oriki*, the anthropologist Karin Barber explains that through attending to what people say (or produce themselves) we learn how people constitute their society. Hair is an embodied visual language and can be understood as one of these indigenous 'texts'; another would be the *bata* drum that mimics the tonality of the Yoruba language.

Understanding these can 'lead to the heart of a community's own conception of self: without which, any description of social structure or process will remain purely external'.[24] Barber investigates the role of *oriki* in Yoruba reckonings of time and culturally significant events:

> At the time of their composition each oriki refers to the here and now. They encapsulate whatever is noteworthy in contemporary experience . . . but because they are valued they are preserved, and transmitted for decades – even centuries.

'Oriki are valued all the more for coming from the past, and bringing with them something of its accumulated capabilities, the attributes of earlier powers.' *Oriki* – much like the hairstyles we can observe from Africa across the Atlantic – 'can thus be a thread that leads back into an otherwise irrecoverable social history'.

> A single performance often contains items composed as much as 200 years apart . . . the items from different historical moments are not usually arranged in chronological order, nor are the most ancient units separated from the newest ones. They might be performed in virtually any order and combination. This is not because a chronological ordering is beyond the scope of oriki performers – the oriki of all the successive Obas

(Yoruba kings) of Okuku and those of the successive holders of the most senior chiefly title are performed in order – but because oriki performances *usually aim at something else.*

The past is recalled for a different purpose.[25]

The weaving that occurs in the braided hairstyles, the aspects of their temporality, their consistency as well as their adaptability, share many similarities with the *oriki* genre. What is this *something else* that *oriki* performances aim at? Simply posing this question highlights a profound difference between a Eurocentric concept of 'history' and Afrocentric engagements with time. It is precisely the kind of investigation necessary if we are to respond with any seriousness to imperatives to 'decolonize'.

The philosopher Elizabeth Grosz interrogates the discipline of 'history' itself: she proposes that to be mired in the past is to be unable to think and act the future. Yet conversely, to be un-anchored in the past, to have no connections to, or resonances with, the past, is also to have no way to see or make a future; it is to have no place from which a future can be made that is different from the present. Well-being requires a judicious mix of the historical and the ahistorical, the timely and the untimely, the past and the *future.*[26]

While such a position remains controversial, even radical, in a European context, it is immediately recognizable among indigenous African cultural practices. In fact, scholars such as Ulli Beier inform us that 'to Yoruba kings, praise singers and storytellers . . . "history" is a means of explaining and justifying the present, rather than enlightening the past.'[27]

As Karin Barber explains:

> the past is not the present, but it must be kept alive in the present, contiguous and accessible to it . . . to explain oriki as merely a means of justifying the status quo, or as reflections of present-day interests, is to miss the point of their most profound significance – their capacity to transcend time.[28]

Braided hairstyles have survived in the diaspora. Later on we will visit San Basilo de Palenque, one the first independent towns in colonial South America, founded by escaped Africans. Some of these styles very closely resemble traditional Yoruba styles such as *koroba* and *kolese*. These styles could be understood as sharing many qualities with *oriki*.

Centuries of accumulated meaning are weaved into braids. The Africans who reached the Palenque often utilized maps they braided into their hair – hiding in plain sight, as it were. The enduring popularity of these styles ensures that the 'past is . . . kept alive in the present, contiguous and accessible'. They operate as a direct bridge between the modern-day inhabitants of the Palenque and their African ancestors. One source describes them as the re-visualization of centuries-old pathways to freedom, a symbolic representation of what was endured on this continent 'that made us cry'. Yet today this pain has been transformed into embodied artworks, symbols of resistance and survival. Barber's analysis of *oriki* applies just as well to any of these hairstyles:

> The past is reactivated to the present . . . the past is evoked in the midst of the activity of the present generation.[29]

Perhaps it is partly this richly embedded meaning that gives *irun didi* (Yoruba braiding) its enduring relevance, that allows hairstyles which were already ancient in the 1600s to appear fresh, futuristic and unique five centuries later.

The same characteristics that are found in braiding and in *oriki* can be seen in many other black cultural art forms. Recursion – where the output becomes the input – exists as much in music sampling as it does in hair braiding. Look at the difference between the European discipline of 'history', which locates action in an irrecoverable time past and in which events are approached as static, are preserved, frozen in aspic, and African methods of engaging the past, which have very different intentions. Examples as diverse as sampling, *oriki* and braided hairstyles can all be understood as 'coming from the past' and bringing 'with them something of [the past's] accumulated capabilities, the attributes of earlier powers', yet while they are of the 'here and now' they bring with them 'the then'. Strand by strand, the past is weaved skilfully together with the present.

THE NATURAL HAIR MOVEMENT

The Natural Hair Movement could be understood as a collective reawakening of black women. It started in the US but soon spread across the diaspora to the UK, France and back to Africa – French-speaking West Africa and South Africa particularly, as well as small communities in places such as Nigeria. Around 2010, my awareness of a change started when I discovered a website called Black Girl with Long Hair (BGLH), founded in 2009 by Leila Noelliste. It was the first time I really saw my hair texture acknowledged, let alone celebrated, anywhere – not only shiny, glossy curls but the matt, springy naps that can be twisted, stretched, coiled and curled into any and every shape imaginable. As the name of the blog suggests, our hair can grow. One of the negative qualities attributed to Afro-textured hair is that it doesn't grow. However, more often than not, this is the result of damaging practices or lack of knowledge. Now, I was presented with all these beautiful sisters rocking very chic fashion looks with their very own natural hair. And if they could do it, so could I! Couldn't I?

Many women insist that their decision to go natural is not explicitly political. The fact that they even have to state this, however, shows how far from the norm black hair is still considered to be. Which other group of women on earth are expected to transform their features so drastically merely to fit in? While it may not be the expressed motivation for many, my decision to stop relaxing my hair *was* political. I emphatically still *did not want* to have Afro-textured hair, yet I could no longer reconcile my politics with chemically straightening it. I realized that, as a grown woman, I did not know my own hair. I was not familiar with its natural appearance nor remotely in tune with its requirements.

Once you chemically straighten your hair, you can't un-straighten it. It's an irreversible process. The only option is the 'big chop'. I would have to cut it short. Undoubtedly, all the images on BGLH helped but, you know, I just wasn't ready for short hair. The texture was bad enough but, in addition, *willingly* returning to a *short* Afro, conceding victory to a long-vanquished enemy, that was unimaginable!

But at last I stopped straightening my hair. I let my roots grow for a year before I cut off the straightened ends (in hindsight, I wish I'd gone for a close crop; it would have looked fab). The following year I became pregnant, and I finally did the thing.

CHOP!

I had various motivations. They say your hair grows quickly while you're pregnant, but it was more than that. I knew that, if I had a daughter, it was crucial she did not grow up with the same warped concept of beauty I'd held. Moreover, if I was having a boy, such enlightenment was just as, if not more, crucial.

Undoubtedly, there was something in the air, a burgeoning collective reawakening, but it hadn't yet gone mainstream. Let me be clear, though: this was not something I *wanted* to do, rather it was something I felt *compelled* to do, if not a punishment, exactly, then certainly a sacrifice, a political statement. Despite those bomb-ass-looking women on BGLH, I still felt it wouldn't suit me, at least not as much as my long, sleek locks. But, down for the cause, I resigned myself to a future as a frumpy militant feminist. It is extraordinary for me to remember that, even at this stage, I couldn't imagine myself as attractive with natural hair.

The knock-on effects of my decision to go natural have been vast and unforeseeable. My re-acquaintance with my natural hair coincided with the birth of my son. My body was capable of things

I had never dreamed possible. Working with it, rather than against it, I felt my relationship with reality begin to transform in incredibly meaningful ways. It was a combination of events. Certainly, breastfeeding and motherhood were central, but my acceptance of my hair and the subsequent events that unfolded because of that acceptance were perhaps no less so. Subtly, over time, I moved away from tolerating my hair to enjoying it, to loving it. I wonder if my hair's new-found freedom, volume and height shifted the energy around me. It is said that many African groups have associated the height of our hair as significant in relation to divine power. The developments with my hair have been important in my ongoing reconnection to my body and its relationship to the natural world. I have a far stronger sense of completeness and a deeper understanding of the processes that work extremely hard to disconnect us both from our own bodies and from nature itself. Entire industries feed off our engineered insecurities to peddle products designed to interrupt our connection with ourselves and the universe. My relationship with my hair has been fundamental to this awakening. Oh, and my scalp is no longer agony to the touch. Bonus!

No gains are ever absolute, but it does appear that big changes are afoot. Globally, there is a movement of black women saying, 'We are enough.' We want to be accepted for looking like ourselves. This in turn is having an impact on mainstream media and the imperative has come directly from us. Until recently, we just did not see natural hair on our screens. There were a handful of black women represented, but in the few instances they were granted visibility they would either have 'good hair' or would be wearing a weave. Textures such as my own remained unseen, forbidden. That finally seems to be changing. The release of *Black Panther* in 2018 made history for many reasons. According to *Forbes* magazine, *Black Panther* is the third-biggest-grossing film of all time and became the third film to earn more at the North American box office than James Cameron's *Titanic*. No mean feat, given that earlier refusal to cast black leads in mainstream films was often justified by the played-out myth that black stories do not sell. But the film remains remarkable in almost infinite ways. It is undoubtedly a feminist milestone: the female characters are tech geniuses and warrior commanders and, in addition, the way they look is unprecedented in Hollywood. This is the first time a Hollywood production has created an onscreen world populated almost entirely by black women with type-4 hair. This was powerful not least because it showed our hair as beautiful but, more than this, because it was presented as *normal* – a space we have historically and very intentionally been excluded from. Growing up, I was made to feel like an abomination. I know that seeing women with hair like mine representing a spectrum of nuanced characters up there on the silver screen would probably have made me feel proud. It would certainly have made me feel far less alone.*

* I remain sceptical, however, about the final message of *Black Panther*, namely that Africa's future success and prosperity lie in its role as an enthusiastic participant in the exploitative neoliberal world order, but that's another story.

2

Ain't Got the Time

*Caring for myself is not self-indulgence, it is self-
preservation, and that is an act of political warfare.*

Audre Lorde

Over the course of my life, I have spent what must amount to years
having my hair done, from Brazil through Nigeria, the UK and the
US, to Trinidad and Tokyo, in homes and in salons, bouji and
back-a-yard, staring at my own reflection and that of the women
above and behind me whose blue-black, dark-black, red-black,
yellow-black, light-black hands apply creams and potions, stitch-
ing lines and tracks of weave to my crown in the service of an
alchemy that transforms what grows on my head from one thing
into an almost entirely unrecognizable other.

My bum has gone numb sitting on stools in various living
rooms, my own and others', listening to the shrieks of children and
the high-octane melodrama of Nollywood while I have extensions
attached to create meticulous braids that tumble down my back.

As a young child I spent long hours on the floor wedged between
the strong legs of strangers, my head cradled in their lap. These
early childhood memories are vague in detail but strong in atmosphere. It is very warm. The earth is red. Everything else muted
browns and beige. Dust motes lend the air gossamer-like materiality. We are in a small wooden building. My head is positioned in
the lap of the hairdresser. I think I am facing towards her. I'm
certainly with my mother. My aunt, my father's sister, is perhaps
with us, too. I have a lot of hair. Deft fingers divide it with mathematical precision. I am not particularly tender-headed but nor, if

West African women braiding each other's hair, 1940s.

I'm honest, am I used to having my hair thoroughly combed. I am certainly not used to having my head yanked in this undeniably violent fashion. My scalp is on fire. I instinctively pull against the direction of my torturer.

> 'Sit still or I will slap you!'
> The tears spring to my eyes.
> 'Stop crying or I will slap you.'

Nor am I used to such commands. The tears freeze before they have a chance to flow. In desperation, I make pleading eyes at my mother. She casually looks away. She does not leap to my rescue. The ordeal eventually ends and my hair has been transformed into a style I can now identify as suku. Not exactly the hair of my dreams; I had wanted long, silky, swishy princess hair. Yet the memory is not an unhappy one. While the experience may not have been entirely comfortable, I've always enjoyed having my hair braided. I like the sensation of feeling it parted, the sharp teeth of the comb making

Ouch. The calm before the storm.

contact with a scalp that is otherwise carefully protected, courtesy of the thick, dense hair that grows from my head.

There is something terribly reassuring about hands that know exactly what to do and how to do it. Confident hands that recognize my hair, hands – even when they are those of a stranger – that nonetheless identify my hair texture as familiar. A world apart from the reluctant hands of white stylists, whose fear of touching often feels at best underscored by the fascination of encountering an exotic and at worst by distaste. The same could be said of the clueless hands of white boyfriends who have tried to 'run' their fingers through a texture not designed for that particular activity. In fact, I love my head being touched, but only by those who know that any attempt to 'run' anything through it will result in snagging and pulling and most likely mash up whatever fabulous hairstyle I've taken pains to achieve.

Generally, black people know our hair takes time and effort to do so they don't usually try and put their grubby hands up in it. I

(*clockwise from top left*) *Ipako elede* (bristles at the back of a boar's neck); *suku* (basket); *kolese* (creature without legs); *korobo* (bucket).

think there is also more of an awareness of boundaries and personal space, as well as the enduring, if these days mostly implicit, awareness that our hair has a spiritual significance. Look, but don't touch. (White people, take note.)

IRUN DIDI

For centuries, cornrowing (*irun didi*) was an everyday feature of Yoruba and more generally much African life. Hairstyles existed as markers of social status and distinction, your occupation, your marital status, membership of a royal lineage, perhaps to demonstrate which *orisha* you were a priest or priestess of. A lot could be told about a person, as well as the values, ethics and priorities of their culture, by their hairstyle.

Traditionally, the majority of Yoruba women learned how to plait or braid their own hair, a practice which stretches back into antiquity. In addition to domestic knowledge there existed professional hairdressers, known as *onidiri*, who were generally faster and exceptionally skilled and were highly respected as artists.

Irun didi are created by recursively braiding the hair to the scalp. This can be done in a seemingly infinite array of styles. Despite the limitless options, there are particular styles that have remained popular for millennia. These are known as cornrows or canerows in English.

The words and terms that we use to describe ourselves remain central to the ways we relate to our bodies. Certainly, if we want to set about the work of decolonization we need to consider language. The discrepancy between the generic term 'cornrowing' in the US and 'canerowing' in the Caribbean and the UK betrays the sad history of slavery. The varying regional names reflect different crops, for instance the sugar cane that was cultivated by the enslaved in the Caribbean. However, in the Yoruba language, canerowing was subdivided into different styles such as *ipako elede* (literally, the bristles at the back of the boar's neck) or what is now considered the classic cornrow, *kolese* (a creature without legs).

Unlike the English names, which directly reference an enslaved past, the Yoruba names originate in a world that exists prior to the one in which slavery became the dominant signifier of black life. The names serve as a powerful reminder that we have identities that existed before, beyond and outside the legacy of slavery.

African hairstyles fulfil innumerable functions and operate on multiple levels. At its most basic, a braid can be understood as a length of material – fibre or hair – interlaced from three or more strands. It is made by a repeating process that creates a pattern. Depending on the style and the size of the braids, an entire head of hair can take a long time – hours, even days – to complete. I'm reluctant to describe this process as time-consuming because I'm keen to disrupt our deeply ingrained (yet recent and culturally specific) myth of time as a commodity. It makes a lot more sense to imagine braiding as a sociable time during which the business of living is conducted. It is a process that brings people together and facilitates intergenerational bonding and knowledge transmission. Women might talk politics or a mother might inform her daughter on sexual mores. And the physical proximity of the exchanges only heightens the intimacy and sense of occasion. The social meaning encoded into braids' multiple layers brings with it centuries of accumulated information, beliefs and practices. Braiding operates as a bridge spanning the distance between the past, present and future. It creates a tangible, material thread connecting people often separated by thousands of miles and hundreds of years.

IRUN KIKO

Although highly developed in southern Nigeria, *irun kiko* is a far more recent innovation then the ancient *irun didi*. Scholars suggest it wasn't introduced into Yorubaland until at least the 1960s, although there is evidence of something comparable during slavery; not as a style itself but as a method of manipulating the hair, for stretching and curling. This 'wrapping' was a process whereby the hair was detangled, parted and wrapped with cotton or a similar fabric. Once the fabric was removed this produced hair which was knot-free and curly. Women would then wrap a length of material around the threading to preserve it until Sunday when they would remove both the wrap and the thread, and style their freshly stretched hair as they pleased.

In an interview, Gus Fester, a former slave born in 1840, told how at camp meetings slave women

> took dey hair down out'n de strings fer de meeting. In dem days all de darky wimmens wore dey hair in string 'cep' when dey 'tended church or a wedding. At de camp meetings de wimmens pulled off de head rags, 'cept de mammies. On dis occasion de mammies wore linen head rags [bandannas] fresh laundered.'[1]

Likewise, Amos Lincoln explained the purpose of threading:

> d'gals uster dress up come Sunday. All week dey wear dey hair all roll up wid cotton dat dey unfol' off d' cotton boll. Sunday come dey comb out dey hair fine. Dey want it nice an' natural curly. Monday dey put d' cotton string back so it hab all week t' git curly ag'in.

Another interviewee, Olivier Blanchard, concurred: 'I t'ink it eel fish w'at dey strip the skin off dey back and wrap dey hair 'roun' wid it. Dat mek hair pretty and curly.'

This could be taken as early evidence of the influence of European beauty ideals that associate looser curls with prettiness.[2]

There exists an almost infinite number of threaded styles, but each is the product of three stages. The first involves the delineation of patterns on the scalp; the shapes within the pattern are twisted and wrapped with black thread or, more recently, with a type of black rubber. The structures created are rich in meaning.

Their names represent everything from metaphysical states of being to significant cultural and social events in the Yoruba/Nigerian world. Popular styles include Ogun Pari ('the war has ended'; in celebration of the end of the Biafran war on 5 January 1970), Eko Bridge (an impressive bridge built in the 1970s in Eko, the Yoruba name for Lagos), the Onile Gogoro (skyscraper) or the Kehin Soko ('turn your back on your husband'). Make of that one what you will!

IRUN BIBA

White people, please don't assume that everybody's hair can be worn down or that asking 'how long is your hair' is a universally meaningful question. *To reiterate*, ours grows up! A traditional Yoruba woman would never leave her hair 'down' (and it would make more sense to say 'out' anyway) in the manner that women with European textures wear theirs.

On the occasions when a woman was not sporting *irun didi* or *irun kiko* she would wear *irun biba* (loose braids). Because of the texture of our hair, leaving it 'out' and unplaited for too long results in moisture loss. Loose braids would be worn as a holding style until a woman was ready to make more formal cornrows.

There is a strong continuity between these traditional practices and some of the low-maintenance 'protective styles' (as we call them today) that black women wear between styles. When we twist our hair between styling, to achieve a 'twist out' look, we are engaging in much the same age-old practices as Yoruba women who made *irun biba* (loose braids) with their hair, or enslaved women with their early version of threading.

Afro hair requires manipulation; it longs to be touched (although not by inquisitive strangers!). While it is not entirely necessary to twist it every night (there are some who would disagree but, hey, like I said, I'm slack), you cannot get away without twisting it for too long. The hair will 'shrink' and become increasingly matted and tangled. Generally, black women have to do a lot of forward thinking. When it comes to our hair, impromptu is really not the one!

While these are practices that have been around a long time, they become more, or less, popular during certain periods. Without a doubt we are experiencing a renaissance of braided styles. Go to any black area in London and everywhere you will see interpretations and modern twists on traditional styles that would have been unusual only a couple of years ago.

With the growing numbers of black women who have stopped relaxing their hair, the frequency with which you see us with these 'in between' protective styles is steadily growing. There is a renewed sense of confidence in being seen with natural textured hair, as well as in wearing simple, casual, braided styles. I am always struck by the fact that there is nothing assimilationist about most of these looks and how little effort to conform to European aesthetics exists in them. These are unapologetically black styles.

BLACK IS BEAUTIFUL I:
*A-DÚ-BÍI-KÓRÓ-ISIN**

Thinkers from James Baldwin to W. E. B. Du Bois to Frantz Fanon and Ngũgĩ wa Thiong'o remind us that the most destructive consequence of colonialism was not the control of the land but the control of the minds of the people. It is during the colonial era that we begin to see the effects of the widespread indoctrination of the type of 'West is best' attitudes that are responsible for much of what is considered aspirational in today's Nigeria. Beauty ideals remain a pertinent example. The World Health Organization estimates that 77 per cent of women in modern Nigeria use skin-lightening creams. While a belief in the superiority of white skin is not innate,

* 'One whose dark skin is as beautifully shining as the seed of the Akee apple'.

there exists a popular and entirely spurious claim that insists on a historic and worldwide preference for light skin. It's a dangerous myth because it continues to subtly perpetuate the idea that lighter skin is objectively superior and that, deep down, on some evolutionary level, everybody knows it. This is untrue.

Yoruba people have skin colours of different shades, some lighter, some darker. Until the imposition of European beauty standards this characteristic alone was not enough to confer or deny beauty. You might be beautiful and have lighter skin but you would not be beautiful *because* you had lighter skin. A person who was fair in complexion might be called *a-pon-bépo-re* ('one who is as red as palm oil'), while a person with darker skin could be *a-dú-máa-dán* ('one whose dark skin is beautifully shining') or *a-dú-bíi-kóró-isin* ('one whose dark skin is as beautifully shining as the seed of the Akee apple').[3] The desire to conform to an aesthetic which values light skin and straight hair is the result of a propaganda campaign that has lasted more than 500 years. It is the imposition of a system that denigrates anything that is perceived as 'too African'.

The only way Afro hair can fulfil the criterion of 'beautiful' is if it is transformed and made to resemble European hair in some way. It wasn't always this way. Yoruba proverbs such as *Irun ni ewa obinrin* ('A woman's plaited hair is her beauty') reveal that it was the intervention of plaiting that conferred the beauty; or the Mende 'She is hair' demonstrates that while hair has long been central to beauty, the context was very different.

Sylvia Boone explains that indigenous judgements on hair refer to its quantity and volume. Beautiful hair is celebrated as *kpotongo*, which means 'it is much, abundant, plentiful'.[4] In reference to hair, *kpoto*, the root word, means long and thick; for the Mende the significant feature of hair is that it grows, and *kpoto* denotes an abundant, numerous quality of growing things, which is why it is also used in relation to fruit on a tree, rice, or objects that can be gathered together and tied. In the same way, braiding, threading, plaiting and weaving are used to style African hair. Other Mende words relating to hair develop the metaphor of hair as flora, the one ornamenting a woman's head, the other decorating the Earth's surface.[5]

Hair that is undesirable is not considered so because of its texture or its lack of similarity to European hair. 'Coarse', 'nappy' and 'tough' don't exist. Instead, undesirable hair is *kpendengo*: hair that is 'stunted, not growing robustly'. The opposite term, *papoongo*, indicates thick growth, luxuriance, like on a farm or in a forest.[6] Again, beauty originates from the bounty of the Earth rather than from the extent to which the texture resembles that of your oppressor.

Styles that suited the texture of African hair and played to its strengths were those admired by potential love interests. Boone learned that both elegance and sexual appeal were achieved through hair 'shaped into beautiful and complicated styles'. In contrast to straight blonde strands or indeed the 'good hair' that seemingly occupies Eurocentric minds today, traditional braided and threaded styles were the height of sexual allure!

The concern was not to achieve either long flowing locks, or tumbling, wavy 'princess hair'. In fact, for the Yoruba one type of 'princess hair' was a cornrowed style called *moremi*.

Moremi takes its name from the clever and courageous Moremi, a twelfth-century princess (see, for better or worse, black girls can be princesses) from the kingdom of Ile Ife, the cradle of civilization, according to Yoruba belief. Fed up with the raids of the forest people, Moremi allowed herself to be kidnapped and taken as a prisoner of war. Her fabled beauty caught the attention of the enemy king, who took her for his wife. Upon learning the secrets of the enemy army, Moremi stole away, returning to Yorubaland, where she revealed logistical information to the Yoruba, who used it to defeat their enemies in battle.

SORORITY

She needed what most colored girls needed: a chorus
of mamas, grandmamas, aunts, cousins, sisters,
neighbors, Sunday school teachers, best girl friends,
and what all to give her the strength life demanded of
her – and the humor with which to live it.

Toni Morrison, *Song of Solomon*

Hair braiding is a social time. For Hagar, a pivotal character in Toni Morrison's *Song of Solomon*, the absence of this necessary chorus of black women has dire consequences. Without it, Hagar lacks the emotional resources to survive the heartache that eventually kills her.

Hagar dies of a fever, but one that is brought about by a manic chain of events kickstarted when Milkman, the object of her obsession, rejects her love. Milkman's rejection is fuelled in no small part by the ravages of colourism, that internecine violence that we black people continue to enact upon each other.

The source of much of Hagar's emotional inadequacy is located in the lack in her life of the networks of kinship, solidarity and support that were central to many traditional societies in Africa. These relationships were prioritized through the extended family, through age-grade institutions, and men's and women's associations like Mende examples of the Sande and the Poro. Black communities have with varying degrees of success managed to reproduce versions of traditional African communities. In her essay 'City Limits, Village Values' Toni Morrison contrasts the 'Gopher prairie despair' depicted by white fiction writers with the affection black writers typically express for the intimate, communal life built around 'village values'[7] (or one thinks of the quilombos* in Brazil or San Basilo de Palenque in Colombia).

* Brazilian hinterland settlements founded by escaped slaves of African origin.

In real life, too, the absence of this necessary chorus of black women can be costly. There was much that was wonderful about growing up in Ireland, but, beyond the explicit racism and the hostility I experienced, the most painful part was the isolation: no mamas, grandmamas, aunts, cousins, sisters, neighbours or best girl friends who might understand or relate to what I was experiencing. I felt a profound sense of loss. Having been uprooted from any extended family and the possibility of black friends when we left Atlanta, I found myself relocated from an affluent, black, sunny suburb to a cold, homogeneously white, often hostile, socially conservative Catholic country.*

Now, many white people – even anti-racist progressive liberals – seem able to conceive of blackness only as an experience defined by racism and unmitigated misery, a condition from which we would gladly liberate ourselves if only we could. I think this partially accounts for why people would occasionally, and with a palpable sense of generosity on their behalf, say to me, 'I don't even see you as black, Emma,' as though this were the greatest compliment they could bestow upon me.

But while I am Irish, I am also black (certainly I was called 'nigger' frequently enough to remain quite convinced that most of the 'colour blind' crew – when they weren't feeling charitable – did indeed very much see me as black). So yes, I am black. I am Yoruba. And that means something. Not least it means a culture, and a history, one which I am nothing less than in awe of, despite ceaseless efforts to make me feel ashamed of it. Don't tell me you don't 'see race'; my blackness is something I have no desire to erase, regardless of how much lesser, or how inadequate, it has been wilfully imagined as.

---

* It frustrates me when people interpret my descriptions of life in Ireland as evidence that I am not Irish. I am an Irish woman. I am deeply connected to and rooted in my Irishness. My critique of problematic aspects of the culture or elements of it that were once painful for me doesn't make that any less so, unless, of course, you don't really accept me as Irish in the first place.

Growing up, I desperately missed living in a black community. I have close white friends today, but, back then, I never felt entirely comfortable in those girly friendship groups that characterize teenage life. I did have some nice friends, but there was always a gulf. Sometimes the cause was quite extreme: there were certain friends whose homes I was simply not allowed to visit, and who were strongly discouraged from associating with me. With others it was subtler: a friend's brother nicknaming me 'Brown Sugar', or another, on a day I remember particularly clearly, shouting, 'Look, it's Emma's cousin!' of any random black person that happened to pass. Or the memory of another 'friend', the niece of the missionary nun in fact, admonishing me for making 'everybody feel uncomfortable' on an occasion when I related that I had just been called a black bitch (again). And I certainly can't recall any one of them, ever, not once, standing up for or defending me against anything I was experiencing.

The world responded to us differently, too. Real talk, I'm quite petite but I have a full bum and shapely thighs. Clothes fit me in a different way and I *hated* it. At that time, physically augmented white women were yet to popularize my features, so there were different consequences for me dressing like the others: 'Oh my God, Emma, you actually look like a prostitute, it looks much better on Becky.'* Sadly, I'm not quoting 'Baby Got Back'. It's an almost verbatim account from my very own life, although names have been changed!

In her 2004 essay 'Irish and White-ish', Angeline Morrison discusses the particular tone of Irish racism: 'The vast majority of racist insults had some kind of sexual overtones . . . this is a specific character of Irish racism . . .' The sexuality of immigrants, particularly but not exclusively black ones, 'has long been represented as exotic, taboo and dangerous'.[8]

---

* I did not have a friend called Becky. It is a generic name for white women who exhibit stereotypical 'white' behaviour.

When I hit fourteen or fifteen I started to get a lot of attention from boys and men. Young girls are conditioned to attach self-worth to these treacherous shifting sands, even when, in my case, it was also accompanied by assumptions about the sexual availability and perceived licentiousness of black girls. Despite the troubling aspects of this attention, it also engendered a lot of jealousy. This might manifest itself in someone saying, 'He's not even into her, he just knows black girls are easy,' something I'd be gleefully informed of by a concerned pal. In short, none of it was really the stuff enduring friendships are made of!

These days, I am lucky enough to have a diverse group of friends, including many wonderful Irish women, but, among them, I'm so grateful for my relationships with other black women, and excited, as the black Irish population grows, about the opportunity for friendship with other women who are both black *and* Irish, something I never foresaw. Living without black female sorority is like living without oxygen. It is a condition I could never return to.

Before we get too carried away, let's pause for a reality check. My intention is not to romanticize or attribute superhuman character traits to anyone. Regardless of race, people are people. Some are great, some are not . . . If I'm honest, shout-out to the group of girls I met in my first year of university; they taught me that in every so-called 'race' there are unreconstructed arseholes. With the benefit of hindsight, I can consider it all more critically and think about the ways in which young women are set up against each other, and how, for straight women, competition centred around the attention of men seems to have been such a recurring theme.

Here it was again, although now there was a shift in the narrative. No longer did boys like me because 'Black girls are easy.' In fact, having crossed the Irish Sea to the UK I was no longer straightforwardly even a black girl any more. In Ireland, people didn't distinguish between 'half black' and black; certainly, I don't ever remember getting only half the abuse because I was half white. In any case, in that environment, proximity to whiteness did not feel like a meaningful reality – but these things are all contextual, aren't they? Similarly, in the US, while I was perceived as light-skinned, I was nonetheless a light-skinned *black* girl.

Now, living in the UK, I became mixed race; and 'They only like her because black girls are easy,' became 'They only like her because she's mixed race,' or, if it was other mixed-race girls, 'He only likes you because you're lighter than me,'* ad infinitum . . .

So I'm under no illusions about any sort of assumed universal black female or indeed female solidarity. The feminist poet Audre Lorde bequeathed us many powerful words, not least among them these: 'Black women are programmed to define ourselves within this male attention and to compete with each other for it, rather than to recognize and move upon our common interests.'9

But, happily, those relationships of mine were not representative, and soon, with the memories of those rookie experiences behind me, I started to meet all types of black women. A new-found pleasure for me in these friendships was hairstyling. When I left America I had been removed from a world where I would have had that chorus of cousins and black girl friends, so this development was something for me to cherish. My new friends hooked me up, showing me how to attach weave (early 2000s, so this was still those black-glue bonded tracks; remember them?) and, more importantly perhaps, how to remove them.

A seventeenth-birthday present from my mum – a trip to Moss Side in Manchester to get my hair relaxed and extensions added – ended in disaster when it became time to remove the tracks. Entirely clueless about how to get them out, I sought advice in a top Dublin hair salon. As you do. Except you don't. The stylist

* Bearing in mind that I wasn't the lightest in this particular group and, unlike me, the others all had 'good hair'. In fact, the lightest, in addition to possessing almost waist-length hair, had pulled the top trump of hazel-green eyes. My point is that racial appearance was a source of conflict because of competition over male attention.

suggested acetone. I declined his sage advice but ended up literally *ripping* them out instead. All these years later, I still have a bald patch. I cringe when I remember this, both for my lack of knowledge and the brutality of my action. After I had moved to London and the dream of black girl friends became a reality, my homie Alesha showed me how to remove the weave with nothing more corrosive than baby oil. It slid out like a dream.

Over the years, my friendships with black women have only deepened. This is something that seems to be happening generally, too. There is much more care and attention being paid to black women's identities. We are experiencing a time of profound change, a reconnection with our shared mutuality – a 're-memory', as Morrison might describe it. In her research with the Mende women, Sylvia Boone explains that offering to plait another woman's hair is – in today's parlance – a 'squad goal'. It is an invitation to friendship.

> A beautiful distinctive style is considered a gift of love . . . It is one woman saying to another, 'I like you. I appreciate you. I have thought about you enough to imagine a style that will suit and enhance your features. I am not jealous of you. I *want* you to look beautiful, so that you will attract love, admiration, and all of the good that these bring. I am willing to stand or bend for several hours working on your hair, expecting no remuneration. My sacrifice proves that I want the best for you.'
>
> Thus braiding someone's hair is indicative of ideal care and love, the concrete contribution of one woman to the success of another.[10]

Why are these expressions of black female solidarity becoming more pronounced again today? Perhaps it is a combination of factors: a recognition of what we have lost and the will of the global decolonization movement to try to address this; a reclaiming of our inherent beauty and worth as we embrace our hair and other maligned features; renewed activism, the loud, resounding cry that black lives do indeed matter and the subsequent self-care conversations; LGBTQ gains, the decentring of patriarchal norms and the competition they encourage; the rejection of respectability politics and the new networks of support and solidarity that are emerging through social media.

I also know that we must do everything within our power to nurture this nascent revolution, to ensure that it does not devolve into performative showboating on social media, and more importantly, as factionalism deepens, we must not turn on each other. As Lorde urges us, 'We have to consciously study how to be tender with each other until it becomes a habit, because what was native has been stolen from us, the love of Black women for each other.'[11]

As social creatures, we all need to be touched. Breastfeeding, babywearing, hugging, holding hands, all of these tactile exchanges have much to offer us in terms of emotional stability, well-being and happiness. Many African cultures are traditionally quite tactile, although perhaps they are not perceived as such. One central expression of this is found in hairdressing culture: attending to our uniquely textured hair was an important and enjoyable part of the culture. How did it come to be re-imagined as *burdensome*?

WORKIN' 9 TO 5

Most ordinary people, irrespective of race, struggle to maintain a good work–life balance, or one in which their self-care needs can be easily met. We are chronically 'time poor'. Yet, instead of causing outrage, if not revolution, this enforced scarcity of time is re-imagined as progress. The appropriation of our personal time becomes evidence of aspirational metropolitan living, the idea of 'the grind' almost fetishized.

Almost everyone but the very rich can relate to this absence of personal time. In today's society most of us feel the intense pressure of this. However, where lack of time relates specifically to hairstyling, the balance is tipped in favour of our straight- or wavy-haired sisters. While white women can quite reasonably rock the tousled, just-got-out-of-bed, shabby chic effect, the hair that grows from my head does not accommodate such a laissez-faire approach to grooming.

For black hair, the costs of not having enough time are higher. Can you imagine running a brush through your hair and done? As I write this, I'm feverishly making impossible calculations about how I'm going to get my hair done tonight, in preparation for tomorrow morning, trying to manufacture time out of a schedule that just doesn't permit it.

Our society operates more or less around the demands of the nine-to-five work day. In this context, it is black women who are told we need to straighten our hair, or feel we need to, because we simply do not 'have time' to maintain it in its natural state.

It is black women who are demanded to do the labour required in making ourselves look presentable. But this is a culturally specific presentability which isn't easily achieved without, at worst, risking cancer or fertility issues, or, at the very least, chemical burns. Why is it that the only way black women can look 'professional' is contingent on producing a poor facsimile of white women's hair? What more poignant example is there of the necessary assimilation required in conforming to a culture not designed for certain bodies, not designed for my body to fit into easily?

The slave system was certainly not concerned with the provision of time for black women to do their hair, and the industrial working day we have inherited isn't much more sympathetic. Capitalism has repurposed time with the accumulation of capital as the central aim. Anything that disrupts the maximization of profit becomes subversive. For black women, when our hair became a burden, reclaiming the time to do it became in itself an act of rebellion. In fact, one of the most practical justifications for relaxing black hair is that far less time is required to maintain it.

The labour regime of Southern field slaves is the one we identify as the archetypal slave experience. Working hours were delineated by how much light there was. Africans worked from can see to can't see. If the moonlight was bright enough you would pick cotton through the night. In such an environment adequate care of the hair was all but impossible.

It was only on Sundays, the 'day off' (which was in reality the day for activities such as the subsistence farming many needed to survive), that slaves could find any time for grooming and styling, with whatever implements they could locate. In the words of a former slave, James Williams, 'the onlies time the slaves had to comb their hair was on Sunday. They would comb and roll each other's hair and the men cut each other's hair. That all the time they got.'[12]

We know that black hair needs to be carefully combed, parted, and braided or twisted to prevent it from matting, knotting and tangling. Once it becomes tangled, which it does easily, the process of detangling can be time-consuming and painful, and this would have been exacerbated by a lack of necessary equipment available to the enslaved Africans: 'we carded our hair 'caze we never had no combs, but de cards dey worked better. We used de cards to card wool wid also, and we jes wet our hair and den card hit. De cards dey had wooden handles and strong steel wire teeth.'[13]

The 'cards' referred to above sound innocuous. They are not. They are nasty, sharp instruments used to prepare fleece for spinning. Recently, I was filming at Cromford Mill in Derbyshire. The British Midlands was a central location in the Industrial Revolution and Cromford Mill was the place that revolutionized both cotton manufacturing and the very concept of the factory. Given the implications for the manufacture of cotton on the lives of the enslaved, it was a fitting location to have my first real-life encounter with a cotton card.

The formerly enslaved Aunt Tildy Collins describes the use of cotton cards on enslaved children in an attempt to comb their hair straight:

Us chilluns hate to see Sunday come, 'caze Mammy an' Gran-
mammy dey wash us an' near 'bout rub de skin off gittin' us
clean for Sunday school, an' dey comb our heads wid a jimcrow [colloquial name for the cards].

You ain't neber seed a jimcrow? Hit mos' lak a cyard what
you cyard wool wid. What a cyard look lak? Humph! Missy,
whar you been raise – ain't neber seed a cyard? Dat jimcrow
sho' did hurt, but us hadder stan' hit, an' sometimes atter all
dat, Mammy she wrap our kinky hair wid thread an' twis' so
tight us's eyes couldn't hardly shet.[14]

The use of the term 'Jim Crow' for a tool used to comb is
thought-provoking. In the 1870s and 1880s Jim Crow laws man-
dated racial segregation in all public facilities in the former
Confederate States of America. This was upheld by the United
States Supreme Court until 1965. This choice of a name that
emphasizes the 'separation' associated with the parting and detangling of black hair has its antecedents in Yoruba, where one of
the names for a comb is *ooya*, which means to be apart or separate.[15]
Accordingly, if someone sends a comb to a lover or friend, it means
that they have separated from them.[16]

The Jim Crow card had sharp metal claws and is clearly not
designed for personal grooming. In fact, curry-combs, as they
were also known, doubled up conveniently as a means of punishment. I remember reading an account of a fatigued black child
being submerged in a vat of boiling sugar and, when he was
removed, the comb raked across his raw, cooked skin. This was a
deterrent against 'crying off sick', because time is money and
money is time.

Yet as opposed to being the burden she imagined it to be, when
Susan Bordo learns about black hair culture through her daughter,
she is amazed to discover the beauty of the practices and their
potency:

As I became used to setting aside at least two hours for doing my daughter's hair, I became addicted to the pleasure of unbroken physical closeness the ritual afforded. As she grew into a more and more independent and active child, I knew that I could count on at least two hours every week when I'd have her on my lap, her little body leaning against mine, sometimes (as I got better at combing) even falling asleep as she had when she was a baby. At first I was intimidated by every ouch, at the same time as it seemed like such a lot of work to take the time to do it carefully and gently, working from the ends on up. But I discovered that there is a kind of Zen to it. Once you give yourself over to it, everything else recedes into background as the closeness of one's child, the taking care, the permission to touch and smell, and attend to her, becomes an absolute centre, a place of peace and safety.[17]

So many rich practices have been warped. But something we should think about more is the way in which black people have been robbed of the time they once enjoyed in abundance. We jest about 'black people time', but African concepts of time deserve further consideration. It is only as recently as the colonialism imposed in the late nineteenth century that the continent was brought under the tyranny of the 24-hour clock and its handmaiden, time management.

A powerful global narrative has been constructed in which urban life, industrialization and wage labour, in addition to the never-ending growth of consumer and financial markets, are an on-going goal. Allegedly this is 'development'. A more truthful version would be that these are the very things that remain analogous to the decimation of both human and natural resources.

The narrative of African racial inferiority might be well established, but it is relatively new. There is a huge shift between the earliest accounts of European observers and those who followed, first with slavery and later with colonialism on their minds.

PRE-COLONIAL KINGDOMS

Descriptions of African hair provide a meaningful site in which we can observe some of these changes. While seventeenth- and eighteenth-century Europeans were often impressed by what they found on the continent, records from the nineteenth and twentieth centuries reveal a markedly different interpretation.

When early European – let's be generous (always stay gracious) – 'adventurers' arrived in West Africa they were astounded by the wealth, abundance and beauty of the land and the people. We know that by 1300 AD the Yoruba people had built walled cities surrounded with farms. They had developed extensive trade and exchange networks with both their neighbours and those much further north. They bartered cloth and kola nuts for the goods they needed and desired. There was a lively exchange of ideas, arts and technology, with institutions such as the Islamic University in Timbuktu. By the fifteenth century, the Yoruba had established the Oyo Empire, located in what is today western and north-central Nigeria. Over the centuries, Oyo expanded until it occupied a huge geographical area, becoming one of the largest West African states. It was successful because of the outstanding organizational and administrative skills of the Yoruba people, and because of the wealth it gained through trade and its powerful cavalry. But great power is rarely benign; much of Oyo's later wealth was consolidated through its own involvement in the slave trade. While the Yoruba make up one of the largest groups kidnapped and transported to the New World as slaves themselves, earlier on they had participated in the trade, accounting in no small part for the might of Oyo.

To the south-east, the kingdom of Benin constituted another powerful empire. The Portuguese, who were the first recorded Europeans to arrive on this part of the continent, in the fifteenth century, were astounded by what they saw. More Europeans followed. A Dutch writer called Olfert Dapper produced the following report:

> Benin City is at least four miles wide. The city has wide, straight roads, lined by houses. The houses are large and handsome with walls made from clay. The people are very friendly and there seems to be no stealing. Inside the city is the king's court. It is large and square and surrounded by a wall. The court is divided into many palaces with separate houses and apartments for courtiers.[18]

The walls of Benin City were reputedly the world's largest earthworks constructed before the mechanical age. *New Scientist*'s Fred Pearce points out that Benin City's walls were at one point 'four times longer than the Great Wall of China'. Pearce describes a city that 'extended for some 16,000 km in all, in a mosaic of more than 500 interconnected settlement boundaries. They covered 6,500 sq km and were all dug by the Edo people . . . They took an estimated 150 million hours of digging to construct, and are perhaps the largest single archaeological phenomenon on the planet.'[19]

Benin City was laid out according to fractal patterning, a design culture which is also strongly evident in African braiding patterns, discussed in more detail in Chapter 6. Ron Eglash notes that Benin and nearby villages were also designed in perfect fractals, while the rooms of houses, and the houses themselves, were comprised of shapes repeating in mathematically predictable ways.[20] Benin was also one of the first cities in the world to have public street lighting, provided by huge metal lamps fuelled by palm oil. The lamps were especially concentrated near the Oba's Palace, in order to assist traffic to and from the residence after dark. In 1691, the Portuguese ship captain Lourenco Pinto observed:

> Great Benin, where the king resides, is larger than Lisbon; all the streets run straight and as far as the eye can see. The houses are large, especially that of the king, which is richly decorated

and has fine columns. The city is wealthy and industrious. It is so well governed that theft is unknown and the people live in such security that they have no doors to their houses.[21]

Another outstanding feature that caught the attention of early European observers in West Africa were the hairstyles. The Benin bronzes created between the sixteenth and nineteenth centuries, which the British kindly 'liberated' from the kingdom following a punitive expedition in 1897,* reveal the same level of attention to ornate and intricate braided hairstyles that we still observe in West Africa and its diaspora today.

Cado Mosto's 'Voyages' (1455) are remarkable for being the oldest extant European references to African men and women's hair. Describing the Jalofs of the south side of the Senegal River, we hear that 'Both sexes go bare-footed and uncovered, but weave their hair with *beautiful tresses*, which they tie in various knots, though it be short.'[22] 'Some let their hair grow long, plaiting it like a Horse's Mane on which they string Coral or Pipe-Beads. Many (especially up the river) wear on their crowns a good number of horse-bells.'[23] Peul women 'like yellow amber, drops of gold or glass of that colour: they make chaplets and knots of them, dressed upon cotton, which they stick in their hair, and looks quite pert and genteel'.[24]

There are many references to attention to detail in the hairdressing culture of the Wolof, Fuli and Mandingo along the Senegal River, who 'dress their hair which is short, very prettily, with grisgris (amulets), silver, leather, coral, copper etc.'.[25]

John Thornton notes that

when Europeans first came into contact with western Africa in the late fifteenth century, they commented on the myriad hairstyles worn by the people they met. Various combinations of

---

* By the 1860s Benin was already in decline. In 1897 the British attacked and razed it to the ground, marking the end of this once proud kingdom, little of which remains today. After the British soldiers stole the art, most of it ended up in British art collections.

braids, plaits (often with shells, beads, or strips of material woven in), shaved areas, and areas cut to different lengths to make patterns adorned the heads of people, creating a stunning effect.[26]

In 1602 the Dutch explorer Pieter de Marees 'published a plate . . . showing sixteen different hairstyles of various classes and genders in Benin alone'.[27]

Complimentary accounts are relatively profuse. It is apparent that, on the part of the European observers, there is no sense of African hair being ugly or inferior. Equally, the people themselves clearly have their own indigenous beauty standards. What the earlier accounts seem to show is that the project to deny and obscure African civilizations has not at this point begun. There was as yet no need to refuse the humanity of African people, because European economies had not yet become dependent on that narrative. At this stage, we see a world in which Africans can be perceived as human beings and, as such, their beauty can be acknowledged.

TIME IS MONEY AND MONEY IS TIME

Black hair culture provides a unique lens through which to re-examine what might be valuable from the African past and to assess the impact of an alien and destructive way of life on African people.

We're all familiar with the old adage 'Time is money and money is time,' but where did it come from? And, if we stop to think about it, what does it really mean, and what does it reveal about the things our society values and those it disregards?

Once European objectives became characterized by the pursuit of enslavement and colonization, there was a dramatic shift in tone in descriptions of Africans. Colonization in the twentieth century produced a new and enduring European obsession with African 'idleness'. *The Prevention of Idleness: The Labour Circulars*, published in South Africa in 1925, stated that

It is in the interests of the natives themselves for the young men to become wage earners, and not to remain idle in their reserves for a large part of the year.

The pamphlet goes on to make the case for the compulsory labour that the British colonial authorities were enforcing on black South Africans. The pamphlet acknowledges that compulsory labour is *not* beneficial, that it is in fact damaging to African people. Moreover it is noted that compulsory labour serves 'exclusively the interests of European settlers and private employers': the group who insist on the government keeping the wages below subsistence level. Despite this explicit awareness about the losers and the beneficiaries of compulsory labour, it continued to be enforced.

This deleterious system is presented as superior to the 'idleness' that the British claimed existed before it. This type of discourse can be identified as a precursor to today's conversations about 'development' on the African continent; a narrative that requires the pathologization of African cultures for its legitimacy. The real causes of poverty, those brought about under the policies of Structural Adjustments to Poverty Reduction Growth Facility (PRGF), an arm of the International Monetary Fund (IMF), are obscured.* Instead, African countries are deemed to be failing due to their inherently deviant natures. This agenda is, in part, the explanation for the mendacity that characterizes the portrayal of the African past.

The deeply ingrained 'truth' that black hair is too time-consuming,† does not make sense in an indigenous context. For the Yoruba, time was understood in relation to the task that had to be done. Until

---

* These policies impose harmful market liberalization on African countries, and adherence to them is the main condition for receiving debt relief. Governments are prevented from investing in national industries, and adequate spending on education and healthcare becomes impossible. These policies, in effect, make the concept of African 'independence' mythical.

† Even brilliant classic hair texts like *African Hairstyles* and *The History of the Afro Comb* use this type of language. Describing hairstyling as arduous has become a default setting.

European forms of capitalism took root, time for most people was your own. The day began at sunrise and ended at twilight. Each compound had a sundial to measure the periods in between. When the sun was not visible, the amount of work done, or other cues from nature – the cries of birds or the behaviour of certain animals – would provide the farmer with the information he needed.

The scholars Iyakemi Ribeiro and Amâncio Friaça describe the daily routine as made up of a mixture of labour activities, socializing, songs and religious acts. The day was defined by tasks to be accomplished, rather than by predetermined units of time.

The Yoruba operated according to a four-day week; the most popular god in a locality would mark the beginning of a week in that area. If we think about phrases like 'time is money', 'saving time' and 'buying time', it's apparent that time in the Western sense has been re-imagined as a commodity, which through purchase one 'owns' or 'possesses'. In *African Religions and Philosophy*, John Mbiti explains that in African cultures time was quite a different prospect, and as such was measured in different ways. It didn't matter if a hunting month lasted twenty-five days or thirty-five: the event of the hunting itself was privileged above a prescribed unit of time. Mbiti describes Western time* as something that must be 'utilized, sold or bought'; but in traditional African time, time has to be created or produced. In traditional African metaphysics, 'Man is not a slave of time; instead he "makes" as much time as he wants.'[28]

When time is not a commodity, not *possessing* the time to do your hair – especially where heavy emphasis was placed on well-presented, immaculately groomed hair – would be oxymoronic.

---

* Although this appropriation of time happened in Europe as well. We see the same processes in full force in Britain when universal education was introduced in 1870. The imperative behind this wasn't to create a nation of scholars, and it certainly wasn't to make society more equal. It was introduced to transform the children of artisanal workers and farmers into compliant factory and shop workers; teaching them to be punctual, docile and sober, instilling 'values' that could be used to coerce them into exploitative labour.

Black hair is not problematic or deviant. Depending on your way of life and your priorities it is not even 'time-consuming'. Certainly it grows the way it grows for a reason. The relatively sparse density of Afro hair, combined with its elastic helix shape, increases the circulation of cool air to the scalp and helps regulate body temperature. In addition, the dryness of Afro hair means that it remains springy, unlike hair with a straighter texture that becomes drenched in sweat causing it to stick to the neck and forehead.[29]

The time it takes to do Afro hair is, quite frankly, the time that is required to do it. And it is in this fact that a very powerful truth is revealed. Our hair continues to be a space in which the fault lines between an imposed European system and black bodies' resistance to that system are exposed and played out in real time. Our very bodies are positioned as seemingly at odds with the 'British values' imposed by colonialism. As such they are subject to regulatory procedures.

The idea that nothing exists alone is a cornerstone of African thought. The importance of the relationships *between things* is emphasized in African metaphysics. In contrast, British consumer culture located value and worth in the desire for the *consumption of things*. Aspiring to the lifestyle necessary to acquire such things was the central principle of this new 'civilization'.

The increasing monetization of African society, accompanied by the incentive to accumulate material objects for accumulation's sake alone, was evidence of civilization. This example of the 'Hottentots' of the Cape of Good Hope* is instructive:

English habits and English feelings seem to be rapidly gaining ground . . . The stores established at Bethelsdorp and at Theopolis must be extremely useful as, *by the artificial wants they create*, they excite the people to increased industry.[30] [my italics]

---

* Good Hope for some, perhaps, not so much for others.

Colonialism was essentially the creation of an infrastructure to facilitate and legitimize the theft of resources from the colonies, and for Europe to accrue the profits.*

Prior to the introduction of artificial wants and the requirement to pay crippling colonial taxes, African people had a lot more time to style their hair, an aspect of self-care that seemingly infuriated the British: 'The *idle* husbands put [their wives] upon braiding, and fettishing out their wooly hair (in which sort of ornament they are prodigious proud and curious), keeping them every day, for many hours together, at it.'[31]

I don't know about you, but a lifestyle of abundance that leaves me with more than ample time to get my hair did and chill with my homies sounds much more appealing than a world of running out of money ten days before pay day, direct debits, overdrafts, hour-long rush-hour commutes and the whole nine-to-five situation, but hey, that's what we call progress, right?

To meet the demands of the British Crown, African farmers had to seek unskilled, poorly paid wage employment. The Nigerian scholar A. G. Adebayo argues that any examination of the underdevelopment of Africa is incomplete without understanding

---

* That infrastructure has not been dismantled. If anything, it has been made more efficient. When the British prohibited the slave trade among British subjects in the region in 1807 they also began to lay the groundwork for the colonialism that was soon to follow. In 1861 the British annexed Lagos Island, establishing the Oil River Protectorate in 1884. British power in the region grew over the nineteenth century, but occupation wasn't official until 1885, when the leaders of Europe met to carve up the continent among themselves at the Berlin Conference, a process known colloquially as The Scramble for Africa. Lest there be any confusion regarding the nature of British interest from 1886 to 1899, much of the country was ruled by the Royal Niger Company as a commercial concern. In 1900 what was known as the Southern Nigeria Protectorate and the Northern Nigeria Protectorate transferred from company hands over to the Crown. Under Frederick Lugard, the two territories were amalgamated as the Colony and Protectorate of Nigeria. It was Lugard's wife Flora Lugard (née Shaw) who named the territory Nigeria. Today globalization, international trade, international (under) development, all continue to operate according to the same logic that Europe got on lock back in the day.

how taxation was used to uproot the people, extract their resources and remove from them not only a part of their income but also the investment capital they might have saved.[32]

As recently as 150 years ago, wage labour seemed both degrading and perverse to the people of what was about to become Nigeria. The schedule that most of us grudgingly accept today – starting work at a certain predetermined time (not of your own choice), eating at a predetermined hour dictated by a boss, finishing work at a regimented time (ordained from on high) – was seen by my great-greats as akin to slavery. It was considered anathema to work for a person who was not a blood relative. Compounding these affronts on freedom and autonomy, the British imposed fines for lateness and unauthorized absence. These were deducted from what were already meagre or 'starvation' wages.

THE INVENTION OF WOMEN

'But woah, steady on, Emma, African cultures are inherently oppressive, sexist and patriarchal.' This common, progressive-liberal concern is an almost knee-jerk response whenever I start to talk about gender in the African context. I'm curious, though; we've seemingly accepted that gender is a social construct, but if this is true wouldn't it would be constructed differently at different times as well as places? If we have accepted that it is a construct, why would we understand the Western category of 'woman' as universal and historically consistent?

We might consider the fact that the group that came to be known as 'women' during the colonial era were probably not historically conceived of as a cohesive group, united through a shared biology; or that, united now as 'women', this group's fate actually took a turn for the worse under the European administration.

The post-colonial scholar Walter Rodney writes that colonialism introduced a system whereby:

> Men entered the money sector more easily and in greater numbers than women, women's work became greatly inferior to that of men within the new value system of colonialism: men's work was 'modern' and women's was 'traditional' and 'backward'. *There-fore the deterioration in the status of African women was bound up with the consequent loss of the right to set indigenous standards of what work had merit and what did not.*[33] [my italics]

In *The Invention of Women*, Yoruba sociologist Oyèrónkẹ́ Oyěwùmí goes further, making the argument that gender was not an organizing principle in Yoruba culture. Accordingly, lineage and seniority were far more important than the presence or absence of a vagina in determining an individual's position in society. This argument is supported linguistically by the lack of gender in Yoruba pronouns and by the fact that Yoruba names can be used for both men and women. Among the various attacks women were now subjected to, wage labour was one that was hugely damaging.

The gender distinction noted by Rodney 'led to the perception of men as workers and women as non-workers and therefore appendages to men'.[34] This was dangerously misleading. African men, unlike their European counterparts, were paid a pittance, ensuring that women's labour was now more necessary than ever before, yet at the same time it was becoming newly devalued.

Wage labour demanded migration away from ancestral lands, to new colonial, commercial centres. This had a deleterious effect on the 'structure, cohesion and function of the family, the community, and interpersonal relationships'. As Oyěwùmí explains, women accompanied their husbands, moving away from their kin groups. That most powerful of resources – the chorus of 'mamas, grandmamas, aunts, cousins, sisters, neighbors, best girl friends' – was being disassembled.

The case of Madame Bankole, a subject in an ethnographic study of Yoruba migrant families, is illustrative:

> In 1949 she married . . . another Ijebu man . . . He was transferred
> frequently from place to place, and she went with him, changing
> her trade each time. From Warri in the Western Niger Delta she
> transported palm oil to Ibadan and re-sold it there to retailers.
>
> Then from Jos and Kano she sent rice and beans to a woman
> to whom she sublet her . . . stall, and received crockery in
> return that she sold in the North. She also cooked and sold
> food in the migrant quarters of those towns. From 1949 to
> 1962 she moved around with him.[35]

Beyond the apparent entrepreneurship that characterizes Yoruba business culture, we observe a dramatic change in Madame Bankole's status:

> Madame Bankole, has *become a wife*, an appendage whose
> situation was determined by her husband's occupation. The
> combination of male wage labour and migration produced a
> new social identity for females as dependents and appendages
> of men. For example, in spite of the fact that Madame Bankole
> was not dependent in economic terms, there was a perception
> of her dependency built into the new family situation. The
> 'anafemales' had moved from being aya to wife.[36]
>
> A corollary of women's exaggerated identity as wives was that
> other identities became muted. As couples moved away from kin
> groups, women's identity as offspring (daughters) and members of
> the lineage became secondary to their identities as wives. Though
> Madame Bankole retained a dominant pre-colonial occupation in
> Yorubaland, the fact that she had to fold up shop whenever her
> husband's job demanded shows that she and her occupation were
> secondary. The family itself was slowly being redefined as the
> man plus his dependents (wife/wives and children) rather than as
> the extended family including siblings and parents.[37]

In the changing colonial landscape, hairdressing was a trade that women on the move could practise in any new town, but this informal economy often represented a departure from the past. Niangi Batulukisi, a researcher of African design, explains:

> Without denying the skills of contemporary individuals, we have to emphasize that in the past there were no professional hairdressers like those who practise in the African cities of today. Among those who follow the old traditions, a person's choice of a coiffeur or coiffeuse is dictated by a friendship or family relationship, since giving someone the responsibility for your hair is an act of trust. (The fear that some of your clippings might fall into the hands of a person who wished you evil, and could use it to do you harm, justifies the greatest possible care in selecting the person who will do your hair.)
>
> In this tradition, the craft of hairdressing, which is practised by either sex, requires training with an experienced stylist. The young apprentices work only on children and on youngsters their own age; adults or children are worked on by other adults. The long styling session, lasting anywhere from several hours to several days, permits the stylist and the client to exchange private information, or to talk about the life of the village. A mother might instruct her marriageable daughter about her future role as a wife, and so on.[38]

GIFT EXCHANGES

Building on the work of the post-colonial scholar Gayatri Spivak, Joanne Sharpe proposed that 'Western intellectuals relegate "other", non-Western (African, Asian, Middle Eastern) forms of knowing' and knowledge acquisition to the 'margins of intellectual discourse' by dismissing them as myth or folklore.[39] Yet if we peek beyond the confines of European intellectual discourse, if we listen to the subaltern* speak, we might be surprised. In extensive research on indigenous African mathematics, the American mathematician Ron Eglash describes the 'egalitarian algorithms' that exist in African technologies. From here he makes an exciting proposal – *generative justice* – which offers an intriguing alternative to the distributive systems of both capitalism and state communism. While the name 'generative justice' might be new, the concept is ancient, and we need look no further than African hair culture for examples of how it operates.

Those on the political left continue to advocate top-down distributive approaches to manage resources, but many of these approaches are played out. Eglash suggests that in the last thirty years or so, new forms of social justice have started to emerge, and these can be understood as bottom-up systems. The parallel that exists between bottom-up, socially just approaches and the more communally orientated, non-monetized or semi-monetized African societies is fascinating. Considering gift exchanges in African societies, Eglash explains:

> Contemporary cases which draw on the idea of gift exchange include open source computing; where the . . . software of big corporations is replaced by code freely generated and distributed, or the food justice movement, or indeed the maker movement, which puts technologies such as 3D printing into the hands of lay people and also encompasses peer to peer distribution of music, art and other media, as well as grassroots activism for sexual diversity across the globe.[40]

---

* The concept of the subaltern was established through the work of the philosopher Antonio Gramsci. It was developed by Gayatri Spivak, whose ideas were further advanced in Joanne Sharp's *Geographies of Postcolonialism* (2008). Sharp proposed that Western intellectuals relegate non-Western knowledge to the peripheries and that, in order to be heard and known, the 'subaltern' who is the colonized or subjugated person must adopt Western ways of knowing, thought, reasoning and language. These processes mean that colonized subaltern people cannot express themselves other than by conforming to the colonizers' imposed norms.

The Divine Chocolate company makes for a creatively instructive case study. Many of you may be familiar with the Adrinka symbols used by the Akan of Ghana to represent the philosophies underpinning their traditional culture.

For example, the *funtunfunefu* below shows two crocodiles who share a single stomach. The symbol represents the fundamental gift-economy principle: 'By feeding you, I feed myself.' In 1993, an animist priest, Nana Frimpong Abebrese, organized local cocoa farmers according to the principles integral to Adrinka philosophy: they would operate as a collective in which the common pool of resources would benefit the group. After receiving a loan from the UK Fairtrade company Kuapa Kokoo Ltd (the 'good cocoa farmer'), Abebrese was able to provide twenty-two villages with weighing scales, tarpaulins and other basic equipment. Her mission was to empower low-income farmers, increase women's participation and develop environmentally friendly cultivation of cocoa. In 1998, the UK-based chocolate company Divine Chocolate was launched, with the *funtunfunefu* and *asase* symbols celebrated on the packaging. Kuapa Kokoo has been a huge success, with 65,000 members in around 1,400 villages. Profits from their 45 per cent ownership of Divine Chocolate are reinvested in village projects to provide water, health and education, as well as to work against the practice of child labour and to adapt to climate change.[41]

Rather than investing back into the communities and the

environment it exploited, the colonial system established by the British required women to work in unfavourable conditions in the informal economy, in order to sustain their families. Extractive systems such as the form of capitalism that began in the colonial era cannot operate without these 'generative processes', such as women's unacknowledged labour and the exploitation of the environment. Under capitalism, the cost of these generative forces remains invisible (until we experience a crisis like global warming and they can no longer be ignored).

SANKOFA*

Pliny the Elder said, 'There is always something new out of Africa.' Thousands of years later, the Yoruba Nobel Laureate Wole Soyinka urges us to remember the same: Africa 'has indeed a history, and a present of surprises', and these surprises not only 'extend our concept of human creativity, but illuminate many conundrums of human existence and destination'.[42] We can look to indigenous culture for innovative responses to contemporary issues.

African practices and beliefs may have been decimated, but some things, it would appear, are unvanquishable. Do not be fooled by the futuristic appearance of African hairstyles, or misled by the fact that they remain at the cutting edge of fashion. Many of the hairstyles we are talking about are ancient.

Yoruba art 'would stand comparison with anything which Ancient Egypt, Classical Greece and Rome, or Renaissance Europe had to offer'.[43] In the 1950s, cave paintings dating back to 3,000 BCE discovered in the Tassili Plateau of the Sahara depicted women with neat cornrows. Many hairstyles of Ancient Egypt closely resemble those still found in sub-Saharan Africa today, and we can

---

* *Sankofa* is another popular Adrinka symbol in Akan and subsequently many Afro-diasporic cultures. It means to take what was valuable from the past and repurpose it for the present.

see traditional Yoruba hairstyles featured in art and sculpture that is over 2,500 years old. If we observe the 2,000-year-old terracotta figures from the Nok civilization (an early Iron Age population found in the north of what is now Nigeria that vanished around 1,000 BCE), we find them again. Recognizable hairstyles are also visible on artwork produced in the mighty pre-colonial state of Benin.

Unlike the bronzes, these styles aren't going anywhere. In the 1960s the photographer and great chronicler of traditional Nigerian hairstyles J. D. 'Okhai Ojeikere lamented that by the twentieth century many traditional hairstyles were being replaced by wigs emulating European hair. However, the US Black Pride movement of the 1960s and '70s in many ways arrested this development. African returnees who had gone to college in the US came home sporting the Afros that were a defining feature of black life in the US. I have photographs of my father and his siblings (who attended the HBCU Morehouse college in Atlanta) rocking their 'fros back in Nigeria in the 1970s.

While weave might be dominant in Nigeria at the moment, nothing lasts for ever. Indeed, today, even more so than in the 1970s, trans-Atlantic exchanges are more about reconnection than rending apart, and the conversation around black hair is reaching a tipping point.

The images that flooded my Instagram feed in 2017 evoke memories of my childhood and my grandmother, who always wore traditional Yoruba braided hairstyles. As a wealthy, Western-educated Nigerian woman, I now read this as something of a radical act. It's far more common to see women of her status attempting to distance themselves from these styles, which were associated with being 'bush', primitive and unsophisticated, a far cry from the European ideal so many still aspire to.

In 2014, Chimamanda Adichie caused a storm in the blogosphere when she rocked *irun kiko*, a traditional threaded style, to

Black British activists at FEPAC in Nigeria (1977) wearing 'traditional' hairstyles.

the opening of *Half of a Yellow Sun*, the film version of one of her novels. It caused many Nigerian women to reconsider a style they had been conditioned to be ashamed of, at the same time introducing it to a whole new audience in the diaspora.

By 2016, the style had gone mainstream, sported by Beyoncé's dancers in her visual album *Lemonade*. A year later, her younger sister, Solange Knowles, released *A Seat at the Table*. It was to become her first No. 1 album, and its popularity was in no small

My grandmother in Atlanta, around 1980, holding one of my cousins.

part due to the hit single 'Don't Touch My Hair', in which Solange popularized a phrase many black girls are so familiar with, bringing it to a huge new audience. In the video to the single, Solange wears a style inspired by the *irun kiko* method.

A method of braiding or a style that is waning may enjoy a resurgence when it is adopted by later generations seeking to reconnect with oppressed traditions. Such styles are diverse, intricate and detailed, demonstrating the care, effort and significance that has been accorded to hairstyling throughout both time and geographical space.

Think about ancient/modern African hairstyles in comparison to old-fashioned European hairstyles. For Caucasian hair, styles from just a hundred years ago are period hairstyles – they look historic – not to mention styles that are hundreds of years or indeed, millennia old!

In traditional African understandings of time, the past is not necessarily seen as finished or dispensed with. Instead, the past is ever present, while the future is part of a feedback loop informing both the present and the past. Black art reflects this temporality. It is the source of the disregard for chronology that Toni Morrison displays in her work. It is the reason that the hairstyles worn by our ancestors still bang in 2018 and the reason they will bang in 3018.

With such long-standing antecedents, these hairstyling methods are unlikely to disappear (the end of the world notwithstanding). Adaptability is a defining feature of West African cultures and their diasporic descendants, an inherent tendency to be syncretic, to mix and blend. The ability to take what you are given and fuse it with what you've got, even in the most challenging of circumstances, explains the enduring appeal of so many black expressive forms. That is one of the reasons why so many cultural traditions whose genius is black in origin are copied and reproduced the world over, with frequently anodyne results. In the face of an onslaught lasting more than five centuries, West African cultural tropes have not only survived but have emerged as the engine driving much of Western popular culture. Although the origins are often obscured, peek a little further and you may find African roots.

SELF-CARE AND RECLAIMING MY TIME

The importance of having 'personal time' is now being widely embraced. The new emphasis on self-care represents a long-overdue recognition that a person's health and well-being is crucial. Healing from traumatic life experiences, eating properly, keeping fit, making time for personal grooming – none of these are extravagant or unreasonable aspirations.

'Reclaiming my time' is a phrase coined by Democratic politician Maxine Moore Waters, who was listed by *Time* magazine in 2018 as one of the hundred most influential people in the world.* She has been an outspoken critic of Trump, and many in the UK may have become familiar with her through the #impeachhim campaign, or the now iconic Reclaiming My Time. For those unfamiliar with the phrase, here's how it went down. On Thursday 27 July 2017 Waters questioned Treasury Secretary Steven Mnuchin on the topic of President Trump's ties to Russia. Mnuchin launched into a rambling response, attempting to placate Waters with empty platitudes and flattering words. Waters was having none of it. 'Reclaiming my time,' she interjected, and redirected Mnuchin to her question. Again and again she repeated it:

RECLAIMING MY TIME

The footage went viral.

Those three words had a resonance that went far beyond that room and became an invocation far greater than the sum of its parts. On one level, the exchange was an example of a senior black woman (one of only twelve who serve in the US Congress) exerting power over a white man as he tries to dupe her. Such a demonstration of institutional black power remains rare enough, and if the phrase had operated only on this level alone it would have been enough to account for its popularity.

But it runs deeper than that. The phrase alluded to the centuries during which white men have silenced black people, and black women in particular. Those three simple words were a subversion. They represented the reversal of the weight of generations of accumulated violence, of centuries of free black labour that still remain unpaid. Waters' three-word incantation is a symbolic reminder of exactly who is responsible for the debt that can never be repaid,

---

* Waters, a Democratic politician, is a high-profile advocate for social-justice issues ranging from opposing South Africa's apartheid regime to opposing the Iraq War and repeatedly calling out Donald Trump.

the sin that can never be atoned for. The simple phrase makes it clear – in no uncertain terms – to whom the debt is due. Waters condenses a huge and structural historic injustice into an allegorical three-word phrase that then plays out in the micro in an exchange between herself and Mnuchin. The result is gripping.

'Reclaiming my time' redirects us to what was once an abundance of time possessed by the people who would come to be known as Africans, and the subsequent repackaging of time according to the demands of the 24-hour clock, a distribution of time that serves the objectives of colonial exploitation and capitalist extraction.

'Reclaiming my time' is also a perfect point from which to reconsider African spiritual belief systems in which time is cyclical or repeating, concepts of time in which the unborn, the living and the ancestral exist in a perpetual cycle of communication. This is the basis of Afrofuturism, where the present informs the past and the future informs the present. Here, time flows in a direction different from the linear, finite understandings that underpin time in Judeo-Christian societies, where existence is divided between two distinct states of being, life and death, and you are offered the carrot of a (possible) afterlife if you play your cards right and conform to rules that reflect and serve the interests of Anglo-American patriarchal forms of morality and capital accumulation.

On a practical and basic level, reclaiming my time is rejecting a lifestyle that prevents us from doing our damn hair. Reclaiming my time is taking the time to practise self-care, time too often denied in a brutal world designed to grind us down.

On 23 January 1826, a group led by Captain Hugh Clapperton became among the first Europeans to gain access to the Yoruba kingdom of Oyo. Clapperton's descriptions are thought to be the first written European accounts of the interior of Yorubaland. What is most remarkable about them is the peace and order that Clapperton comments on. Today, Western embassies issue travel warnings to citizens wishing to visit Nigeria, emphasizing the risk of kidnap, theft and other forms of violence. Clapperton and his team were able to travel with an efficiency and ease that would be almost impossible today.

> I cannot omit bearing testimony to the singular and perhaps unprecedented fact, that we have already travelled sixty miles in eight days, with numerous and heavy baggage and about ten different relays of carriers, without losing so much as the value of a shilling public or private; a circumstance evincing not only somewhat more than common honesty in the inhabitants, but a degree of subordination and regular government which could not have been supposed to exist amongst a people hitherto considered barbarians.[44]

We have no way of knowing what might have happened in the continent had millions of the most active and able not been shipped away, if traditional family and kinship structures had not been decimated, and the people hadn't been uprooted from land which had for centuries provided for their needs. We do not know what might have developed if foreigners had not imposed a world of taxes and artificial wants, producing a new reality where scarcity replaced abundance. What might that land look like without the imposition of a system where working became necessary for survival but where there would never be enough work to meet the population's needs? Sadly, we do not know what 'Nigeria' – Flora Shaw's invention – might now look like, if it had never been thus named, or what might exist if the British hadn't quashed spiritual practices that were far more flexible, fluid and humanitarian than the didactic forms of Christianity which have since taken root. (Wakanda perhaps?)

In the cult classic text *The Undercommons: Black Study and Fugitive Planning*, Fred Moten and Stefano Harney remind us that there remains a huge debt to be paid. I am an advocate for reparations. While there is little that can compensate for the seismic cultural, economic and spiritual loss created by the transatlantic slave trade and subsequent events, reparations are necessary in going someway towards restoring balance. However, reparations should not be an endpoint, and as such I am fascinated by Moten and Harney's case for refusal, a refusal of the very values of the system we have had imposed upon us. I'm excited by the idea that real power lies not in asking, or even in demanding, but in refusing: 'Refuse that which was first refused to us, and in this refusal, reshape desire, reorient hope, reimagine possibility, and do so separate from the fantasies nestled into rights and responsibilities.'[45]

This first refusal, followed by a recalibration, is work that needs to be done urgently. We need to re-imagine the way we think about progress, about modernity, about success, about development, about 'civilization'. We need to think about the way we frame demands for inclusion and representation and seriously rethink the way we attribute – or more often *do not* attribute – value to indigenous knowledge systems. And yes, we need to reject many of the beauty standards we subscribe to, those that privilege lighter skin, thinner noses or 'good hair'.

One of the easiest ways to demonstrate our nascent freedom is to wear our natural hair not only in homage to what it announces externally, but moreover to wear it in recognition of the more internal work, demonstrating our engagement with the history and the knowledge encoded and transmitted via braided hairstyles.

These hairstyles emerged out of a cultural and material world in which black people were central, a world that was open and accommodating of difference, a courtesy that has rarely been afforded back. Our unique hair texture allows us to be the living embodiments of a complex visual language, the scope of its concerns social, technological, philosophical and spiritual – a visual language that was designed to be transmitted by our features. That integration of the metaphysical and the physical is the reason why, when we wear these styles, it is with a finesse that Kim, Kylie, Iggy, Becky and co. can only dream of, try as they might to claim it as their own, try as they might.

3
Shhhh . . . Just Relax

Beauty shops
could have been
a hell-of-a-place
      to ferment
            a . . . . revolution.[1]

Not so long ago I was on my way to the Black Cultural Archives in Brixton. When I emerged from the Underground somebody tapped on my shoulder. I turned around and saw a black woman in her early forties wearing a platinum-blonde wig.

'Your hair is beautiful, natural – it's good to see.'

My heart sings. I am still overjoyed by such encounters. I will always rejoice in the camaraderie of black people celebrating one another. *Especially* when it's in mutual appreciation of features we've been conditioned to detest. The fact that these exchanges happen regularly – with both men and women – feels like something of an antidote to the negativity that characterized my childhood experiences of my hair.

This positivity couldn't be further from the culture I grew up in, where my hair was an object of ridicule. Oh, how I longed for straight hair! Yet while I remember these feelings intellectually, the *feeling* of those feelings fades with each passing year.

The society I come from is one in which speaking positively about oneself was not done. Now, I'm all about self-deprecation. I've spent far too long in Ireland and the UK not to be. And in our current climate of rampant narcissism, there is much to be said for keeping those tendencies in check. Yet this was an environment where cultural norms violently suppressed anyone having 'notions' about themselves. But because it was also an environment characterized by a pervasive and constant refrain of black inferiority, there was little I could do to contest the negativity I was bombarded with. Navigating the tension between the two and developing a healthy sense of self-worth seemed impossible. While my mother was not one to offer much praise (to my face – wouldn't want anyone getting notions), she did drill it into me to walk straight with my shoulders back. As a result, I had really great posture when I was younger. Apparently, even this was a problem: *Who does that young wan think she is? Does she think she's better than us?* Eventually, my shoulders slumped accordingly.

These days, however, I'm struck by the distance between that attitude and the imperatives in black popular culture with their emphasis on and encouragement of being a 'queen' , where regal bearing is recognized and applauded, where your glow is not seen as threatening; on the contrary, it enhances the shine of your whole squad.

We can see the antecedents of this in Yoruba culture. When I hear a family's *oriki*, they are singing of the greatness of a particular family but not necessarily to the detriment of any other family. Our greatness is not at the expense of yours.* It's a phenomenon that can be observed in a mother's traditional morning greeting to her child: the child has a short *oriki* of their lineage sung to them when they wake up. This serves two main purposes. Firstly, it grounds the child within a trajectory of the achievements of their forebears. Secondly, it gears them up for whatever tasks they have to accomplish in that day. To me, it seems the most beautiful and profound type of affirmation.

So, yeah, my hair look dope. I'll keep going. It is big, thick and abundant. It's also keeping me warm on this bone-numbingly cold

* I'm not trying to romanticize blackness; we all know that petty jealousies exist between people regardless of race. Nonetheless, there is generally a more acceptable culture of 'bigging yourself up', and this stands in stark contrast to the self-flagellation expected of one in the Dublin of my childhood. I remember one of the worst slags at the time was being labelled a 'shaper', someone who 'threw shapes' – basically, anybody who walked around in a way that was perceived to be showing off.

winter's day and it smells like a dream. The scent of shea butter, incense, sage and perfume linger; it's like a magnet for good scents.

Gassed from the compliments to my hair, I reach the archive. Excitedly, I dig into the first box I have asked for and there it is, a headline from a 1990 edition of *Afro Hair and Beauty*.

WHO LETS YOU DOWN?
YOU OR YOUR HAIR?

Anxiety grips me. All the self-loathing from my childhood is thrown into sharp relief. Afro hair may well still be stigmatized today, but I'm instantly reminded that a huge cultural shift has occurred since this article was written. What follows is a battle-ground of chemically ruined hair. It describes a world of shame and punitive measures, one I recognize only too well.

The disciplinary thread that often runs through black cultures can be at least partially located in black people historically having to prove not only their worth but their humanity. This attitude of 'discipline and punish' went beyond haircare, regulating the entirety of my being. The condition of my hair then couldn't be more different from that of the radiant crown that adorns my head now; the self-doubt that plagued me then couldn't be further from the assuredness I now feel in being myself. But moments like these remind me that I am still vulnerable.

Despite all this, equating natural hair with good and straight hair with bad is not helpful. As Willie Coleman reminds us, some-what affectionately:

> Used to be
> ya could meet
> a whole lot of other women
> sittin there
> along with hair frying
> spit flying
> and babies crying.

Because, if I'm honest, I remember 'hair frying' with something approaching a tiny degree of affection myself. That very particular smell of freshly relaxed hair, the sizzle as the straighteners finished off the look – I can't deny that it reminds me of how fly, how unstoppable I would feel sashaying out of that salon. The power of Coleman's poem exists in the tension between the pleasure and the pain of relaxing our hair. I appreciate that she challenges the binary system that defines natural hair as 'conscious' or, in more recent parlance, 'woke', while straightened hair is imagined as the default setting for self-hating, internalized oppression. This distinction is not as obvious as it seems. Within a traditional West African aesthetic, the idea of artifice was often highly valued, and we know that hair was rarely, if ever, left out in anything resembling a natural Afro. The range of styles and textures that can be achieved with Afro hair – from relaxer, to weave, to intricate braiding patterns – is evidence of the expertise and creativity that black people, particularly black women, have demonstrated through their hair over millennia.

The extent to which hairstyles conform to European beauty standards is of course not immaterial, but we should also keep in mind that an enduring characteristic of African cultural practices is their seemingly inherent ability to adapt responsively to changing circumstances and the new realities of the environments in which they take place.

This Afro-diasporic cultural tendency does not merely copy, rather it innovates, melding the old with the new and creating something entirely original in the process. Black women might wear their hair straight but that fact alone does not manifest a slavish reproduction of European aesthetics.* The hair may be worn in gravity-defying constructions or in unnatural colours. Often the price paid for this innovation is the label of 'ghetto', until

---

* While I wish to bring some nuance to the conversation about relaxer on one level, it remains impossible not to attend to the realities of assimilation and conformation to European ideals that are also at play.

it is appropriated and becomes alchemically redefined as high fashion.

The temporary decline in black American hair salons, brought about by the 'natural' look of Black Power, may have represented the loss Coleman speaks of, but these salons were not the first time in history that black women came together in service of dressing their hair. We know that women gathered to braid their hair in spaces that functioned similarly to the hair salons, where their descendants would meet centuries later to straighten their hair. Whatever the style, whatever the social convention or prevailing aesthetic, hairstyling has been an essential component of a strong visual language that has been passed down through the generations across Africa and her diaspora.

But what exactly is it that we are talking about when we speak of relaxed hair? It's an innocuous term for a brutal process. This use of euphemistic, gentle language for practices that are anything but sets the tone for how hair and beauty products would be sold to black people over the course of the century since the relaxer was invented.

Despite having my hair chemically relaxed for about fifteen years, I knew or cared little about what was going on on my head. Although I had an awareness that it was toxic and associated with multiple and significant health problems, I remained undeterred. I knew that chemical burns were a recurring reality. After almost every relaxer I would be left with at least a couple of scabs on my scalp. But these were almost badges of honour, testimony to the fact that the relaxer had taken. Because I associated these scabs with straighter, softer hair I did not perceive them as negative. I, like most of my peers, conveniently ignored the links between cancer, fertility issues and the development of fibroids and the chemicals used in straighteners. The cognitive dissonance required to do so horrifies me now, but the stories that we construct to justify all manner of violence we perpetuate against ourselves (and others) are frighteningly powerful. Nonetheless, I'm going to turn now to look at a process whose details I chose to overlook for all those years.

IT'S A DOG'S LIFE

In 1909, Garrett Augustus Morgan was in his Cleveland, Ohio, workshop experimenting with a solution to ease friction in the sewing machines in his tailor's shop. When Morgan's wife called him to dinner, he unthinkingly wiped his hands clean on a piece of cloth. Returning to his workshop, he was astounded to discover that the fabric was standing straight up! Curiosity piqued, he applied the mixture to the fur of a neighbour's dog.

Rover was transformed. Lo and behold, the first documented evidence of a hair relaxer being used! Not the most auspicious of origin stories, but it is what it is.

Morgan established the G. A. Morgan Hair Refining Company, and the wealth generated from his hair-straightening business allowed him to go on to invent the gas mask, the traffic signal (that's right, invented by a black dude) and the self-extinguishing cigarette.

The technical term for the process we refer to as hair relaxing or perming (yes, just like perms for white hair, but the intention here is to straighten, not to make curly) is 'lanthionization'. Relaxers deform the elliptical shape of the hair, breaking down the chemical bonds of the hair shaft and restructuring it in a new way. Hair can be relaxed professionally in a hair salon or domestically with over-the-counter relaxer kits. Similarly to applying hair dye, the hair that has been treated grows away from the scalp, requiring a retouch every eight to twelve weeks so that the regrowth is the same texture. Section by section, the solution is applied to the base of the hair shaft with a little brush. The 'cooking' process alters the hair's texture by damaging its protein structure. As a result, over time, the hair can become weakened, resulting in brittleness and breakage. Relaxing has been known to trigger alopecia in many, which results in hair loss and baldness.

Next, the hair is rinsed. Different formulas exist, but the relaxers must be alkaline so the hair is neutralized or acidified with a suitable shampoo immediately afterwards. Hair conditioner is important, as the process strips the hair of its natural oils, again contributing to potential problems.

Cosmetic products are not strictly regulated. As a result, many brands of hair relaxer contain phthalates, which are listed in a number of US states as chemicals of high concern, because they may disrupt endocrine (hormone) systems and can have adverse effects on development and reproduction.

I didn't know any of this when I was pregnant, but I do remember thinking, *Now feels like the time to quit this mess.* I also recall my stylist discouraging me from doing so. She explained that if there was ever a time I needed to feel good about my appearance it was now. Disturbing advice and a clear example of the way in which straight hair is associated with confidence and self-esteem.

THERE AIN'T NO BLACK IN THE UNION JACK

By the mid-twentieth century the US had a long-established history of hair straightening, but the situation in Britain was somewhat different. Relaxers weren't readily available here until after the post-war Caribbean migration. Beryl Giddens, an early migrant, recalls that when she told her uncle about her plans to migrate from Guyana to Britain in the 1950s his primary advice was hair-related: 'walk with your pressing comb'. At this time, Beryl explains,

> There was nowhere you could have gone into to have your hair done in a white salon . . . they could not even comb our hair.

And they were so scared of it, they said, 'We can't do your hair,' and often they never tried, and so I had people who used to come, you see the girls now cutting their hair off, that's just what they resorted to, just cut.

By 1955 a Trinidadian migrant, Carmen England, née Maingot, who later helped set up the Notting Hill Carnival, had opened what is listed in the *Hairdressers' Journal* as probably the first black hair salon in Britain.

England's 'straightening salon' was located in salubrious South Kensington in the Royal Borough, and catered to a well-heeled crowd. The emphasis was on straight hair, but England allegedly remained committed to the hot comb (the non-chemical alternative for straightening), because it required more constant upkeep than chemicals and was therefore arguably more lucrative.[2]

Migration from the Caribbean continued, and with it demand rose, especially for salons that specialized in chemical relaxers. In 1957 another Trinidadian, Winifred Atwell, opened Atwell's in Railton Road, Brixton, south London, where much of the growing black population was concentrated. When she was growing up, Atwell's family had owned a pharmacy and Winifred had to follow in the family trade. Yet, in addition to studying pharmacy, Winifred was also a gifted pianist. In 1946 she moved to London, where she had gained a place at the Royal Academy of Music. By the time she opened her salon she was a celebrity. Atwell was the first black person to sell a million records in Britain, and her stardom was further solidified in 1954 when she became the first black person in the UK to have a No. 1 hit. This she achieved with the twee 'Let's Have Another Party'. It exemplified the type of sanitized, non-threatening output that white audiences of the day demanded from black performers, and Atwell became a huge star.

The *Hairdressers' Journal* covered the opening of the salon, remarking that a huge throng of Winifred's fans congregated outside in the rain for hours, chanting: 'We want Winnie,' while local traffic ground to a halt.[3]

Atwell's high-profile performances (the Queen and Princess Margaret were among her legions of fans) demanded professional hairdressing. Following one hair-related disaster after another, she decided to open her own salon. Before long, the entrepreneurial Atwell had launched Opus, her own range of hair-straightening products and cosmetics. She even manufactured a range of stockings for those with darker skin. By 1960 Atwell was successful enough to have upgraded from Brixton to the rarefied atmosphere of Mayfair. Her new salon was situated on New Bond Street and counted among its neighbours the famous Vidal Sassoon.[4] However, by 1967, as tastes in music changed and her popularity waned, Atwell decided to move to Australia, where she still enjoyed widespread popularity.

Australia had at the time an openly racist immigration policy, so it might seem unusual that a black woman would willingly move there. The *Sunday Mirror* reported on the news:

> Pianist Winifred Atwell has been given permission to settle down in Australia as an immigrant. She has been told this officially in spite of the country's 'White Australia' policy. An Australian immigration official said yesterday that she had been granted residence because she was 'of good character and had special qualifications'. Immigration Minister Mr Phillip Lynch said: 'We will not stand in the way of an international artist of such repute.'[5]

In the 1950s there was a significant rise in the informal market for black hairstyling, but this was largely in the hands of untrained individuals. When it comes to braiding, in my experience it is those without 'formal' hairdressing training who have achieved the most outstanding results. However, when it comes to the application of chemicals, the reverse holds true. By the time I moved to the UK I had experienced way too many nightmare scenarios of perms applied over kitchen sinks to go anywhere but to the most certified of salons. Back then, people didn't have the same choices.

Much like the rest of society, the British hairdressing world of the 1950s and '60s was openly racist. Many salons couldn't cater for or simply refused to treat black hair. Such decisions were generally justified by the argument that a black clientele might be off-putting to other customers. Salon segregation continued but, as the years progressed, excuses became more coy. Racism was rampant, but its agents were increasingly reluctant to admit it. However, cartoons such as this 1963 beauty from the *Hairdressers' Journal* leave one in little doubt of popular attitudes at the time.[6]

The fashion of the 1950s and early '60s was defined by straightening. Whether straight hair was to be achieved by hot press or chemical straightener, both methods had potentially dire

"Don't cut too near the bone!"

consequences in the hands of untrained professionals. To overcome this knowledge deficiency, in 1958, Roy Lando, a Jamaican man who had trained in the US, set up a salon and training school. Lando offered six-month courses leading to a Diploma in Hairdressing. The industry continued to expand, and by 1967 The Mamore School of Hairdressing claimed to be the largest in Britain training black hairdressers. The Mamore School further distinguished itself by training both black and white students.[7]

Until the 1980s there were a good variety of black companies both manufacturing and distributing their own products. Unlike today, the black hair industry in the UK was primarily in black hands. Jamaican-born 'Len' Dyke and Dudley Dryden's Dyke & Dryden was one such successful black British business. However, like all the others, Dyke & Dryden was eventually overwhelmed – in its case by American competitors – and finally sold out to Illinois-based Soft Sheen in the 1990s.

Today, the lucrative black hair business is almost entirely dominated by South Asian men. While the reasons behind this are multiple, one of the biggest cited is retail infrastructure. South Asian businesses were well established and able to transfer their business model to take over the hair-care market. This allowed them to buy in bulk, facilitating a monopolization of the market and effectively driving out competitors.

Aesthetically, until very recently the tyranny of straightness dominated. The expectation was that even the merest suggestion of frizz, the sight of a wave or, God forbid, a curl, needed to be smoothed out. As recently as the mid-noughties textured hair still evoked adjectives such as 'frizzy' and 'wild' and was felt to require the type of taming that most brands – from Shea Moisture, to Mixed Chicks or indeed Madam C.J. Walker – continue to instruct us to comply with. But until the natural-hair movement, the pressure was almost by default to present a sleek facsimile of whiteness.

As Susan Bordo writes:

> Every transformation on [TV shows] *The Swan* and *Extreme Makeover* includes a mandatory straightening for the black contestants. Late-night and early-morning infomercials for ceramic wands and miracle straightening lotions feature emotional before-and-afters of both black and white women with tousled and 'natural' hairstyles miraculously transformed into sheets of sleek and shine.
>
> What is most incredible about these commercials is the women's reactions. They weep and speak of miserable lives redeemed, of dreams of beauty realized, of nothing short of deformity corrected, salvation achieved. Having straight hair has achieved a trans-racial beauty status.[8]

Until very recently, the message was loud and clear: you could be black and beautiful (that was just about permissible), but you could not have tightly coiled Afro hair and be one of the beautiful people.

DAMNED IF YOU DO, DAMNED IF YOU DON'T

The politics surrounding black people and hair straightening are characteristically contradictory. In *Hair Story*, Ayana Byrd and Lori Tharps discuss the fact that early approximations of European hair – as a type of performance of respectability politics – did little to influence white opinion favourably. It often had quite the opposite effect:

> The free Black populations sprinkled about in cities like Boston and Philadelphia were wont to wear the same fashions and hairstyles as their White contemporaries, only to find themselves ridiculed and satirized in the press, in the theatres and on the streets. Blacks were actually accused of being pretentious in their adherence to White fashion standards.[9]

Shane White and Graham White note the prevalence of this type of attitude:

> If unkempt hair seemed vaguely offensive to whites, hair that was groomed and elaborately arranged must also have seemed out of place, suggesting, as Gwendolyn Robinson has pointed out, 'an attention to cosmetic detail only permitted by the enjoyment of a free and independent status.' This impression of unreadable signs and ambiguous meanings can only have been strengthened when blacks dressed, as they often did, in ways that whites considered inappropriate. Their thick hair and dark skin must have seemed to clash discordantly with the items of formerly expensive clothing and cast-off military apparel that slaves were sometimes able to acquire. Hair shaped like a fashionable wig must have looked even more out of place when combined with an ensemble of shabby, nondescript garments and a vocabulary of gesture and bodily movement whose meanings whites could not easily decipher . . . [European Americans'] confusion at the appearance of blacks could easily be displaced into ridicule, a patronizing mockery of black pretensions and lack of 'taste'. What whites failed to detect were the signs of an emerging African American culture, a series of borrowings and blendings that, always changing over time, at least obliquely challenged the hegemony of blacks' oppressors.[10]

Centuries later, the white aesthetic rejection of relaxed hair remained. Going to the School of African and Asian Studies (SOAS) to study African Studies, I had mistakenly assumed there might be something of a black cultural life at the university. For the most part, my cohorts were of the white-hippy variety. Coming from Ireland, I was of course intimate with white people, but this tea-drinking, poi-swinging, drum-playing, often dreadlocked variety was new to me. Despite their affected lack of pretension, their privilege was palpable and, although I didn't have the language to articulate it at the time, their gap years in African countries and in India made *them* seem like the experts and me like the ignorant Westerner. It was really disorientating. In truth, I didn't even really want to be there. I had originally applied to Spelman, the all-girls historically black college and university (HBCU) in Atlanta. These institutions were established in the late 1880s to facilitate the education of black students denied access to white institutions. Alas, it wasn't to be; unable to afford the international tuition fees, SOAS was plan B outta Dodge.

SOAS social life certainly didn't quite live up to my dreams of becoming a cheerleader on an all-black campus, but one of the things moving to London did offer me was hair options. Once I got there I seized the opportunity to do two things: 1. Date lots of cute black boys (had to make up for those lost years in Ireland, didn't I? Jk.) and 2. Get my hair properly straightened. I steered clear of the local salons, heading straight for the boujie west London variety, where the stylists prided themselves on achieving mobility for the hair.* For those who've relaxed their hair, you know the world of difference that exists between the rigid facsimile of European hair and the fluid, swish-swish achieved when it's done by an expert and set properly afterwards. Now I certainly did not have the money to live that life, but I would forgo anything to manufacture it. To my mind, it was comparable to a necessary medical treatment needed to keep a chronic condition in check.

Imagine my surprise when my white-hippy peers pretty much unanimously slammed my hair. I mean, they were far from my target audience but I still found their responses interesting: 'Oh, no, Emma, it looks so much better out!' Say what? Let's bear in mind that at this stage I didn't have the first clue how to care for or maintain my natural hair, so that shit was a mess. Nonetheless, its appearance elicited countless assertions about how cool it looked.

And this was strange to me. Would they tell a white person that their tangled, uncombed hair looked great? Unlikely. Is it something to do with a desire for the exotic, with wanting to see

---

* The best had been trained at Splinters, a renowned black hair salon in Mayfair, where in the 1980s the great and the good of black society had their hair done.

difference, whether, objectively, it looks good or not? Or perhaps it is informed by the way the Afro conforms to a Western rather than an African aesthetic, one that would be especially appealing to white hippies. Speaking about the fate of the Afro in the 1960s and '70s, Kobena Mercer explains:

> The Afro operated on terrain already mapped out by the symbolic codes of the dominant white culture. The Afro not only echoed aspects of romanticism but shared this in common with the counter-cultural logic of white youth in the 1960s. From the Beatles' mop tops to the hairy hippies of Woodstock, white subcultures of the 1960s expressed the idea that the longer you wore your hair, some-how the more 'radical' and 'right-on' your lifestyle or politics.[11]

But while rich-kid hippies might approve, there exist sanctions in the mainstream world for hairstyles that are too black. Often it can seem like a lose–lose situation. Almost as though the world is racist. So, the moral of this story is: DO YOU BOO. Black and mixed-race people exist in a system that has been designed with our marginalization as central to its operating logic. It almost doesn't matter what we do. Being a woman who is mixed, who is black, who is Irish, whatever way I choose to live my life, no matter what way I choose to present myself, somebody – and this I can guarantee – has a problem with it, has a problem with me.

The comments are as staggering as they are contradictory, but I've heard them all. In different contexts I've been told I'm too black, I'm too white, I'm too stuck-up, I'm too light-skinned, I think I'm too nice, I'm too posh, I'm too street, I'm too Irish, I'm not Irish enough, blah blah fuckin blah. The best option is to do whatever feels authentic to me. I see no need to conform to any limited definition. There is a great freedom in that. So I just do me, whatever feels right. And so should you!

Yet I remain aware that my freedom to say any of this – let alone put it into action – is in large part facilitated by the sacrifices, work and efforts of those who went before me.

Structural inequalities remain, but in many ways these are obscured by gains in social freedom, particularly in terms of creative expression for (certain sections of certain) minorities. As long as we situate our cultural production within the terms of engagement of market relations, and while our identities remain commodifiable, as long as our contestations can be made into content and be absorbed into the status quo, many of us can, for the most part, continue within that delineated boundary to do what we please.

But even during what were at least perceived as far more socially restrictive times there have always been black people who have dared to live by their own rules, who have carved out communities of unimaginable possibilities for themselves, often at the risk of potentially huge social sanctions.

BLACK HEIR

If I close my eyes I can practically smell the perfumed air: aftershave, whisky, pomade and cigar smoke combine in a heady concoction. I'm in a darkly panelled room. It's packed. The great and the good of the black cultural renaissance converge alongside rogues, royalty, waifs and strays, brought together by chance, new opportunities and a sense of adventure. Chandeliers diffuse light throughout the room, highlighting multi-hued blackness: tawny yellows, golden browns and midnight blues. Lean figures strike modish poses, oblique against the plush furnishings. Important allegiances form and dissolve, transforming the political, literary, sexual and racial landscape for evermore.

In the smoky atmosphere hard edges soften, as do strict moral codes. Glamour is non-negotiable. Honey-tongued men dressed for heartbreak whisper into willing ears framed by sharply marcelled waves. Cupid-bow lips issue assent between insouciant puffs on cigarette holders. Anything can happen and everything often does. The new strains of jazz – the soundtrack of the decade – infuse proceedings. This is hip. This is where it's at! Bold and beautiful, and black and brave. Harlem in the 1920s. The centre of the universe. What a time to be alive!

If I could be reborn at any point in modern history, it would be the Harlem Renaissance, a period when an explosion of black literary and cultural talent was ushered into being, not least by the combined energies of an earlier group of educated black professionals known as the Talented Tenth.

Yet these days I am a little less naïve than I once was. The thing about elites is that they are, as a result of privilege and stratification, often comprised of snobs. And I tend to find elite pretentions insufferable.

The Talented Tenth believed that if the world could bear witness to their refinement the result would be universal social acceptance for all black people. Ensuring access to these rights for themselves would eventually extend to the other (socially inferior) 90 per cent of black life. W. E. B. Du Bois, who coined the phrase 'Talented Tenth', was a huge advocate for the arts, particularly literature, understanding it as one of the most powerful tools to demonstrate the positives of African-American cultural life.

Before long, an industrious group of individuals were establishing and supporting an array of literary initiatives, events and awards. African-American publications came on board. Wealthy whites, in thrall to the earthy delights of Harlem, got involved as patrons, while networks emerged between black literary talents and the bohemian white Greenwich Village writers.

It worked. From this environment there emerged an outpouring of stellar black creative energy. The era produced writers including Langston Hughes, Nella Larson, Zora Neale Hurston, Countee Cullen, Jean Toomer and Claude McKay. To this day, the period remains associated with a multitude of beautiful and compelling African-American literary works.

Prior to the renaissance, Du Bois had written *The Souls of Black Folks* (1903), a seminal text in articulating the black experience of dislocation in the West. He famously writes:

The Negro is a sort of seventh son, born with a veil, and gifted with second-sight in this American world, a world which yields him no true self-consciousness, but only lets him see himself through the revelation of the other world. It is a peculiar sensation, this double-consciousness, this sense of *always looking at one's self through the eyes of others*, of measuring one's soul by the tape of a world that looks on in amused contempt and pity.[12]

Yet despite its noble aims, accusations of elitism and colourism plagued the movement. Critics ranged from the working-class Jamaican activist Marcus Garvey to members of the in-crowd itself. Langston Hughes challenged what he saw as an assimilationist attitude and agitated to change the tone and direction.

Du Bois himself became far more radical as time went on. A committed communist, he was one of the most prominent advocates of black liberation, not just in the US but globally. Du Bois is recognized as the father of Pan Africanism and was hugely influential on post-independence African leaders such as Kwame Nkrumah, the first president of Ghana. In fact, hounded by the American authorities, Du Bois would spend his final years in self-imposed exile in Ghana, where he passed away on 27 August 1963, the eve of Martin Luther King's legendary 'I Have a Dream' speech.

While these contestations of Hughes and others were to a degree effective, the Harlem Renaissance remained a culture extremely aware of skin shade and hair texture, with entry into its upper echelons (with some notable exceptions) often predicated upon conforming to the light-skinned/good-hair gang. Yet here, as ever, the politics remained complicated and at times contradictory. While features that were the product of mixed ancestry were prized, there was a stigma associated with recently identifiable 'race mixing', for example having a white parent. It remained more desirable to have acquired such features from light-skinned parents (which required mixing further back) than via one black and one white parent. While evidence of 'mixing' was the recipe for beauty and success, mixing that was too recent was distasteful.

At the centre of this decadent and image-conscious world was a glamorous young heiress and socialite called A'Lelia Walker. Her parties were legendary, providing a safe and discreet environment where the scene's brightest stars could get up to get down. Membership was a diverse cross-section of black life and inclusive of many men and women who would today be described as queer.

Despite the systemic violence and racism that continued post-emancipation, the official abolition of slavery in the US in 1865 created economic opportunities previously unimaginable for any-body black. Thus, in the early twentieth century, we begin to see the emergence of the first black millionaires.

Black heirs (excuse the pun) were thin on the ground in the first place, but for a young black woman to have inherited such fabulous wealth as A'Lelia did was simply unheard of. The source of her fortune? Black hair, of course. Vast creative energy is poured into black hair and its cultural expression. Du Bois (who himself had wavy, almost straight hair) described Negros as 'always looking at one's self through the eyes of others'. Chemical hair straightening was seen as an example of this tendency and one of the most pro-nounced displays of internalized oppression. Yet it was also one of very few avenues that could provide financial liberation to black women at a time when such opportunities were practically non-existent. With all the business acumen of the West African marker traders she was descended from, A'Lelia's mother, the famous Madam C.J. Walker, had identified a gap in the market and made a financial killing.

Madam was a formidable figure, a self-made black female mil-lionaire at a time when pretty much all conceivable odds were stacked against her. She is eulogized as the mother of black com-mercial haircare, as well as the first self-made American female millionaire. Yet evidence suggests that the real mother of black commercial haircare, the woman who inspired Madam herself, is someone whose name remains far less familiar. It was Annie Turn-boe Malone, and she was Madam Walker's former employer.

What is the truth? Was Madam Walker a shrewd opportunist whose dizzying rise to fame and riches remains firmly mired in accusations of dishonesty? Her staggering achievements and entre-preneurial acumen cannot be denied. Her rags-to-riches narrative is kept alive by family descendants, namely great-great-granddaughter A'Lelia Bundles, a television executive and writer named after her socialite great-grandmother.

But Walker cut her teeth as one of Annie Malone's agents, just prior to setting up shop herself. Both her 'wonderful hair-grower' and her business model bore little difference from the products and model of Malone's hugely successful Poro Company. These details are not emphasized in her PR-friendly legacy. However, writing in the *New York Review of Books*, Jill Nelson notes that it is sus-pected that Madame 'met Edmund L. Scholtz, proprietor of the Scholtz Drug Company in Denver, who offered to analyze the ingredients in Pope-Turnbo's formula and suggested that, with a few minor changes, she could create her own product line'.[13]

While Malone might have been in many ways the originator, Walker was arguably superior when it came to marketing. As Nel-son continues, 'what distinguished Walker was her aggressive use of almost any occasion, public or private, as an opportunity for sales and publicity.' In a precursor to the personality-driven mar-keting of today, in which YouTubers, bloggers and influencers sell their life stories, part of Walker's genius was to use her own life as the central point of her marketing strategy.

Her ability to self-mythologize (in contrast to the far more reti-cent Annie) was pivotal to the success of her brand. The packaging on Walker's products utilized astonishing before-and-after pic-tures of herself, her short Afro hair elevated to the holy grail: those sleek, flowing locks – that 'good hair'.

The fact that Walker, a dark-skinned woman with unambig-uously African features, had achieved such miraculous results also

went a long way to creating faith in the powers of her product. However, the power of mixed ancestry and 'good hair' was perhaps even more potent. A'Lelia did not have children and therefore there was no heir to their great fortune. The problem was solved through A'Lelia's adoption of thirteen-year-old 'Fairy' Mae Walker, the 'perfect walking advertisement: for Madam's hair products'. The circumstances of exactly how or when the Walkers met Mae are not known, but her grandmother, whom she frequently visited, lived in the same neighbourhood. A'Lelia Bundles says that it was 'Fairy Mae's braids – long thick ropes that reached below her waist – that had caused Madam Walker to notice her'.[14] Mae was a 'bright and curious child' whose impoverished family could not afford for her to continue her education. 'With Madam Walker's interest, however, it seemed that her hair – an inky version of Rapunzel's locks – would provide a path from poverty.'[15] Fairy Mae's looks were a marketing coup. As Bundles explains, she was not 'delicately featured or light-skinned', with the 'looks favoured by the black elite'. But if she had been, she would certainly have been less appealing to the masses of 'ordinary' women C.J. Walker was targeting. Like most black people in the

Americas, Mae was of mixed ancestry, but in her case it was more apparent in her hair texture than her complexion. Although Fairy Mae was dark-skinned, her grandmother was a 'mulatto' and her grandfather half Cherokee, his own father a 'full blood Cherokee Indian'. The result of this mixed heritage was 'beautiful . . . heavy crinkly hair that made people stare, sometimes with admiration, sometimes with envy'.[16] As Jill Nelson writes, in adopting her, A'Lelia had promised Fairy Mae's mother that they would see to her education, but the demands of displaying her most prized asset, her long thick hair, were such that she would not return to school until she was seventeen.

The world of big business, marketing and PR was a far cry from Madam's beginnings. She was born Sarah Breedlove,* in 1867, on the same Delta, Louisiana, plantation on which her parents had been slaves. By the age of seven she was orphaned, by fourteen she was married, by seventeen she had had her first and only child and by twenty she was a widow.

Prior to her employment with Annie Malone at Poro, Walker supported herself and her infant daughter by working as a washerwoman. Until that point there is little to distinguish Walker's story from the lives of millions of other impoverished black American women whose employment options were restricted to sharecropping or domestic work, the same labour their parents, grandparents and great-grandparents had endured for the previous three centuries. Walker's rise to fame took more grit and determination than most of us can begin to muster in our imaginations. According to the official story, Breedlove, distraught and deeply ashamed of her looks, 'prayed in desperation' to cure her 'frightful appearance'.[17]

Because of poor nutrition and damaging hair-dressing methods, a lot of black women in the early 1900s had broken and damaged hair (I mean, I still had broken and damaged hair in the

---

* Quite a romantic name, although, I suppose, without the gravitas of her adopted moniker, which was suggested to her by her second husband, an advertising agent named Charles J. Walker.

1990s, so there you go). It was a world far removed from the nutritious diets and the rich butters (shea butter, or *òrí*) and oils (coconut oil, or *àdí àgbon*) applied to the hair that resulted in thick, lustrous locks for their ancestors in West Africa.

Breedlove's petition to God was successful: 'a big African man appeared', fortuitously revealed the recipe for a magical elixir with unspecified ingredients all the way from 'Africa', and Walker set to it. Her hair, now favoured through a lucky alliance between God and African magic, miraculously grew back. The rest, as they say, is history.

Today A'Lelia Bundles is keen to change the focus of her forebears' achievements away from the straightening of hair. Walker herself applied a similar strategy. Yet as Byrd and Tharps point out, Madam C.J. Walker's success was undoubtedly the result of her method of hair straightening. Nonetheless, in her lifetime Walker marketed her tonics and hot combs as necessary treatments promoting *healthy* hair, rather than focussing on the process of straightening. In what would become a common trend in the advertising of black hair products, Walker purposely associated straight hair with health and cleanliness. By extension, straight hair became, perversely, associated with 'naturalness'. Walker was so widely associated with the hot comb that she is often credited with its invention. However, unless Madam was also a white Frenchman named François Marcel Grateau, this is untrue. The Parisian revolutionized hairstyling in 1872 when he invented heated irons that could curl and wave hair. The comb could also be used to achieve a bone-straight look, in emulation of the ancient Egyptian images that were in vogue in Paris at that time. Despite its French origins, the hot comb was quickly adopted by black women in the US who sought a method to tame their kinks. Before long, the hot comb was a staple of black hairstyling culture. Until very recently, any salon I went into would have a requisite set, although these days seeing that equipment would probably be enough to ensure that I never returned.

Elizabeth Cardozo, the owner of Washington's most successful salon in the 1950s, paints a graphic picture of black hair salons in the first half of the twentieth century.

> When we started, most black hair shops had gas stoves. Every hair operator had her own gas stove and you would put these hot irons on the gas stoves and most black businesses had a very heavy grease . . . most of the manufacturers felt that the only way to handle a black customer's hair was with this very heavy grease which was made of yellow petroleum and mineral oil and beeswax.
>
> And it sort of laid the hair down . . . the weight alone! And by the time they used these heavy pressing irons, the hair was really controllable. Unless you got a drop of water to it.
>
> But because they had gas stoves and this, what I call axle grease, the shops were always smoking . . .[18]

A frequent side effect of using the traditional hot comb is burning and the damage associated with it. Hot combs were generally heated to over 65° C, and in a domestic setting this was usually done straight off the stove. Anyone familiar with the process knows that, because you straighten right down from the root of the hair, regular use increases the likelihood of severe burns and even scarring. When we consider the Hieronymus Bosch-like hellscape conjured by Cardozo, is it any wonder that the hot comb represents yet another instrument that invokes feelings of stress and anxiety in me?

While her legacy might not be as well preserved as that of her former employee, Annie Turnboe Malone (née Turnbo) is one of the people largely responsible for creating the earliest commercial hair straighteners for black women. And it was Annie who utilized the pyramid scheme typified by Avon sales, whereby women recruited other women as salespeople and made a commission from their recruits' sales as well as their own. This system enabled Annie to transform her company into a hugely successful national concern.

Malone's parents' story was even more dramatic. Malone was

the daughter of escaped slaves. We are so bombarded with stories of black pain that we almost become desensitized to the horror, but let it sit with you for a moment: escaped slaves. If you can't imagine it, I assure you there is nothing like reading an escaped-slave notice describing someone that could be you to help sharpen your powers of imagination. I've read two recently to that effect: Escaped: a bright mulatto with a sullen countenance (I actually have a relatively cheery countenance, but I suspect slave Emma might have felt differently); and a well-spoken mulatto, with a port wine stain on chin and neck, who may attempt to pass as free. Reading that one, my hand automatically went to the port-wine stain that covers my own chin and neck. It was the strangest feeling. The realization that, regardless of any of my talents, abilities, personal hopes, dreams or ambitions, had I been born a mere century earlier, I might have been the property of another human being – well, that feeling has never really left me.

We are further assisted in the imaginative process by the similarities between the Turnboe family's escape and the journey of Sethe in Toni Morrison's troubling masterpiece *Beloved*. While writing *The Black Book*, Morrison says, she came across the story of Margaret Garner, an enslaved woman who in 1856 escaped from Maplewood Plantation in Kentucky to Ohio with her husband and four children, and it was this story on which *Beloved* is based. Around the same time, Annie's parents took a similar route, escaping out of Kentucky and down the Ohio River.

Margaret Garner didn't get her freedom. A day later the family was apprehended. But Margaret was determined. Her family would return to Maplewood only over her dead body. Grabbing the closest implement, Margaret murdered her two-year-old daughter with a butcher knife. She was overpowered while attempting to do the same to another child. Valuable property must be protected at all costs, and the posse of white men subdued her. Her subsequent trial transfixed the nation.

Margaret is documented as saying, 'I'd do it again,' Morrison told the *Paris Review*. A detail I was not aware of, and one which the casting of Oprah Winfrey in the film adaptation obscures, is that Margaret was a 'mulatto'. Black women were systematically raped by white men during slavery and well into the twentieth century. As a result, many of the enslaved were mixed race. The world of plantation slavery divided 'livestock' into different categories, based on their quotient of black blood. A mulatto had one black African parent, one white European parent; a quadroon had one black and three white grandparents; an octoroon was one eighth black, and so on.

The historian Gary Nash explains that, in the US, 'raising the social status of those who laboured at the bottom of society, and who were defined as abysmally inferior, was a matter of serious concern. It was resolved by ensuring that the mulatto would not occupy a position midway between white and black. Any black blood classified a person as black; and to be black was to be a slave.'[19]

There is overwhelming evidence to suggest that John P. Gaines – Margaret's previous owner, before he sold both her and the plantation itself to his younger brother, Archibald K. Gaines – was Margaret's father.

Lucy Stone, a white feminist and anti-slavery campaigner, documented the trial. She commented that Margaret's two older boys were listed on the census as Negro and possessing visibly African features. However, her two youngest daughters, the nine-month-old baby and the two-year-old whose life she look, looked virtually white. The implication was that Archibald K. Gaines was not only Margaret's uncle and owner, but also an incestuous rapist and the father of the two almost-white little girls.

On the closing day of the trial Lucy Stone took the stand to defend Margaret. Stone highlighted the sexual abuse that was the unspoken factor in the case. Calling upon the court to remember the faces of Margaret's children and to compare them to that of A. K. Gaines, Stone told the packed courtroom:

The faded [pale complexion] faces of the Negro children tell too plainly to what degradation the female slaves submit. Rather than give her daughter to that life, she killed it. If in her deep maternal love she felt the impulse to send her child back to God, to save it from coming woe, who shall say she had no right to do so?

In *Reminiscences*, Levi Coffin, a Quaker abolitionist, noted the commissioner's reply: this was 'not a question of feeling to be decided by the chance current of his sympathies; the law of Kentucky and the United States made it a question of property'.[20]

Margaret's fate was sealed.

This was the true horror of Maplewood Plantation and the true horror that America has been built on. Despite the relative material advantage and privilege that lighter skin could and often did confer, it can never be historically assumed. The American social historian J. C. Furnas explains that interracial children in the US generally fared far worse than in other New World countries. Whereas in colonies like Haiti, mulattos occupied a middle caste between black and white, in the US and other English-speaking colonies, terms like 'mulatto' referred to appearance rather than status. The United States had passed laws ensuring that mixed-race individuals occupied the same legal status as blacks, regardless of whether one was a recent arrival from Africa or indeed descended from several generations of African-Americans. Furnas continues that there was 'not an old plantation in which the grandchildren of the owner are not whipped in the field by his overseer'.[21]

While mixed-race slaves might have been over-represented as 'house Negroes', the assumed benefits of this status are debatable. In Margaret's case, both she and her children were probably the product of rape. This type of horror was generally compounded by the threat of living among resentful white female family members seeking to avenge a husband's infidelities.

A WOMAN SCORNED

White women were known for meting out vicious punishments, and the shaving of female slaves' heads was one of the most common for minor transgressions like 'talking back'. Many African-American women had their heads shaved and 'it was almost invariably white women who meted out the punishment.'[22]

James Brittian recalled his grandmother, an enslaved woman who had been born in Africa and who had hair that was 'fine as silk and hung down below her waist', hair that made the 'Old Miss' jealous of her and the 'Old Master'. The mistress, who was 'mighty fractious',' had Brittian's grandmother whipped, and her hair cut off. 'From that day on,' he recalled, 'my grandma had to wear her hair shaved to the scalp.'

There was also the case of one Judge Maddox, owner of a Texas plantation, who 'brought home a pretty mulatto girl' with 'long black straight hair'. Suspicious that the young slave had not been bought for doing the fine needlework her husband claimed, Madame waited until the judge was away, 'got the scissors and cropped that gal's head to the skull'.[23]

White and White note that, generally, it was similarity between their own hair and that of enslaved women that made white women deeply uncomfortable. Hair texture often signified that

> husbands, brothers, or sons had been illicitly visiting the slave quarters or suggested that, if something were not done soon, the temptation for them would be too great. As a result of the warped sexual dynamics of an antebellum plantation, the mutilation of an African American female's hair was usually an action directed at whites rather than at the victim herself, although doubtless its import was not lost on the slaves in the quarter. Whatever the motivations for these incidents may have been, they occurred frequently enough to become part of the

remembered fabric of slavery, passed on from generation to generation. In her autobiography Sarah Rice recalled her mother
telling her about Sarah Rice's great-grandmother. As a slave,
she had had 'gorgeous hair,' which she had styled into ringlets,
'[b]ut her mistress didn't like it and took her and cut it all off'.[24]

The jealousy and fear that white women felt was deemed serious
enough to have a direct impact on legislation. The Tignon Laws,
which were signed into being in 1786 by Esteban Rodríguez Miró,
the governor of the then Spanish colony of Louisiana, are an explicit
demonstration of this. The fabulous, ornate hairstyling of black
women was causing much consternation for white women, who felt
it bestowed unfair advantages in vying for the attentions of white
men. Feelings were running so high that the governor intervened,
decreeing that black women must, by law, cover their hair in public
on the grounds of maintaining social order. Can you imagine?
Black kinks and curls, apparently so jeopardizing to the status quo,
attesting to the various levels of social control that have for centuries been enacted upon black women's bodies. It was decreed that
Afro hair now had to be hidden from sight by a tignon, an African-
inspired head-wrap. Of course, the law failed spectacularly; black
women responded by demonstrating their creativity in the face of
stricture, sporting elaborate and beautifully decorated head wraps.
This served to make them only more alluring to male suitors.

This history was unknown to me. Growing up hating my
appearance, it would never have occurred to me that there had
once been – and not that long ago – a time, soon to re-emerge –
Hello Kardashian-Jenners! – when white women wanted to look
just like me, because that would be crazy. Right??

The shaving of heads was relatively minor; far more terrifying viola-
tions existed. I came across one account from Brazil where a white
mistress suspected her husband was having sexual relations with an
attractive mulatto slave noted for her beautiful eyes. Wifey responded
by removing the eyes of her 'competitor'. A woman scorned, eh?

Other accounts describe mixed-race house slaves corrupted by proximity to the toxic culture of their captors. They had better clothes, the hand-me-downs of their owners, and they often had better food too, as they might be allowed eat their owners' left-overs, but, often separated from black culture, they lacked the cultural resources of those less divorced from their African trad-itions. For mixed-race slaves, like Margaret Garner, proximity to whiteness, without the protection that whiteness brought, could be nothing less than deadly.

What makes the Garners' story even more upsetting, if such a thing is possible, is how close Margaret had come to freedom. Nine other escapees who made the journey with the Garner family all got away, disappearing into the free black population. Missouri was a border state during the American Civil War and as such was the destination of many black refugees fleeing the unimaginable conditions in the South. Who knows what Annie's mother, Isabella (Cook) Turnbo, was running from when she too, like Margaret, escaped from slavery in Kentucky, fleeing down the Ohio River with her children. Unlike the Garners', the Turnbo family's escape was successful, and they found refuge in Metropolis, Illinois. It was there that Annie was born in 1869, the tenth of eleven chil-dren. If, like the Garners, they hadn't made it, and Annie had never been born, the course of the history of black hair might have been radically altered. It makes you think, doesn't it, about all the ones who never got away. Who knows what might have been? Who knows what we have lost?

BAD AND BOUJIE

Frequent illness meant that Annie didn't graduate from high school. She did, however, spend enough time in formal education to discover a great aptitude for chemistry. Combined with her interest in haircare, this would eventually lead not only to the development of her own products but to the creation of a huge business empire.

The story behind Annie's invention is not as dramatic as a secret recipe revealed by an African god, but perhaps it constitutes a more likely origin for the products that would make both Annie and Sarah multimillionaires. It is impossible to claim that Madam was selling the product earlier than Annie, but A'Lelia Bundles is keen to emphasize that Annie didn't invent anything either. She writes that 'the real secret was a regimen of regular shampoos, scalp massage, nutritious food, and an easily duplicated, sulfur-based formula that neither of them had originated. Home remedies and medicinal compounds with similar ingredients had been prescribed at least since the sixteenth century.'[25]

Nonetheless, Annie's products provided a welcome respite for black women. They were an alternative to the goose and bacon fat, the heavy oils and God knows what else that damaged both scalp and hair but were relied upon to regulate 'unmanageable' kinks.

Malone's community-based business model developed out of her inability as a black woman to access normal distribution channels (talk about lemons into goddamn lemonade). This success arguably led to her position as the first black female millionaire, a title often accredited to Walker. The truth and the story remain complex. It is reported that it was none other than the savvy Walker who encouraged Annie to copyright her products under the name Poro,* part of a bid to discourage counterfeits and unregulated imitations.

---

* The choice of the name Poro is itself fascinating. The Poro is the highly influential, powerful men's secret society started by the Mende people of modern-day Sierra Leone, as mentioned in Chapter 2. There are numerous stories about why Malone adopted this name for her company, and one of them is that it was chosen because of these West African origins. To me, the connection seems too likely to dismiss. It is revealing that Malone would choose to emphasize her connections to West Africa at a time when association with the continent was usually a source of shame.

While Walker's reputation has certainly been more enduring, it remains a matter of dispute which woman was truly wealthier. Madam Walker certainly lived far more lavishly. And why not? She endured back-breaking labour to achieve her status. Walker was a one-woman advertising and promotional tour traversing the US, Cuba and the Caribbean. Segregation and Jim Crow made such travel around the US extremely risky, but Madam was unstoppable. Five years shy from working as a washerwoman, Madam, née Sarah Breedlove, had established an entirely black-owned business, complete with a factory and a beauty school staffed almost entirely by women. By 1912 Jim Crow had become little more than an inconvenience for her. No more filthy trains for Madam – she bought herself a seven-seated touring automobile, complete with chauffeur.

Bad and boujie, Madam was intent on displaying her wealth to the world. It was just the beginning. In December 1916 she made a spectacular announcement and left polite society reeling. A black woman had purchased a four and a quarter acre estate, and in Irvington-on-Hudson, no less. According to *The New York Times*, many doubted the story's veracity. At that time, the picturesque village only nineteen miles from downtown Manhattan was America's most prime real estate. Madam announced that her fantasy abode, Villa Lewaro, which had been designed by Vertner Tandy, the first African-American architect registered in New York, would 'cost . . . no less than $100,000, and it is going to be very swell'. One can only imagine what Madam's new neighbours – the Carnegies, the Rockefellers, the Tiffanys; names representing the epitome of American wealth, class and taste – must have thought.

Meanwhile, Annie Malone had been busy too. By 1918 she had established Poro College in St Louis, a five-storey multipurpose building. It contained a manufacturing plant, a shop where Poro products were sold, business offices, a 500-seat auditorium, dining and meeting rooms, a roof garden, a hotel, a gymnasium, a bakery and a chapel. The cosmetology school and training centre offered black women educational opportunities that were rare for the time.

In addition, Poro College provided an important space where black Americans could gather for functions. No expense was spared and the lavish interiors gave their white counterparts – from which black people were barred – more than a run for their money.

By the end of the First World War, Annie was a millionaire, yet she lived humbly. Both Walker and Madam contributed generous sums of money to their respective communities. Annie invested most of hers through donations to institutions, such as the St Louis Colored Orphans' Home. She was generous to a fault, which ultimately negatively affected her personal finances.

Annie Malone's multimillion-dollar Poro business empire was put at risk in 1927 when her husband filed for divorce and demanded half of the business. Seeking a fresh start, Malone relocated to Chicago in 1930, where she was still dogged by financial troubles and lawsuits, quickly followed by the Great Depression, yet she remained in business. In the mid-1950s, there were still thirty-two branches of the Poro schools operating across the nation. Malone continued to support charities both in St Louis and

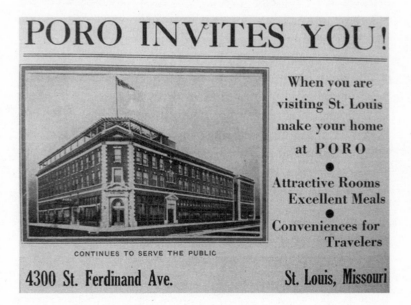

PORO INVITES YOU!

When you are visiting St. Louis make your home at P O R O

•

Attractive Rooms
Excellent Meals

•

Conveniences for Travelers

CONTINUES TO SERVE THE PUBLIC

4300 St. Ferdinand Ave.   St. Louis, Missouri

nationally. It is reported that at one time she was supporting at least two students at every African-American land-grant college* in the country, while her $25,000 donation to Howard University in Washington, DC, was at the time the largest financial contribution by an African-American to an African-American college. She died in Chicago on 10 May 1957.

Madam had died almost forty years earlier. On 25 May 1919 she passed away from hypertension aged just fifty-one. While her company was also hit hard by the Depression, it was so many years after her death that her fun-loving daughter A'Lelia took the fall for the failure. She was certainly not the businesswoman her mother had been, although she did have a knack for publicity. Her greatest PR achievement was the 'Million Dollar Wedding', the most ostentatious black wedding of the Jazz Age. In 1923 A'Lelia arranged for Fairy Mae to marry Dr Gordon Henry Jackson, the grandson of one of the nineteenth century's richest black businessmen. No matter he was 'a violent man thirteen years her senior', or that she was allegedly in love with someone else. A'Lelia Walker wrote to the company's general manager, F. B. Ransom, 'This is the swellest wedding any colored folks have ever had or will have in the world . . . While its purpose certainly is not for the advertising, God knows we are getting $50,000 worth of publicity. Everything has its compensation.'[26]

The marriage lasted only three years, but the splendour of it all (9,000 wedding invitations were sent out) did temporarily boost sales. It was not, however, enough to save the company, and by 1930 Walker revenues had fallen so drastically that A'Lelia was forced to auction the art for which Villa Lewaro was famed. A year later, aged only forty-six, she suffered a cerebral haemorrhage while at a party. Her funeral in Harlem was as spectacular as her life. Over 11,000 people attended, including Langston Hughes, a close personal friend, who recited the following poem:

* Land-grant colleges were set up as educational institutions with a particular emphasis on subjects like agriculture, science and engineering. They were established on federally controlled land that was granted to individual US states for this purpose.

So all who love laughter
And joy and light,
Let your prayers be as roses
For this queen of the night!

By 1932, the year after A'Lelia's untimely death, Villa Lewaro had been sold.

The legacies of both hair dynasties live on. The Annie Malone Children and Family Service Center in St Louis is located on a street named Annie Malone Drive in her honour, and Walker has been reinvented for the twenty-first century. The Madam C.J. Walker website extols 'America's first female self-made million-aire' who 'created a beauty culture that enriched and transformed the lives of millions of women'. This contemporary incarnation targets a high-end mainstream consumer. Promotional materials feature all races and hair textures. Their Instagram account is populated mostly by white and mixed-race women and is almost devoid of women who might have resembled Walker herself. Madam Walker 2.0 is owned by SunDial, which also owns both Shea Moisture and Nubian Heritage. The products are stocked exclusively by Sephora, themselves owned by LVMH Moët Hen-nessy Louis Vuitton, the world's leading luxury-goods group.

Before the arrival of these two dynamos at the turn of the twen-tieth century, manufacturers of black haircare products were overwhelmingly white men. The burgeoning beauty industry in which Walker and Malone were trailblazers revolutionized earn-ing and employment opportunities for generations of black women in an industry that is today worth $2.5 billion (not including wigs and accessories). Byrd and Tharps note that at a time when unskilled white women earned about $11 a week, a Walker agent might be earning $15 a day, and that at Poro's peak in 1918 the company employed 240 staff members and 68,000 sales agents nationwide.

Nonetheless, the politics of their products remain complicated. On the one hand they were pioneers, able to achieve previously unimaginable success, but the ideal they promoted was one that positioned whiteness as the benchmark not only of beauty, but also of class and success. It preyed on the trauma of a people only one generation, if that, removed from centuries of enslavement.

Before the emergence of the black-hair capitalists, white manufacturers had been little more than openly insulting. Words like 'kinky', 'snarly' and 'ugly' were commonplace. Savvy black entrepreneurs, on the other hand, understood how to advertise rather than antagonize. But while they tweaked the language, the sentiment remained the same. And the intention behind the products – regardless of whether they were made by white men or black women – was identical: the achievement of straight hair.

The key difference now was that the language became not only more palatable but positively empowering. With its emphasis on health, beauty, personal success and the uplift of the entire race, this new narrative, designed by black people for black people, was meeting a huge demand.

The wealth generated by Annie Malone and Madam C.J. Walker was staggering, but they were certainly not the only black women generating a handsome livelihood as hair capitalists. As their success waned there were others ready to capitalize on an ever-changing but consistently lucrative market.

BLACK EXCELLENCE, RESPECTABILITY, ANTI-BLACKNESS AND CLASS

Compiled to address the relative absence of black women in the archives, the 1976–81 Black Women Oral History Project is an extraordinary resource. It contains the testimonies of women of note at local, national and international levels. When I discovered it, one collection in particular jumped out at me, that of the Cardozo sisters.

In 1928, Elizabeth Cardozo Barker, a young single mother of two, founded the Cardozo Sisters Hairstylists salon. Later, her sisters Margaret and Catherine came on board to help run what would eventually become Washington's most successful beauty salon. Elizabeth credits both Madam Walker and the Poro Corporation for creating the landscape in which black commercial haircare could flourish. But she notes the gap left by focusing primarily on straightening what she describes as the 'harsh, kinky textures'. Elizabeth notes that these women had showed little interest in developing products or solutions for the in-between or straight hair possessed by some Negro women.

Unlike 'ordinary-looking' black women, the ones 'who looked like domestics', the Cardozo clan were part of an illustrious progeny whose achievements were inarguably entwined with their position within the light-skinned Negro elite. The sisters were the children of Francis L. and Blanche Warrick Cardozo. Their paternal grandfather was Francis Lewis Cardozo, the son of Lydia Weston, a free woman of colour who was herself a slave owner, and Isaac Cardozo, a Sephardic Jew.

In 1858, their grandfather Francis matriculated at Glasgow University,* and ten years later he was elected Secretary of State in South Carolina, making him the first African-American to hold a statewide office in the United States.

The achievements of the sisters' generation were no less impressive. Their brother, Dr William Cardozo, was a paediatrician who went on to become a pioneer in the treatment of sickle-cell anaemia. Their first cousin Eslanda Cardozo Goode Robeson was a

---

* To put the black world of that time into perspective and to illustrate the range of conditions mixed-race African-Americans might find themselves in, Francis Cardozo's achievement took place a mere two years after Margaret Garner felt that murdering her infant daughter was a better option than returning into slavery.

cultural anthropologist, actor and civil rights campaigner who married the actor, singer and activist Paul Robeson.

Their maternal grandmother, Emma Warwick (née Jones), was the great-granddaughter of a woman who had reputedly been an Ethiopian princess before she was enslaved. Grandma Emma was an award-winning wig maker who owned salons in both Philadelphia and Atlantic City, catering to an exclusive white clientele. The Cardozos grew up in the salon, coming of age immersed in its rites of passage. Childhood days were spent making human-hair wigs for dolls and drying the long hair of the white patrons with palm-leaf fronds.

The Cardozos represent the epitome of what might today be called 'Black Excellence'. Yet to varying degrees their transcripts reveal what an oppressive construct that can be, predicated along the fault lines of respectability politics, with an imperative towards assimilation into oppressive power structures and frequently diffuse with rampant, internalized anti-blackness. This shows that, despite the advantages of their class, they were hardly the most inspiring candidates for black uplift.

The internalized and deeply entrenched anti-blackness that exists in black communities is often denied. The sisters make outward claims of concern for and solidarity with the black community, but contradictory attitudes remain apparent in their narratives. Fascinatingly, much of what they really think about blackness – perhaps only on a subconscious level – is revealed through their descriptions of hair and hairdressing culture.

Elizabeth explains that their mixed ancestry has resulted in the different grades of hair possessed by each sister. The fact that the siblings all exist on different points of the spectrum between 'good' and 'bad' hair is what motivates them to create different methods for dealing with the various textures – sort of like a nineteenth-century Mixed Chicks (a hair-product brand), although, unlike Mixed Chicks, the Cardozo sisters' systems and products took into account the kinkier textures too. (Mixed Chicks products simply don't work on my hair. They clearly have a very particular definition of mixed-race hair, and it isn't mine.)

But Elizabeth's attitude to the more African hair textures is apparent when she describes the way in which she deals with different types of hair:

> I didn't treat all hair as though it were kinky. I treated the hair as it deserved to be treated and some of the medium hair, hair that is a little more on the side of straight than kinky, looks so much better if it doesn't have the life pressed out of it. And they were very pleased with the fact that they left looking so much more natural.[27]

This echoes the Madam Walker strategy of associating heavily processed straight hair with looking natural. Such processes inform the deeply internalized sense that our hair is so inadequate it is healthier when it is damaged. It also advances the nonsensical Eurocentric association of straight hair with cleanliness and health. With a self-delusion I recognize, Elizabeth Cardozo could actually claim that 'The chemicals made our hair better.'

The Cardozo sisters cut their teeth in a salon frequented by whites. Their own clientele extended to both white women and, in the parlance of the time, 'Orientals'.

Yet Elizabeth hastens to add that the Oriental customers are few and far between. They didn't tend to bother much with the salon at all, because 'oriental hair is beautiful to start with'. Considering how many black women continue to weave Asian women's hair on to their heads, one of the many things that saddens me reading Elizabeth's account is the depth to which her attitude and the beauty standards it normalizes remain potent to this day.

Black women, on the other hand, with their chronic malaise, required ongoing treatment and booked lifetime appointments (in fact, the business was famed for its long-term booking system).

Despite haircare requiring the expertise that can be found only in local salons, Elizabeth cannot disguise her distaste for the black businesses that operate in the informal market:

> I went to the best black hairdresser in the community, Madam Caitlin. She was better than anyone at the schools but Madam ... *had a living room and customers seemed quite satisfied to sit there for hours, play cards and gossip. That was the kind of place, I was not going to have.* [my italics]

While she cannot deny that Madam Caitlin is the best hairdresser around, neither can she hide her contempt for what she considers the crass activities that are encouraged on her premises. This paradox often characterizes anti-black discourse, the thirst for black expertise or cultural knowledge existing side by side with a refusal, or an inability, to confer any worth on the creators of the work. Elizabeth needs to learn from Madam Caitlin, but she cannot hold her in high esteem. Cardozo has a very different type of establishment in mind for herself.

> We train them in the hair work and we also train them to act as professionals.
>
> For instance like a trained nurse would act. And not like some hairdressers have often acted, loud and noisy and talking over the customers and talking their personal business.
>
> In other words we tried to show them that the only way to uplift them from the status of little better than domestics was for them to uplift themselves and that was fairly easy when Mrs. [Margaret] Holmes was there ... Nobody resented that but she walked around with her queenly air, which nobody resented, and they seemed to love her ... so without any noise, or undue talking or irregularity of any kind ...

Real talk, we've all had first-hand experience of the wasted hours and mounting frustration when we turn up for a 2 p.m. appointment that still hasn't started at 3.30. Nonetheless, I want to pay my respects to the conviviality of the black hair shop. Unlike the Cardozos, I possess great affection for the cut and thrust of black hair salons, the gossip and the drama. In the UK, I love the blending of West African and Caribbean culture that defines the space: the afrobeats, the bashment, the 90s R'n'B. My conversations with other customers and my stylists, most of whom I've now known for years, run from colonialism through colourism and the role of the Chinese in Africa and the Caribbean to identity, melanin, love and loss. Equally, if I don't want to talk, I don't.

These can be important spaces, and the urge to sanitize them in the way the Cardozo sisters did, in pursuit of a Victorian-style 'respectability', is an imperative that is pronounced in the white-washing of black cultures.

The Cardozos' accounts reflect a tension that existed during the nineteenth and twentieth centuries between middle-class and working-class black women, who often had significantly different priorities. In her research on African-American women in Detroit, the historian Victoria Wolcott suggests that middle-class black women at times weaponized racial-uplift ideology, using it to distinguish themselves from poorer black people, whom they castigated for not conforming to the same standards of cleanliness, religious virtue and sexual wholesomeness. They often urged poorer African-American women to become 'respectable'. Working-class black women often had different priorities with regard to improving their situations, primarily by creating opportunities that might lead to their escape from the never-ending drudgery of domestic labour.[28]

Elizabeth might have financially improved the fortunes of the black women she trained, but, at the same time, the paternalism that formed the cornerstone of her activities was characterized by a distinctly colonial attitude.

As ever, these contestations, ostensibly about hair, are in fact about so much more. The attitude of the Cardozos towards African hair, to 'ordinary-looking' black women, as well as their distaste for aspects of black culture, reflect issues that we are confronting today no less than we were a hundred years ago. Tightly coiled African hair remains stigmatized and visual representations of blackness are largely dominated by mixed women of African descent whose mixedness makes them more palatable, while black culture is appropriated yet demonized and presented as deviant and inferior.

Their were political implications too. In her 2014 book *Pageants, Parlors, and Pretty Women*, Dr Blain Roberts argues that the natural made a political statement with which women like the Cardozos disagreed. Catherine makes this position clear. From her perspective, civil rights activists, never mind the more radical Black Power proponents, were skivers, work-shy troublemakers: 'You didn't have to exert any self-discipline. You were simply black and that was it, that was the important thing.'

As Roberts explains, Catherine favoured a moderate, integrationist approach to civil rights work. To Catherine's eyes the younger generation was exploiting unjustified demands based on superficial petitions of blackness and were failing to demonstrate the discipline, hard work and respect that she believed were prerequisites to gaining concessions from whites.[29]

While arguably representing what today might be termed black excellence, Catherine, as a member of an elite group, represents precisely the class of person that Black Power activists such as Stokely Carmichael claimed were operating contrary to the demands of black liberation. In contrast to what the Cardozos might have believed, groups such as the Black Panthers were not organized around shallow appeals to blackness. Central to their mission was a vision of international anti-imperialism and revolutionary socialism. Appealing only to blackness – without any political framework beyond identity – would lead to the assumption that women like the Cardozos automatically share a fundamental set of interests with all

African-Americans. In reality, the Cardozos occupied a class position that situated them in a very different position to the black majority. Catherine's argument that work will set you free is the worst kind of strawman. It represents the typical 'pull yourself up by the bootstraps' rhetoric of the (relatively) privileged, who disavow the structural impediments that prevent members of marginalized groups from achieving their true potential, regardless of their attitude. The hair salon is a site where we can observe a microcosm of national issues, witnessing how, once again, black hair proved a battlefield where cultural and racial tensions were reproduced. While each generation may have a tendency to believe that they are the 'first generation to . . .' I have never seen this conceit as pronounced as it is today. In truth, there is little new under the sun. In many ways, the burning questions being asked during the late 1960s and the early '70s were more pertinent, and certainly more radical than the discussions we are having today. Black organizers such as Stokely Carmichael and Charles Hamilton stated: 'We reject the goal of assimilation into middle-class America because the values of that class are in themselves anti-humanist, and because that class as a social force perpetuates racism.'[30] Carmichael argued that the major flaw in the Civil Rights Movement's ideology was integration, the attempts of black citizens to fit into the institutions of white America, the very institutions that were responsible for the oppression that black people faced. Radical black activists felt that the successes of the Civil Rights Movement primarily benefited an elite group of black individuals who gained the legal ability to succeed in white institutions. The integration effort was little more than integration into the middle-class, white power structure and value system.

To those with more assimilationist tendencies, the Afros or 'naturals' worn by black activists were anathema. They were also bad for business. Catherine identifies the rise of the 'natural' as accelerating a decline in the beauty salons. She is emphatic that she would never wear her own hair in such a way. The immediacy with which she links her disavowal of the natural hairstyle to a rejection of Black Power is remarkable: 'I would never have assumed that hairdress because I just thought it was an affectation. Particularly in view of my color [very light-skinned].' Yet as her elder sister Elizabeth pointed out, all of the sisters had varying degrees of kinky hair which they disguised. Nonetheless:

CATHERINE: I just felt it was just something, it was a way out of the way ... We went through a terrible time at that time, I think because we were so divided, so schizophrenic ... divided as to what our thinking was, most of the black power people, because they wanted everything, we wanted everything, but we didn't want to have to work for it ... we found that the things that were handed to us on a silver platter, we couldn't handle. We simply could not handle it.

INTERVIEWER: What were you referring to when you mentioned things handed on a silver platter?

CATHERINE: Civil Rights.

There you have it. All our skinfolk are not kinfolk. Catherine's class position shaped her response to black liberation, despite the fact that she was African-American. Throughout their interviews, the sisters emphasize their insistence on 'professionalism', but their use of the word seems to bear a strong resemblance to colonial accounts of civilizing missions.

In contrast to 'unprofessional' places, where 'gossip' occurs, the Cardozos take every pain to ensure that their salon would never become 'a hell-of-a-place / to ferment / a revolution'. Nonetheless, the Cardozos were businesswomen. Whatever reservations they might have harboured about the ethics of the aesthetics of the natural, they knew which way the tide was turning and they were determined not to be left out. In the face of dwindling returns, natural-hair services were added to the Cardozos' roster. It is precisely this type of calculating decision that leaves me at times suspicious of the motivations of some of our newly woke faves. But that's none of my business.

The Cardozo family's experiences are far removed from those of typical black Americans of that time. Margaret talks about a trip to Paris with another sister, Emmetta. In the 1930s, the 'beautiful' (i.e., almost white-looking) Emmetta Holmes, née Cardozo, enjoyed a successful modelling career with the *New York Mirror*, an opportunity impossible for a woman who looked identifiably black. Emmetta even had a spell working as one of the iconic Ziegfeld Follies on Broadway. At that time, Ziegfeld wouldn't have hired a Negro performer, so the implication is that she passed as white. Her story reminds us of the power of hair to confer racial status. You see, Emmeta had a secret shame, one that had to be rigorously policed. As Elizabeth explains:

> I was always the best at kinky hair because that was what I had
> started with. If I do say it myself, I could do a beautiful job of

giving what they call the hard-press. With so much skill with that pressing iron and so little grease you'd take a very hard kinky head of hair and you could press it so that it almost looked like straight hair. One of the reasons that made this so important to us, to get that look, was because the sister who was with the Follies had kinky hair. She didn't look like she had kinky hair, because she had the features and everything of a white person or a foreigner. So it was very necessary for her to know exactly what to do or what to have done with her hair.

She had someone who would do it, but sometimes she would perspire, and maybe you know what that will do to pressed hair. She knew exactly how to handle it. I used to say that *she went down under the skin* before it even got to the roots. When you looked at her hair it was a satin finish. It was beautiful. It was real art. I don't think people do that much anymore because very few people want their hair pressed that thoroughly. [my italics]

'She went down under the skin.' A painful image, suggesting something elemental, cruelly disfigured, of blackness kept at bay, the cost of external acceptance in a world not of our own design.

As well as potentially passing as white to model, Emmetta had trained as a hairdresser, which suggests the level of social status offered by the profession:

[In 1927] we inherited a few thousand dollars. We thought we wanted Meta to learn a trade that would keep her occupied and have a little bit of glamour to it, so we decided that she should go to Paris and learn the beauty trade. I stayed there six weeks and at that time it was a very nice time to be in Paris because it was the time of Josephine Baker and all of the beautiful entertainers were in Paris at that time.

Don't forget that France had established itself as the home of the hot press and the marcel wave. It was believed that some of the best stylists in these methods could be found there. The reference to Josephine Baker is significant also. Even this most feted chanteuse was cashing in on the beauty business.

By the 1930s Baker's image was visible on a wide range of products. She capitalized on the craze for all things black. Similarly to Rihanna and Fenty Beauty, which was launched in 2017, Baker's manager saw a gap in the market and was hugely successful. The chanteuse launched 'The Baker Look', which included a skin-darkening product called Bakerskin and Bakerfix, and a pomade for slicking back and glossing the hair (arguably copied from a Madam Walker formula – do we see a pattern emerging here?).

These products were marketed to and subsequently snapped up by wealthy white Parisian women desperate to achieve the famous Baker look. It has been suggested that the success of the Revue Nègre, combined with the influential appropriation of African art by avant-garde artists like Picasso, Matisse, Derain and Braque, as well as Baker's unparalleled popularity, created a 'trend for blackness'. Many argue that this was the source of the tanning craze that started in France and went on to transform Western beauty ideals. The similarities with today are many. One of the most obvious examples is the hyper-visible black female celebrities of today, those whose mixed ancestry is evident in their golden-brown skin or their green eyes. There is evidence to suggest that Baker's father was a white man; certainly, to look at her, it is clear to see that she has significant white ancestry.

Given white women's desire to achieve the Baker look, it is ironic, yet unsurprising, that much of Baker's personal beauty regime was centered around skin-lightening through milk baths and lemon rubs. In this we see the early antecedents of today's beauty ideals, coalescing around light-skinned or white, tanned bodies with the lips and behinds of black women and the straight, shiny, lustrous hair of Asian women. The Kardashian-Jenner clan represent the fullest contemporary expression of this look.

Despite the Cardozos' privilege, details from their lives remind us that we must remain alert to the ways in which race and class intersect and that it can be misleading to conflate the experiences and social position of the black middle class with middle-class white realities.

The convent school the sisters attended had no greater aspirations for its pupils than the production of good house servants. In addition to substandard schooling, throughout her life Catherine was forced to undertake menial and administrative labour. In fact, the Cardozo Sisters business developed out of Elizabeth's precarious financial position. A divorced mother of two young sons, she desperately needed to generate income. Hairdressing that could be done from home provided much-needed income while at the same time solving her childcare issues. In the end, her informal education – the childhood spent assisting her grandmother Emma – turned out to be of far greater value than the schooling that was accessible to black folks, even those who were 'privileged'.

Like other savvy hair capitalists, the Cardozos ran a salon that adapted and modified the natural style to save their business, part of a wider process that ultimately contributed to the commodification of the Afro. As Blain Roberts puts it, 'the trajectory of Angela Davis' famous hair, by becoming a model for wig makers, highlighted this in vivid terms. Manufacturers of beauty products accelerated the trend. From Madam C.J. Walker to Clairol, black- and white-owned brands alike marketed products for use on natural hair.' Roberts argues that 'the assimilation of "the natural" into black beauty culture represented a betrayal of the politics of the styles. The whole point of rejecting straightened hair was rejecting artificial manipulation.'[31] The same argument applies today.

REPRESENTATION OR LIBERATION?

People are quick to highlight parallels between the black activism of the 1960s and '70s with today's movements. In truth, there are major distinctions and, in relation to hair, the different ideologies that underpin both movements have a direct effect on how 'natural' our natural hair looks.

Our Black Power forebears were anti-consumerist, grounded in socialist and Marxist theory. Today, 'activism' is seen by many as a legitimate hustle through which to 'get your coin'. On top of this, we buy products and 'lifestyles' that demonstrate our wokeness; we are persuaded that we can 'shop ourselves free'.

Thus, today's protestations remain largely devoid of any analysis of capitalism. The fact that most forms of inequality find their origins in the neoliberal logic underpinning the industries and institutions in which we want to be represented is largely ignored. Black Power activists, on the other hand, believed that liberation for the black masses and the marginalized, poor and oppressed more generally could never be achieved through the existence of a small elite or the presence of a few 'exceptional Negroes' taking up space in the very institutions that perpetuate exploitation or the corporations that lobby for the policies that legislate against the interests of minorities and the poor. Representations employed in the service of providing a humanizing façade to authoritarianism or a veneer of kindness to capitalism are not only counterproductive – they are counter-revolutionary. Organizers such as Fred Hampton and Stokely Carmichael theorized from a position of exclusion, using their liminality to challenge the moral and ethical legitimacy of the society that oppressed them. They inhabited the 'angry, disreputable places' that Paul Gilroy reminds us remain crucial so that 'the political interests of racialised minorities might be identified and worked upon without being encumbered by an affected liberal innocence.'[32] It is difficult to see the parallels between such an approach and conversations today that frequently conflate activism and involvement in 'the struggle' with diverse representation in the corporate, glossy world of advertising campaigns for brands owned by multinationals.

The natural-hair movement that emerged from this earlier intellectual and political space sought to avoid artificial manipulation of hair as a rejection of consumerism. Today's nat-ural-hair movement has been born out of a different cultural moment: a renewed confidence in our own worth driven in many ways by the revolution in social media. Today we are product-obsessed, and a lot of them are expensive products. 'Natural' products, usually paraben- and sulphate-free, and which claim to use only organic materials, are pricey and often marketed as high-end luxury goods.

In contrast to the picked-out 'fro that reigned supreme in the late 1960s and early '70s, the emphasis today is much more on stretching, making the hair look long and achieving a twisted-out, soft, curly look, one that conforms to a type of femininity more in line with European beauty standards. While the dominance of straight hair might have been pronounced for decades now, the boundaries have recently expanded to include curly-haired girls: 'if it's going to be curly then it has to be the white kind of curly, loose curls or, at worst, spiral curls, *but never kinky*.'[33]

The internet, in its thirst for endless content, has contributed to the creation of a historically unique moment in which there is a continuously eroded distinction between private and public. Identities – particularly traditionally marginalized and inter-sectional ones – have become their own lucrative form of cultural capital. Much like the Revue Nègre in Paris in the 1920s, black-ness is 'in' and there exists a whole system of benefits and rewards acquired by speaking publicly about pain resulting from racism, sexism, homophobia or transphobia. As the acerbically sharp Instagrammer Jill is Black summed it up, 'trauma is trending'.

In this context it can be easy to confuse representation with liberation. But speaking about pain is not the same as dismantling the power structures that create that pain. Seeing our images reflected back to us in advertising campaigns for institutions or brands that further entrench those systems is certainly not free-dom. I have this sneaking suspicion that our kin didn't endure what they did so that we could wear 'THIS IS WHAT A

FEMINIST LOOKS LIKE' T-shirts produced by sweatshop slaves. We have to dream bigger than brand inclusivity as an end goal. Market research has recognized that the general market is becoming increasingly diverse and that ethical insights are invaluable in terms of creating an authentic message. Sundial Brands, the home of Nubian Heritage, Shea Moisture* and the relaunched Madam Walker, were pioneers in coining the new general market concept about ten years ago.

1. *Diversity is the default today, not the exception.* Minorities are already the majority in most large cities . . . The New General Market is inherently social, mobile and disproportionately influential. They are diverse and urban; they value authenticity, creativity and community.
2. Advertising stereotypes is cancerous for a brand. Failure to acknowledge social commentary and cultural norms *appears insensitive.*
3. A committed group of brand advocates are your best brand influencers. *What people buy is more and more indicative of who they are.*

There is the illusion of subversion, or the newly popularized 'disruption', as part of a 'woke' lifestyle that one can now buy into.

But 'subversion' in the service of oppressive power systems and exploitative practices is not subversion, ya dig? As Susan Bordo explains, 'Subversion is contextual, historical, and above all social. No matter how exciting the "destabilizing" potential of texts, bodily or otherwise, whether those texts are subversive or recuperative, or both or neither, cannot be determined by abstraction from actual social practice.'[34]

Revolutionary symbolism emptied of all its revolutionary meaning is appropriated by companies whose social practice is about wealth accumulation. This defanged symbolism is then sold

* For more on Shea Moisture, see Chapter 5.

back to us as evidence of progress. Businesses now know what the new general market demands to see. Yet they still so often get it wrong – 'coolest monkey in the jungle', anyone? Much like an automaton attempting to express emotion, this diversity is still only performative. There is no substance. Like the tin man, it has no heart. When the agents of these processes are black themselves, they are even more seductive and thus even more pernicious. The UCLA Professor of American History Robin Kelley cautions about the black face of authoritarianism and the 'rise of a black political class that serve as junior partners in forms of authoritarian governance'[35] yet at the same time are held up as evidence that things are getting better, because hey, look: diversity. I reiterate: all skinfolk are not kinfolk.

Personal success stories are not necessarily transformative for the group. More often they are merely reflective of one particular individual's aptitude at calculating a way to thrive under capitalism. Usually these individuals are the exceptions, and they often operate from a position of structural advantage vis-à-vis 'ordinary blacks', an advantage that is likely to have emerged from a social, cultural or aesthetic proximity to whiteness (although, of course, not always; sometimes sheer ruthlessness can be sufficient).

In *Style and Status*, Susannah Walker notes a March 1994 fashion editorial entitled 'Free Angela: Actress Cynda Williams as Angela Davis, a Fashion Revolutionary' that appeared in the urban entertainment magazine *Vibe*. In a response that would be unlikely today, the iconic activist Davis penned an essay, 'Afro Images: Politics, Fashion and Nostalgia'.[36] Davis argued that reproducing the photographic images from her high-profile court case in the service of consumerism was incongruous with everything she stood for and represented. It was the 'most blatant example of the way the particular history of my legal case is emptied of all content so that it can serve as a commodified backdrop for advertising'.

Kobena Mercer describes this phenomenon as the incorporation of protest into the fashion industry, advertising and other economies of capitalist mediation.

> Once commercialized in the marketplace, the Afro lost its specific signification as a black cultural-political statement. Cut off from its original political contexts, it became just another fashion . . . Similarly to the 'far-out' logic of long hair among hippies that sought to symbolize disaffection from western norms, it was rapidly assimilated and dissimulated by commodity fetishism.[37]

Fast-forward to 2019. We don't even call this stuff out any more. Instead, we celebrate it as a win for representation.

AFRO, CLASS AND AFRICAN AESTHETICS

> There was nothing particularly African about the Afro at all. Neither style [dreadlocks or the Afro] had a given reference point in existing African cultures, in which hair is rarely left to grow 'naturally'. Often it is plaited or braided, using weaving techniques to produce a rich variety of sometimes highly elaborate styles, reminiscent of the patternings of African cloth and the decorative designs of African ceramics, architecture and embroidery. Underlying these practices is what might be termed an *African aesthetic*. In contrast to the separation of the aesthetic sphere in . . . European thought, this is an aesthetic which incorporates practices of beautification into everyday life. Thus artifice is valued in its own right as a mark of both invention and tradition.[38]

The aesthetic meanings – both of the Afro and straightened hair – are not necessarily what they first appear. The 'militant' Afro of the 1960s and '70s differs from traditional braiding and from hair straightening. The main difference from much of today's natural hair movement, obsessed as it is with twist-outs, curl pattern, stretching and products, is lack of manipulation. The Afro's *raison d'être* was the abandonment of artifice – the decision to let the hair spring forth naturally as the good lord intended. Ironically, while the Afro harked back to natural origins and was a direct rejection of consumerism and liberatory in its politics, it was not necessarily aesthetically African. Undoubtedly a bold black expression, it demonstrated resistance to Western realities. Undoubtedly black, it was nonetheless a Western reaction.

It wasn't to last. By the 1980s 'the natural' was largely a relic of the past. Cultural critic Asali Solomon explains that, 'in general, working-class and low-income black girls and women' had become the trailblazers in stylistic innovation. 'Middle- and upper-income blacks wore more conventional relaxed styles,' in approximation of Euro-American norms, with an 'emphasis on the vertical length of the hair'. Meanwhile, those who came from a lower socio-economic background were generally more interested in a 'style's ability to flout gravity and incorporate extravagant sculpting details. In this way, hair became somewhat a marker of class.'[39]

In her research on the role of hair in racialization in the Dominican Republic, Ginetta Candelario notes the distaste that the Dominican women she interviews show for the heavily processed hair of black Americans. Confronted with images of hairstyles from the 1990s and 2000s, they identify the sculpted nature of African-American styles as distinguishing them from Dominican hair culture. Dominican women place emphasis on hair that looks 'healthy, natural and loose'. Unlike for their African-American cousins, artifice is not the aesthetic. As Candelario explains, the extensive technology, time and effort employed to make hair loose and manageable must not show. The hair is supposed to 'pass' as natural 'good' hair. This has parallels with the marketing ploy of Walker as a 'hair culturist', rather than someone who made millions selling straighteners, and the Cardozos with their 'the chemicals made our hair better' line.

Hair has been chemically straightened here, but there is little that is recognizable from conventional European beauty standards.

African cultures should be noted for their dynamism. Stylistic expressions adapt to the contemporary cultural landscape. With relaxed hair, the centrality of artifice remains, but it has transformed itself to adapt to the European standard that equates femininity with vertical length. The fashion for weave today is often dramatically long, thick, full hair, quite unlike the hair of European women. This is in part due to the fact that the far more luscious locks of Asian women are used as extensions. But in addition (and this is what is more interesting to me) it is perhaps because there remains a working relationship with artifice, one that has survived the ravages of colonization. It is this African aesthetic that reveals itself in 'unnatural' hair colours today, or the innovative shaping and design of the 1980s and 1990s, a creativity that – until its recent acceptance into fashion – was dismissed as 'ghetto'.

Assessed in this light, one could make a strong argument that obviously chemically straightened, heavily processed hairstyles can be located within the parameters of African aesthetics. It is easy to understand that straightened hair that is attempting to 'pass' as European, or at least to conform to European norms, is less easily located within that aesthetic. But what might be more surprising is the fact that it's difficult to interpret the self-consciously Afrocentric Afro as aesthetically African.

In 2018, the film *Black Panther* changed the game. It was way overdue but signifies that we've come a long way in a remarkably short space of time. As recently as 2014 I saw Terence Nance's *An Oversimplification of Her Beauty* and was stunned to see both the leads, Terence himself and Namik Minter, sporting natural 'fros. Woah! I thought, this is radical! Which is in itself completely messed up. Can you imagine a white woman seeing straight hair onscreen in 2014 and thinking, 'Wow, history in the making'?

In 2016 Donald Glover's television series *Atlanta* went one step further. His character's on/off girlfriend Van, played by Zazie Beetz, got out of bed wearing her headscarf, walked to the bathroom mirror and removed it to reveal a head full of bantu knots which she then proceeded to untwist!?!!! I think I spat out my tea, or maybe it was wine . . . anyway, amid much spluttering, I realized that this was a historical moment onscreen. A black woman's daily natural-hair routine – *my* natural-hair routine – performed on international television as though it were the most normal thing in the world. As though we were normal.

The scene was particularly poignant for me because the actress Zazie Beetz is also mixed race and has a similar hair texture to mine, something I have been conditioned to believe was an unfortunate anomaly. And we simply *never* see this texture represented by women, mixed or not. While Zazie and her hair are, inarguably, gorgeous, she still has this to say:

> I have come to love myself, and my hair, and grown into loving my brown skin, but that doesn't mean I don't struggle with my hair too sometimes. I still cry about it, be it the difficulty, or

aesthetically what I wish I had, and it's because you really just don't see it.[40]

As I've grown older I have realized that so many things have been designed to constrain and constrict us – all of us – but especially black and mixed-race women, especially us. However, our emotions, our likes, our dislikes and our desires are not discrete or conclusive and cannot be deduced from looking at us. We are complex. We contain multitudes. And unlike so many of the women before us, we are free. There is no one way to be black and there is no inauthentic way of being yourself.

From Annie Malone to Madam Walker, to A'Lelia Walker and Fairy Mae, to Josephine Baker, to Angela Davis, to Rihanna, to Zazie Beetz, to me, and to YOU. The seemingly contradictory spaces each of us might simultaneously occupy need not be at odds with each other, nor do they need to conform to anybody's limited imaginings of who or what we can be.

4
How Can He Love Himself and Hate Your Hair?

In 2013 I wrote a blog post entitled 'Who Stole All the Black Women from Britain?' It went viral after being shared by the black feminist bell hooks. It opened with the following passage by Eldridge Cleaver. I don't think I've ever cited anything that has provoked such disbelief.

> There is no love left between a black man and a black woman. Take me for instance. I love white women and hate black women. It's just in me so deep that I don't even try to get it out of me anymore. I'd jump over ten nigger bitches just to get to one white woman. Isn't no such thing as an ugly white woman . . . *and just to touch her long, soft, silky hair.* There's softness about a white woman, something delicate and soft inside of her.
>
> But a nigger bitch seems to be full of steel, granite-hard and resisting . . . I mean I can't analyze it, but I know that the White man made the Black woman the symbol of slavery and the White woman the symbol of freedom. Every time I'm embracing a Black woman, I'm embracing slavery, and when I put my arms around a White woman, well I'm hugging freedom.[1] [my italics]

People found it hard to believe that a prominent member of the Black Panther Political Party and not just some (proto-internet) troll could have written these words. They *must* be fraudulent, like the Willie Lynch hoax – the letter that affected to allegedly detail a slave owner's account of the breaking of men and the making of slaves? Sadly not. These are Cleaver's words, the real deal.

'You too can have good hair! Instant Hair. Instant Beauty. Instant Success. He will love you too.' A 1960s US advertisement for wigs. Misplaced anxiety can become concentrated on our hair. A powerful narrative exists that promotes the idea that straight hair has the power to resolve all our problems.

There is a lot to be said about this excerpt, but let's focus on hair for now. Notice that Cleaver doesn't mention the white woman's complexion. The racialized feature that distinguishes 'white women' from 'nigger bitches', the feature that distinguishes freedom from slavery, is hair: *'and just to touch her long, soft, silky hair . . .'.*

'I thought that was your hair, I was finna wife you up.' Of this I was informed by a teenage fling in Atlanta upon his painful discovery, when I took out my braided extensions, that my hair was neither the length nor the texture he desired, nor indeed what he imagined befitted someone of my mixed racial background. The revelation that my hair was closer in texture to the African side of my heritage, rather than the European, was enough for him to rescind his hypothetical marriage proposal. Less extreme than Cleaver, who, quite frankly, sounds like a lunatic, but not entirely unrelated. This was the summer I became fully aware of the value many black men placed on women's hair texture.

There was a girl that summer; all these years later, her name escapes me, but the memory of her fabled beauty remains. The first few weeks I hung out with my new boo and his crew, she was just a rumour who was down in Mississippi, Atlanta temporarily deprived of her shine. Bae finally reappeared, and I still remember the feeling of surprise upon meeting her. I was confronted with the strange fact that there was little about her that might normally be considered attractive. The source of her legendary loveliness seemed to lie almost entirely in her hair, which, bequeathed to her by her Korean mother, spilled, oil-like and silky, blue-black, down her back, distinguishing it – distinguishing her – from the coarse kinks of Africa. This asset alone was seemingly more than enough to usher her into the hallowed halls of hotness.

Even among ourselves, the only way we could make sense of our beauty was when it conformed to European conventions. This discovery hurt me to my core. White people denigrated my hair, but the realization that black people were just as contemptuous – were, in fact, often *more* contemptuous – was too much!

I suppose it was a reality that was first introduced to me when I was a toddler and people would comment that my hair texture was a pity. The next explicit incident I remember was being fourteen and the mother of my only black friend at the time, who was Jamaican, casually informing me, as she braided my hair, that I didn't have good hair and was in a way I was lucky to have grown up around white people who couldn't tell the difference. I couldn't really process what she was saying, but now, back in Atlanta, I was confronted with first-hand evidence. In possession of that knowledge, it was no longer possible to seek scant comfort in self-righteous 'them and us' rage. The 'us' had internalized what the 'them' had dictated. The hate wasn't external any more. Discovering this was an entirely different kind of violence.

An enduring memory of my eventual meeting with this girl was her decidedly glacial response. She was positively hostile. To be fair, I was probably chilly too. While it's all somewhat blurry looking back, we had definitely been set up as competition to each other. Me with the light skin, her with the good hair. I also recall that often during those long Southern summers my popularity with boys seemed to work entirely in disproportion with the distinctly less breezy vibe I got from girls.

Few of us understand how much our behaviour has been predetermined by systems that were put in place far before our birth. Of course, back then, I, like most people, did not realize how we are all, to an extent, characters in a play whose plot we certainly didn't write.

Toni Morrison beautifully reveals the complexities and interrelatedness of black hair, black love, self-worth and competition between women in her 1977 novel *Song of Solomon*:

> [HAGAR:] 'Why don't he like my hair? . . .'
> [PILATE:] 'Of course he likes it. How can he not like it? . . .'
> 'He likes silky hair . . . he don't like hair like mine . . . silky hair the colour of a penny . . . curly, wavy, silky hair. He don't like mine.'

Pilate put her head on Hagar's head and trailed her fingers through her granddaughter's soft wool: 'How can he not love your hair? It's the same hair that grows out of his own armpits. The same hair that crawls up out of his crotch on up his stomach. All over his chest. The very same. It grows out of his nose, over his face. It's all over his head, Hagar. It's his hair too. He got to love it . . . How can he love himself and hate your hair?'[2]

Hagar, desperate to capture the heart of Milkman, believes that the beauty salon, the palace of transformation, will equip her with the necessary 'beauty' to win his affections. Yet, ultimately, her attempts at hair straightening and, more crucially, securing Milkman's love fail, with tragic consequences. The object of Milkman's desire remains unnamed, but we know that she is a lemon-yellow black girl with, perhaps more importantly, good hair. The fact that this exchange takes place on Hagar's deathbed just before she dies – quite literally of a broken heart – indicates the depth to which these issues run. 'He's never going to like my hair,' are the last words the distraught girl ever speaks. Hagar loses. The girl with the good hair wins. That lemon-yellow girl might not be white, but she's the next best thing, and the closer the better, right?

'All your girlfriends had long flowing hair,' she said, her tone thick with accusation. 'What?' She was being absurd, but knowing that didn't make her any less so. Pictures she had seen of his ex-girlfriends goaded her, the slender Japanese with straight hair dyed red, the olive-skinned Venezuelan with corkscrew hair that fell to her shoulders, the white girl with waves and waves of russet hair. And now this woman whose looks she didn't care for, but who had long straight hair . . . *She felt small and ugly* . . .[3] [my italics]

This passage, from Chimamanda Adichie's *Americanah*, hit me like a slug to the chest! The jealousy and inadequacy I have felt upon discovering that all of an ex's girlfriends had good hair, as well as the pointed rage; the sense of betrayal that a black man who purported to date only black women might not have been entirely honest in not admitting that this only extended to a *certain type of black woman*.

Do a little test. Think about the high-profile black men in Britain or the US. If they even deign to date black or mixed women in the first place, look at their partner's hair. You know where I'm going, and if you don't already you soon will. Take a look. Tell me what you see.

HE WILL LOVE YOU TOO

In late 2017 I attended an event on black love and dating, during which I conducted a survey among the audience, over 95 per cent of whom were female. The questions asked how they felt about their hair. How did they describe their own texture? What was their ideal hair? Did men respond to them differently based on the style they wore? Did they feel represented by the natural-hair community?

Almost ninety people took part in the survey. The vast majority of women described their own hair as 'kinky' while using terms like 'soft' and 'curly' to describe ideal hair. Most also noted that the natural-hair movement was dominated by women with curly hair. There was a prevailing consensus that men preferred hair that was either 'straight' or 'mixed-race', 'soft' and 'curly'. Not one respondent answered that men liked kinky hair as a first choice.

A number of respondents felt that, while black men had a preference for ' long, straight' or 'soft, curly' hair, they hated wigs. This hatred of wigs is interesting, given that African aesthetics celebrates artifice. The association of 'naturalness' with beauty is a legacy of Romanticism, the artistic and literary movement that emerged in Europe at the end of the eighteenth century. The aversion to wigs shows how European norms have been internalized in many ways that we don't even realize.

When I asked respondents if they felt men had a preference, one woman described their behaviour as 'slightly schizophrenic; I think they act like they prefer natural, but actually like the long flowing hair.' This type of sentiment was commonly expressed.

> Sometimes, black men want women with straight hair but yet despise weaves.
> Straight hair and bouncy curls. They don't like to see wigs on the stand.
> I think they like everything other than wigs, largely because of when it comes off.
> I feel like black men prefer more of a mixed-race hair texture.
> Yes, they don't want a woman with 'picky' hair.
> Yes – but not always expressed.
> Yes, long, soft and 'pullable' in bed.
> Yes – loose curls, long hair. Of course not all, but a large percentage.
> I think although they may not say out loud, most men do tend to go for women with softer and longer hair.

A tiny minority of answers deviated from this. One respondent felt there was no preference 'as long as it's neat'; another, simply, 'I think hair that flatters a woman.' But these were very much in the minority.

One interesting answer was 'Yep, certain types of men have a different preference, but it's all patriarchy.' I interpreted this as a reference to men who prefer natural hair because they think it conforms to ideas about 'respectable', demure women. The association with respectability is interesting, as often, in the past, natural was seen as unkempt and then militant. The idea of political consciousness is still there in the sense that you are perceived as a more genuine or authentic type of woman. This is not without its problems, veering close to the fault lines of the ho–queen hotep binary and the limitations of respectability politics.

The natural-hair hierarchy means it is easier for those with 'good' hair to go 'natural', and to then be praised as 'natural queens'. Meanwhile, women with the hair texture that is most stigmatized might be more likely to use wigs or weave, and then face discrimination.

While I have had white guys try to 'run' their fingers through my hair, black men tend to know better. Nonetheless, I've still heard a number extol this 'fingers through the hair' malarkey as an ideal. Whether it's the girl with the wind-whipped hair framing her face or the chick wearing nothing but an oversized man's shirt peering coquettishly through her tousled mane and wordlessly reminding you of last night's vigorous hair-pulling, these are norms that have been constructed in a society in which black hair is an anomaly. But because we consume the same media, are force-fed the same images, this is our expectation of what beauty, femininity, dating, romance and sex look like, regardless of what *we* look like.

When I had relaxed hair, attempts to conform to this standard were scuppered by certain activities, especially when dating. No quick dips into the pool or slipping into the sea with me boo, and, particularly during hot and humid summers, too much (ahem) physical exertion was more likely to produce frizz and reversion than sexy chic! But when my hair texture is one of the most versatile in the world, when the way I style it is only as limited as my imagination and white supremacy, isn't it ironic that a hair type that can do so little remains the standard against which all others are judged?

What was encouraging in the survey results was that very few who responded believed that any of this was the result of some sort of natural preference. Almost everybody located the origins of these ideas in colonialism and the prevalence of European beauty standards. Yet if we know this, why do these standards prevail? One or two even went further, highlighting the fact that the way men looked at women and made judgements, of whatever nature, was itself patriarchal.

In his revolutionary text *Ways of Seeing* the wonderful John

Berger reassessed how we evaluate that which we 'see', how we behave correspondingly and how this goes on to inform social relations. According to Berger, our ways of seeing have been greatly influenced by the tradition of oil painting, the primary visual art form characterizing the age of modernity. The reign of oil painting dates from approximately 1500 to 1900. Its governing laws and cultural norms still provide the framework through which we represent ourselves and how we perceive others. In its most current manifestation, this is the visual logic that underpins image-heavy social media networks such as Instagram, a platform many of the respondents referenced as deeply influential on romantic 'preferences'.

One of the primary relationships to emerge out of the tradition of oil painting is that between the spectator and the object on display. Nudes were a prolific genre of oil painting, and it is in the nude depiction of women that we can locate the origin of contemporary female representation, particularly the implication that the female subject is aware of being seen by a spectator. Berger identifies *The Judgement of Paris* (c. 1528) by Cranach the Elder as having been pivotal in the development of these ideas.

With this painting, an enduring theme was introduced. *The Judgement* portrayed what was by now an established idea: that a man – or men – looked at naked women; but it introduced a new and crucial element, that of *judgement*. 'Thus beauty becomes competitive. Those who are not judged beautiful are *not beautiful*. Those who are beautiful are given the prize.' This would go on to have a transformative impact on relations between women and men, as well as between women themselves.[4]

Berger explains that the attitudes and values that once informed oil painting are now expressed through other, more widely diffused media – advertising, journalism and television. 'Oil painting did to appearances what capital did to social relations, reducing everything to the status of objects. Everything became exchangeable because everything became a commodity. All reality was

mechanically measured by its materiality.'[5] The historical period
in which these developments took place is key. Oil painting emerged
as a popular art form at the beginning of European global expansion, African subjugation and the birth of the system of capitalism
that has grown increasingly powerful over the last 500 years.

As Berger argues, this paradigm determines not only most relations between men and women but also the relationship of a
women to herself: ' . . . thus she turns herself into an object – and
most particularly an object of vision: a sight'.[6] For extra potency,
add to this heady concoction a generous dose of white supremacy,
and we have a hierarchy whereby women with certain racialized
features are considered more beautiful than others. As Patricia
Hill Collins puts it:

> Within the binary thinking that underpins intersecting oppres-
> sions, blue-eyed, blond, thin White women could not be
> considered beautiful without the Other – Black women with
> African features of dark skin, broad noses, full lips, and kinky
> hair. Race, gender, and sexuality converge on this issue of eval-
> uating beauty . . . African-American women experience the
> pain of never being able to live up to prevailing standards of
> beauty – standards used by White men, White women, Black
> men, and, most painfully, one another. Regardless of any indi-
> vidual woman's subjective reality, this is the system of ideas that
> she encounters. Because controlling images are hegemonic and
> taken for granted, they become virtually impossible to escape.[7]

European features exist at the pinnacle, with value progres-
sively decreasing the more your features correspond to certain
types of African feature, particularly those found in the parts of
Western and Central Africa from which people were kidnapped
then enslaved.

The binary tradition advanced by French philosopher René
Descartes separated the mind from the body, associating men with
the lofty pursuits of the objective mind. The cerebral and the

intellectual were the man's domains. Meanwhile, women were relegated to the subjective fleshiness of the body. Being just bodies, the way women looked was given far more emphasis then the way men looked.

> Men *act* and women *appear*.
> Men look at women.
> Women watch themselves being looked at.[8]

Many feminist scholars have analysed beauty ideals and considered women's involvement in beauty practices within a political context. As Kathy Davis explains: 'Beauty is integral to the construction of femininity in a gendered social order, and the female sex is idealized as the incarnation of beauty, while the bodies of most ordinary women tend to be treated as inferior and in constant need of improvement.'[9] The competition created by the prizes and rewards bequeathed through the possession of beauty (which is turbo-charged by our society's notions of romantic love and its key institutions: monogamous marriage and the nuclear family, the natural progression of romantic love) creates in turn a fertile market for advertisers.

'He will love you, too,' they whisper. Or perhaps, in this era of commodified female empowerment, it is more likely you will hear them breathe, 'You will love yourself' (as the necessary preparatory state before he can love you fully, of course). In one Madam C.J. Walker advertisement, 'a dreamy woman clad in an evening gown sits at her dressing table applying cosmetics. She is a light-complexioned black woman with wavy hair pinned up in an elaborate style.'*

You, too, may be a fascinating beauty.
Perhaps you envy the girl with irresistible beauty, whose skin is flawless and velvety, whose hair has a beautiful silky

---

* Consider contemporary black performers and how enduring this representation remains.

sheen, the girl who receives glances of undoubted admiration.
You need not envy her. Create new beauty for yourself by using
Madam C.J. Walker's famous preparations.[10]

When we think about how beauty products – in this case black
haircare products – are sold to us, we need to consider the art of
publicity. 'The spectator-buyer is meant to envy herself as she will
become if she buys the product . . . the publicity image steals her
love for herself as she is, and offers it back to her for the price of
the product.'[11]

Just like the poster promises: *You too can have good hair! Instant
hair. Instant beauty. Instant success. He will love you too.* It's all
so beautiful and achievable; you're so close you can nearly touch it.
All you need to do is make the purchase. Buy the product.

For the black market, the sales pitch was rendered even more
emotive through the association of beautification with the process
of black racial uplift. The secret behind the success of the most
memorable hair capitalists was not so much the creation of products
but their marketing. The new narrative developed by black manufacturers capitalized on the desire of black communities to improve
their circumstances through hard graft and general excellence.

The vision of beauty promoted was one that made sense primarily in relation to its proximity to whiteness (although not as much
proximity as media representations might have suggested). In 1929
the *New York Interstate Tattler*, an African-American celebrity gossip and entertainment paper, launched a Lonesome Hearts column
that continued throughout the following decade. Susannah Walker
has shown that its advertisements provide a rare glimpse into the
prevalent beauty attitudes of a largely undocumented world, revealing the aspirations of ordinary African-Americans, which are
usually obscured behind more prolific media representations.

But whether or not the lonely hearts accept or reject the dominant standard, they clearly position themselves in relation to it.
Walker notes that most of the letters highlight quality of hair and

complexion, either of the author themselves or of the partner they desire. Hair and skin are mentioned as frequently as age, and more frequently than weight or height.

Some of the letters make for painful reading, demonstrating the ravages of colourism on people who imagine themselves too far from the ideal to be considered beautiful and, by extension, imagine themselves to be undeserving of love. When a woman describes herself as 'a black girl', a later writer comments, 'I venture to say that she is not as black, or as unattractive as I . . . I don't expect anyone to want to take me places, or to become interested in me, but oh, how I should love to receive a letter now and then . . . I am black, have short hair, very unattractive, a typical Negro type.'[12]

Elsewhere we see defiance of those same norms. At least among a minority, there is a significant distance between what people are told they want and what they actually want. Consider a letter from a male correspondent writing in the same year as the unhappy girl above. The author declares that any girl he seeks 'must be dark', 'she doesn't have to be good looking but she must be dark. In other words, a real Negro is what I wish better than anything else in the world . . . I'm a Negro and I want a Negro pal.'[13]

Black people come in a vast range of complexions, so the idea that darker skin makes somebody more of a 'real Negro' is something that must be unpacked. Nonetheless, the writer's preference does suggest that not everybody accepted the 'light bright' propaganda. In fact Walker highlights the fact that there existed a preference for brown skin over skin that was too light. This certainly differs from the lighter-the-better logic that dictated who won beauty contests or excelled in the entertainment industry. Regardless of complexion, however, the preference for good hair endured. The ideal woman most often described in the letters is one with brown skin, but not too dark, and crucially with good hair. This has echoes of the situation in Spanish-speaking countries like Cuba and the Dominican Republic, where the *jubao*, the person with light skin, tightly coiled hair and African features, is reviled, while the person who has brown skin, more European features and good hair is the desired standard.

MANDEM

The costs of the beauty regime fall disproportionately on black women. Because women's bodies are constructed as objects of sight to be judged, men are more likely to be left out of these con-versations. When I started writing about these painful truths, I had a sense that perhaps it was possible for Milkman to reject Hagar while still holding himself in rather high esteem. When a black man rejects a woman for possessing the same features he himself has, we know that this is often born of the legacy of slavery and colonialism: a toxin that breeds in the resulting ecosystem of black inferiority. At its most pronounced it is the disgusting atti-tude of Cleaver, but few of us have escaped entirely unscathed. We have all of us, to varying degrees, internalized aspects of white supremacy. Hair remains one of the pre-eminent sites where this plays out in constructions of beauty.

Recently, I started talking to men about why so many of them wear their hair closely shorn. I wasn't prepared for what I discovered.

Masculinity is foregrounded in stereotypes about blackness. Obviously, this affects men and women differently. While an emphasis on masculinity might contribute to black men being per-ceived as more attractive – often in limiting and derogatory ways – the association of blackness with masculinity has contrib-uted to black women being stereotyped as less attractive.

One way in which this masculinity might be mediated is by a detour through whiteness. In many ways, black femininity has been read through mixedness and its associated features. Behold the mixed-race/light-skinned black woman, the one with the 'fair' skin and the long, pretty hair. *Voilà!* Femininity achieved! Isn't this the reason that most internationally recognizable black women are generally light-skinned and silky haired? Equally, one imagines, it's the reason that light-skinned or mixed-race men are rarely chosen as representatives of black manliness. The way in which colourism is gendered is often overlooked, but the light-skin and good-hair gang is undoubtedly associated with femininity. Men with these features are often perceived as 'sweet boys' or effeminate in some way. While these features can be perceived positively, they can just as easily be weaponized. For example, they might be used to challenge how authentically black somebody is. A recent high-profile rap beef between Pusha T and Drake commanded headlines in *The New York Times* and left Twitter in flames. Pusha pretty much annihilated Drake. One of the most devastating dimensions of the assault was Pusha's questioning of Drake's blackness. Yet, like Cleaver, Pusha doesn't mention complexion. Once more, blackness or lack thereof is assessed by hair texture.

Confused, always felt you weren't Black enough
Afraid to grow it 'cause your 'fro wouldn't nap enough.

Drake's blackness is in question due in no small part to his hair texture, but the rules are, as ever, complex. A darker-skinned, kinky-haired black man can more easily conform to an accepted attractive trope of blackness than can a female counterpart with the same features. Men may indeed 'act' and women 'appear', but race adds another layer. I naïvely imagined that, by virtue of their masculinity, black men had escaped the stigma associated with possessing tightly coiled hair.

The first time I reconsidered it properly was a few years ago when I mentioned my interest in hair and someone commented that the motivation for many black men to keep it short was simply that they didn't like its texture. I broached the question to a wider audience and the word 'picky' came up again and again. I was shocked by how many men also confessed to using texturizer – essentially a form of chemical relaxer – which instead of making the hair bone straight maintains a 'texture:'; the soft waves or curls associated with 'good' hair. I remembered my Guyanese step-father and the pride he took in his mother's Amer-Indian blood, and the subsequent 'good quality' of his hair. Every night he performed mysterious rituals involving a tub of Sportin' Waves, before donning a satin du-rag, and each morning that shit was waaaaaaved.

I thought about the handful of black indie boys I knew during the heady days of electroclash (lol). They all had chemically straightened hair in emulation of the floppy indie fringes the white boys had. (Even though my own hair was relaxed, I remembered how incredibly dismal I found theirs.) I thought about a young mixed-race boy I know who complained to me that he doesn't possess the softly, curly texture both he and others expect, given his ancestry. I considered the contempt I occasionally heard in the voices of black men when they talked about wigs or 'nappy' hair, and I thought, Yes, of course, Morrison has nailed it again: 'How can he love himself and hate your hair?'

It might be hard to imagine, but between the 1920s and the 1960s a significant percentage of black men in the US relaxed their hair. Comparable with today's belief that type-4 hair is picky or looks African, it was often seen as 'country'; meanwhile, smooth, sleek hair, combed back or brushed up into a pompadour conferred urban sophistication.

In his bestselling autobiography, the human-rights activist Malcolm X, or Omowale,* details this 'conking', or chemical processing of hair among black men.

My first view in the mirror blotted out the hurting. I'd seen some pretty conks, but when it's the first time, on your own head, the transformation, after the lifetime of kinks, is staggering ... How ridiculous I was! Stupid enough to stand there simply lost in admiration of my hair now looking 'white',

---

* Omowale means 'The child has returned home'. This is the Yoruba name Malcolm was given when he visited Nigeria in 1964.

reflected in the mirror in Shorty's room. I vowed that I'd never again be without a conk, and I never was for many years . . . This was my first really big step toward self-degradation: when I endured all of that pain, literally burning my flesh to have it look like a white man's hair. I had joined that multitude of Negro men and women in America who are brainwashed into believing that the black people are 'inferior' – and white people 'superior' – that they will even violate and mutilate their God-created bodies to try to look 'pretty' by white standards.[14]

Despite its prevalence by the 1960s, straightening among black men was hugely unpopular. Undoubtedly, this was due in part to the Black Power movement. But it was more widespread; even black Republicans like James Brown were on board, declaring, 'Say it loud, I'm black and I'm proud!'

By the 1980s, the conk might well have been retired, but so was the Afro, replaced with the use of texturizing products to create the wet-look Jheri curl and the S curl. It would be highly unlikely to see anyone anywhere sporting a Jheri curl these days but, nonetheless, I started to understand more fully that ideas about masculinity did not protect black men from feeling some type of way about themselves:

I have a varied past with hair texturizing and it all boils down to not being content with my type 4c hair. 100% there was [stigma] for me. When I was growing up, all I saw was texturized, short styles. All the black men on TV were doing it (predominantly the RnB artists I would see) and my friends with the less coily hair could achieve it naturally. Black boys and men have long stigmatized one another over their 'picky' black hair. I think it was because it was seen as unkempt, a sign of poverty and Africanness. The guys with straighter, slicker, more Eurocentric hair types were seen (and are still in many ways) as the black beauty standard. Coily 4c hair was a big no-no.[15]

Overall, I heard a lot of this kind of thing. While Drake might have been denounced because his hair texture was not black enough, picky, 'peppercorn', African-textured hair is also discriminated against. Many men also talked about neatness, respectability, pressure from parents, assimilation, the fear that Afro-textured hair when worn longer might be seen as threatening. A black man might be no more threatening than a packet of Skittles,* but the cost of being perceived as such can be no less than death.

Men shared stories of locks shorn, of heads closely cropped to fit into the corporate world. They described environments where, much like black women being prescribed certain hairstyles, they were told that anything other than closely shorn was not permissible. One respondent explained: 'You go through school being excluded for locs, Afros, or braids, it's a constant issue, and by the time you need to go find a job you know in no uncertain terms what's expected of you.' Pressure from women was mentioned too. It's not all one way, ladies. And it was eye-opening to hear how many men simply did not know how to manage their hair. One brother confessed to letting his hair grow to a certain length before asking his dad how to maintain it. Pop's advice? Cut it off. He didn't know himself!

AFRICA

Make no mistake, I am not claiming shame is the sole motivation for black men who have short hair. Many reported far less pernicious reasons; receding hairlines and the time and effort required to maintain longer hair were also common explanations. But

---

* This is in reference to the murder of Trayvon Martin by George Zimmerman. Zimmerman's defence was that Trayvon posed a threat when, in reality, he was a teenage boy armed with nothing more deadly than a packet of Skittles, while Zimmerman stalked around with a Kel-Tec PF-9 pistol. Zimmerman was acquitted of the murder and went on to sell the gun for a reported $250,000, apparently bought as a gift by a mother for her son. And black people are the criminals?

lack of time, as we have seen, is the result of a division of time that does not reflect the norms of black culture or the needs of black bodies.

Black men wearing carefully cropped hair has long historical antecedents. In pre-colonial Africa, both men and women often had closely shorn hair or shaved heads. We know that African aesthetics place a strong emphasis on neat and careful grooming, particularly when it comes to hair. Most Yoruba men shaved their head, moustache and chin until old age, when grey hair (*ewu*) and a beard (*irugbon*) were celebrated as valued signifiers of experience and wisdom.[16]

In the Yoruba community men's hair was used to reinforce political power. The hairstyles men wore were as replete with social meaning as those of the women. The *ilari* (messengers) of the *oba* (king) wore their hair half shaved (*ifari apakan*). Regional variations also existed, for example the messengers of the Oyo Kingdom had their heads shaved every fifth day, leaving a circular patch on the crown that was worn long, braided and dyed with indigo.[17] To attack or kill a royal messenger was an attack on the kingdom they represented. Their hairstyles allowed the *ilari* to be identified in public, effectively bestowing upon them a measure of diplomatic immunity while they conducted the king's business.

Yoruba men's hair in relation to the spiritual world, and the *orisha* in particular, is fascinating. There exist categories of priests of both sexes that serve as intermediaries for *orisha*, for instance Sango, the god of thunder. The female body is said to be ideal for this role because of our incomparable strength and resilience and our ability to bear children without serious injury. In honour of this, the initiation process metaphorically converts the body of a male priest into a female one, allowing the manifestation of the *orisha* during possession. This emphasis on female physical strength exists in stark contrast to European gender norms. Both male and female priests are called *iyawo* (wife). This identifies the priest as a special confidant who ensures regular offerings to the *orisha* and is one of the reasons male priests of Sango wore traditionally female hairstyles such as *suku, koroba* and *kolese*.[18] According to the Yoruba scholar Babatunde Lawal, this is not supposed to have a sexual implication; nonetheless, we should remain sensitive to contemporary readings of a world in which gender and sexuality would have been understood entirely differently.

In the east of the continent we also see gendered European norms concerning hair and, by extension, masculinity and femininity, being blown apart. The Masai men of what is modern-day Kenya wore their hair long and intricately styled, while women tended to shave their heads. Like other African groups, the Masai spent much of their leisure time engaged in hairdressing and self-adornment. The *moran* (warrior) wore his hair extremely long and had it styled by another *moran* during sessions that could last between fifteen and twenty hours. As previously mentioned, we have been conditioned to automatically describe such activity as arduous or time-consuming, but we should continue to disrupt that notion. I remain curious as to what exactly it is that we are expected to be doing with our time? What is more profound or simply enjoyable than this type of activity? What is life for, if not physical intimacy and communion with our bredrin? If, at the end of the exchange, we look better than we did before, issa win.

THE NEW WORLD: BLACK POWER, EIGHTEENTH-CENTURY STYLE

Eighteenth-century Africans' hairstyles were neat, intricate and complex, or short. Yet at the same time in the US, long before the rise of the Afro associated with the Black Power movement, black men were showcasing their natural hair in defiance of anti-black norms.

The historical record presents significant challenges when our interest is in black lives. Black life has not been archived or documented in the same way that white life has. There are no oil paintings that display our wealth and power. We are present, but you have to look for us elsewhere, perhaps in the language you use, in the way you dance, in the food you eat, in the computers you use (more on that to come), in the art you make or the music that is the soundtrack to your life. Black people are there, although recognition is scarce.

When we appear in the New World, our achievements are not those faithfully recorded for prosperity. Rather, we appear in ledgers, books that contain details of livestock, lists of profit and loss. We are possessions, and, as such, there is little need for detail beyond the perfunctory. But every now and then a fleeting glimpse of detail emerges. It's a motley collection, but you work with what you've got: an escaped-slave notice in 1730, a lonesome-hearts advert in 1930.

In their study of slave hair and African-American culture, Shane and Graham White find that newspaper advertisements seeking the return of runaway slaves contained the most detailed descriptions of the bodies of African-Americans at that time. The distinguishing features of black people were considered important enough to record only when it served the interests of white men demanding the return of their property. Outside the considerations of white men, black lives did not matter. In many ways, one could argue that not much has changed.

White and White discover that these abhorrent documents reveal not only the details nobody else bothered to record but that, in eighteenth-century British mainland colonies at least, slaveholders seem to have allowed African-Americans to style their hair as they pleased.[19] Hair culture represented a rare space in which there was a temporary lapse from the regulatory procedures controlling every aspect of black life.

'Eighteenth-century advertisements for runaway slaves were unique in supplying information about a miscreant's name, age,

A Masai *moran* (warrior) styling another *moran*'s hair in the traditional Masai style.

skin color, likely destination and clothing . . . They also, and very frequently, described the escaped slave's hair. What is striking about such descriptions is the great variety of hairstyles included. We learn from them that some slaves wore their hair long and bushy on top and that others cut it short, or combed and parted it neatly, or shaved it at the back or at the front, or trimmed it to a roll. An African-American's hair might be closely cropped on the crown but left long elsewhere'.[20]

White and White argue that the appearance of long, bushy, and/or unkempt hair in the New World might have stemmed from violent restrictions on both the time and the tools that the enslaved had to do their hair, but that this cannot account for the whole story.

Cameroonian men creating a hairdo for an annual dance.

Obviously, blacks were not supposed to be proud of their hair, as they or their ancestors had been in Africa; any suggestion that they were would have sharply challenged complacent white cultural assumptions. In this context, hair worn long and bushy, an arrangement that emphasized, even flaunted, its distinctive texture, may have been, in some cases, an affirmation of difference and even of defiance, an attempt to revalorize a biological characteristic that white racism had sought to devalue. The same comment could be applied to long, bushy beards, which, as eighteenth-century runaway advertisements show, many male slaves possessed.[21]

Occasionally, white people's descriptions hint at such meanings. The 'owner' of the Maryland runaway Bazil notes that his

While Masai men had long, ornate and intricate hairstyles, Masai women favoured shaved heads anointed with red ochre and oils.

slave possessed 'woolly hair, in which he takes great pride', and that Walton, a Virginia runaway, 'commonly combed [his hair] very high'. Ned, a South Carolina slave carpenter, possessed 'a large bushy head of hair, which he wears remarkably high'. These examples might well be read as declarations of pride in their hair. 'Similarly, if Bacchus's master was prepared to acknowledge that his slave possessed "a fine suit of wool", it is possible that Bacchus himself may have shared the same assessment.'[22]

By the nineteenth century, the hairstyles described were far more muted and conformist. We can only speculate on the reasons but, by this point, the pride that was once displayed in defiant hairstyles was gone.

Children of the chief at Toulepleu in the
Ivory Coast, c. 1938.

BLACK IS BEAUTIFUL II

Those eighteenth-century slaves subverted expectations of what
they were supposed to think was attractive, showcasing the very
feature they were conditioned to feel ashamed of. So is this the
solution? Flip the script?

> We are told black African features are ugly.
> We contest it.
> We insist they are BEAUTIFUL.
> Say it loud,
> Say it proud,
> **Black. IS. Beautiful.**

It sounds empowering. It sounds positive. In many ways, it is, but it cannot be an end goal. Visual beauty is not as straight-forwardly benign as we are led to believe. The Black is Beautiful cultural movement of the 1960s ran in parallel with the Black Power movement. It involved an explicit rejection of the Eurocen-tric beauty ideal that denigrated black features while elevating the straight hair and blue eyes of Europeans. Black is Beautiful sought to counteract the narrative that African features are inherently ugly. Instead it reclaimed and celebrated the physical features of black people, encouraging them not to straighten their hair or bleach their skin.

Our society places a huge emphasis on physical beauty. It teaches us that this is a natural consequence of the sense of sight and that beauty is a universal norm.

This is not necessarily accurate. I am not suggesting that Afri-can cultures did not place any importance on beauty. We have seen how people enjoyed and celebrated rituals of beautification and how hair operated as a powerful visual language. But there are major distinctions. Most striking is that the idea of physical beauty as an abstract entity untethered from context existing on its own was perhaps not meaningful in the same way it is today.

In *The Invention of Women*, Oyèrónké Oyěwùmí distinguishes between the Eurocentric worldview and the Yoruba 'world-sense'. The author argues that 'the differentiation of human bodies in terms of sex, skin colour, and cranium size' (a system that has served black people, and black women particularly, so poorly) 'is a testament to the powers attributed to "seeing".'[23]

We hear a lot about the male gaze, but the very concept of 'the gaze' requires further scrutiny. The gaze *itself* is the invitation to differentiate bodies first and foremost based on visible features.

Reality is always only a culturally specific arrangement that we have been conditioned to perceive. Other realities exist. And some of these have privileged senses beyond that of sight.

Different approaches to comprehending reality . . . suggest epistemological differences between societies.

Relative to Yoruba society . . . the body has an exaggerated presence in the Western conceptualization of society.

The term 'worldview', which is used in the West to sum up the cultural logic of society, captures the West's privileging of the visual. It is Eurocentric to use it to describe cultures that privilege other senses.[24]

Oyěwùmí suggests 'world-sense' as a more meaningful way to describe cultures that place less emphasis on the visual, or those which do not understand what they *see* as a standalone way of ascribing value or worth. Our so-called 'natural' tendency to judge a book by its cover and to be entirely influenced by the way someone or something looks is not universal.

BEAUTY BECOMES COMPETITIVE

Talking about the Ashanti, Anthony Appiah argues that it is not typical within an indigenous African worldview to isolate a purely aesthetic dimension. *Fe*, which is an Ashanti Twi word for someone or something beautiful is also used in the evaluation of social behaviour. A child who misbehaves is told that what they are doing is not *fe*. Our European cultural tendency to see something from a single aspect – 'its fineness', 'its beauty' – and to isolate this dimension, represents a movement away from the wholeness of vision that existed in many African cultures. Appiah explains that viewing something as beautiful as the only important way of assessing it would be puzzling to indigenous thinkers. Hair art and other artefacts of adornment allow us to 'appreciate the subtle interplay of the sociological and the aesthetic'.[25] To look at physical beauty entirely isolated from any context made little sense. Beauty was more contextual, and value judgements of what was beautiful couldn't be made in an entirely superficial way. As other senses were privileged as much as sight, there was no need for the old adage about not judging a book by its cover: it was already a given! The beauty standards that emerged from such a world-view were subsequently very different; less standardized, less homogenized and more inclusive. As stated, amongst the Yoruba a person would not be considered attractive or not based on anything as arbitrary as height or complexion. A short person who was attractive might be described as a *kúrú yë jó* (one who is short and perfectly elegant when dancing) but equally they might be *èniyàn kúkurú bilíìsì* (a short devil). While an arched foot was considered a thing of great beauty for a woman, not having an arch was not enough to preclude one from beauty. Those with lighter complexions were not perceived as more beautiful than those who were darker. Both light and dark skin could be attractive but equally both could be unattractive. Even smallpox scars might be deemed beautiful, on the right person: *eni-sàsá-sojú-e-lewà-ferefere* (a person whose facial beauty is enhanced by smallpox spots).[26]

Appiah describes the aesthetic movement in Europe during the latter part of the nineteenth century as one that taught us to see visual art 'for art's sake'. The tendency to imagine that every single thing in existence is quantifiable and can be subject to measurement, the urge to measure things in isolation from their context, is a Western European imperative. It's the logic of dividing, naming and categorizing things, the teasing apart of the very fabric of meaning as part of an attempt to ascribe relative value and worth to a seemingly endless proliferation of sub-categories. Each living being becomes distinctly separated from its relation to everything else. Reciprocity is destroyed and replaced by competition. Beauty becomes oppressive and competitive, an abstract, isolated quality.

In addition to the idea of removing beauty from context and character being seen as odd, we find examples in which beauty that is too extreme is suspected to have originated somewhere beyond the mortal world. The Mende believed that physical perfection was an ideal achieved only by the gods, while the Yoruba associated external perfection with supernatural sources that were not entirely positive, believing that balance was the ideal.

In the Black is Beautiful movement the emphasis on achieving and possessing beauty fell, as ever, disproportionately on women. Black is Beautiful did nothing to displace the oppressive notion that black women had a special duty to their race to be beautiful. Moreover, it defined beauty by conforming to a narrow standard. It also stated that you couldn't be down for the cause if you didn't dress for the part, a type of thinking that is misleading in its attention to style, potentially at the cost of substance.

On the subject of Black is Beautiful, Toni Morrison asks from whom such validation is being sought, before eventually surmising that it is validation from the white gaze. Morrison doesn't need to be told she is beautiful, or to be told that black is beautiful. She knows that it is.[27]

The concept of validation from the white gaze resonates deeply. I am reminded of all the times I was told that I was pretty for a black girl, or that I was lucky I was pretty because I could 'get away with being black'. That perceived beauty was the price I had to pay for the burden of blackness. My worth as a human being was not recognized because of my race but, apparently, the possession of beauty could compensate for my racial inadequacy.

I'm grateful for the different cultures I've lived in and the different positions I have occupied on the spectrum of beauty, in certain times and places beautiful, in others not; and I saw the difference in treatment based on whether or not I was judged as possessing this thing called 'beauty'. I understood then that beauty was not the space for my salvation. It is far too fragile, and my worth as a human being cannot be given, or withheld, based on something so arbitrary.

Yet so much of our identity is invested within the beauty regime. It occupies a huge percentage of our thoughts and social interactions. When we are perceived to possess it, it provides us with a fleetingly enjoyable feeling. Thus, we interpret beauty as a benevolent, positive force within our lives. Sometimes in our fight for inclusion and equality we forget that achieving the position we are fighting for might become something of a pyrrhic victory.

In our desire to see our own beauty acknowledged we forget that the beauty regime is an oppressive construct designed to keep women in a state of heightened insecurity. This doesn't stop at the 'white gaze'. The idea of 'the gaze' itself is Eurocentric and its origins are implicitly white and implicitly patriarchal.

Black is Beautiful doesn't solve the problem of competitive beauty, nor does it operate outside of the paradigm created by Eurocentric values. It 'operates on terrain already mapped out by the symbolic codes of the dominant white culture'.[28]

Of course, today black people have their own oppressive beauty standards – light skin and good hair might be the most pertinent – and there can be huge pressure to conform to these but, generally, beauty was not as standardized and, as a result, these standards remain, to an extent, comparatively forgiving. Certainly, they are often positively encouraging of a lil wiggle and jiggle. Take Osun, the Yoruba goddess of beauty and fertility. Lines from one of her *orikis* describe her as 'A corpulent woman / Who cannot be embraced around the waist'. I can't think of a beauty ideal further from the purge and punishment food culture that I grew up with in Ireland. As Naomi Wolf explains, 'A culture fixated on female thinness is not an obsession about female beauty, but an obsession about female obedience ... Dieting is the most potent political sedative in women's history; a quietly mad population is a tractable one.'[29] The difference exists as a powerful challenge to the tired narrative of black and African women, oppressed in relation to liberated white Westerners.

The current celebration of Rihanna's changing body is a perfect example. Rather than 'getting fat' – that personal and moral failure of women in Eurocentric culture – Rihanna has, from a black aesthetic position, got 'thick', and we love her all the more for it. Her significantly increasing curves are seen as only adding to her allure. I can't imagine there being a sex symbol like her when I was younger. Considering how I used to obsessively regulate my calories in the hope that my 'fat' thighs would disappear, I remain somewhat luke-warm about the inclusion of tall, skinny black women in the fashion gang because they are as stick-like as the white models.

I remember being on a family holiday in Trinidad and sneaking out on a couple of clandestine dates with a boy I met at harvest festival. As we walked he commented on my 'thickness'. Upon my horrified 'Erm, what do you mean?' ('thick' in Ireland meant stu-pid) he broke it down; he was talking about my body shape, and it was most definitely a compliment!

Even though this suitor meant to flatter me, so indoctrinated was I by the European metric of female worth (how little we weigh, how little physical space we take up) that I was even more horrified than if he had been questioning my intellectual capabilities. I man-aged a tight smile and vowed to starve myself.

According to 'Fifty States of Women', a survey conducted by *Glamour* and L'Oréal Paris in 2017, out of 2,000 participants, 59 per cent of black women described themselves as beautiful. In con-trast, only 32 per cent of Hispanic women and 25 per cent of white women described themselves as such. More black women also agreed with the statement 'I am happy the way that I am' when they looked in the mirror.

Dr Jean Twenge, Professor of Psychology at San Diego State Uni-versity, suggests the reason is that, 'Growing up, black women are taught you're strong, you're beautiful, you're smart, you're enough – and that mindset is passed down from generation to generation as a defence mechanism against discrimination . . . The more confident you are, the better equipped you'll be to deal with racism.'[30]

I think it goes deeper than this. The Eurocentric emphasis on thinness has its origins in a particularly punitive and patriarchal construction of femininity characteristic of Anglo-American cul-tures. Perhaps the endurance of a more African-centred tendency to appreciate something or someone by taking into account qualities beyond the isolated imagining of a physical beauty might be interpreted as an antidote to Eurocentric perceptions that have become an increasingly dominant global norm.

Among the lonely hearts from the last century Walker discovered similar nuggets of hope – attempts to challenge the value placed on certain features and the reduction of women to objects of sight alone. One male writer looking for a girl of 'any colour' chastised the contributors for their emphasis on colour and hair texture: 'How in blazes do they expect equality from other races when they don't even practice it among ourselves?'[31]

While some Bob Marley lyrics have become ubiquitous to the point almost of cliché, I find myself coming back to those words from 'Redemption Song', which tell us that none save ourselves has the power to free our minds. This is the rallying call. It is the invitation to 'tear this shit down', to 'reject that which rejected you'.[32] We do not need to further perpetuate psychotic colonial fantasies about who we are. Over a hundred years ago Du Bois wrote about the danger in seeing oneself through the eyes of the colonizer. Yet here we are today, still reproducing the very same norms.

Understanding our past makes it easier for us to identify the future we want to create. So much of what we are conditioned to believe is 'natural' is not. Certainly, it is not universal, nor 'just the way things are'. We have choices in what we collectively recognize as valuable. For me, great possibilities exist in my recognition that the society I live in was designed with my exclusion in mind. Never again will I mutilate any part of myself in an attempt to one day awkwardly almost-maybe fit in. We have the freedom to design a reality of our own making, one that recognizes our humanity and thus reflects our highest needs. We are the ones we have been waiting for.*

---

* This is a line from a June Jordan poem, which Alice Walker took as a title for her 2006 book. She uses it to invoke the power of each of us to make political change happen.

5

Everybody Wants to Sing My Blues, Nobody Wants to Live My Blues

But someday
somebody'll
Stand up and talk about me,
And write about me –
Black and beautiful –
And sing about me,
And put on plays about me!
I reckon it'll be
Me myself. Yes, it'll be me.[1]

Or if we're lucky it might be Kim.

Despite its new name and the recent volume of column inches commanded by the cultural-appropriation debate, it's a story as old as America itself. In the twentieth century, Harlem Renaissance writer Langston Hughes called it as early as 1940 in *Note on Commercial Theatre*, his poetic response to wealthy whites who were flooding into Harlem desperate to 'experience' and repackage the culture of the very same people they and their institutions denigrated, segregated and lynched.

'Father of the Harlem Renaissance' Alain Locke (incidentally, the first African-American Rhodes scholar at Oxford University) summed up the paradox:

It almost passes human understanding how a people can be so despised and yet artistically esteemed. So ostracized and yet culturally influential. So degraded and yet a dominant editorial force in American life.[2]

Yet we seem to believe that everything is new, happening for the first time, and that this is the first outspoken generation, the one that'll achieve the *real* gains. Thus we are condemned to repeat the mistakes of the past, perpetually reinventing the wheel. In this context, confusion as to what cultural appropriation actually is remains rife.

Much like understanding racism, the key to understanding what is and isn't appropriation requires an analysis of power. Cultural appropriation operates as part of a structural power dynamic where the 'appropriating' actors belong to an advantaged group. This group systematically extracts the cultural resources of a subordinate group, erasing the subordinate group's involvement in the process. The structurally advantaged group becomes the primary (financial) benefactor of an innovation that was not theirs.

Thus, individual or isolated examples whereby members of subordinate groups occasionally borrow from structurally advantaged groups do not constitute acts of cultural appropriation. An understanding of power dynamics makes it clear why the wholesale appropriation of black culture that underpins Western popular culture is not comparable to a black woman straightening her hair.

The fact remains that there is no other group of people on Earth whose cultural production has the mass appeal of black culture yet is simultaneously derided while effectively repackaged and claimed by everybody else.

Over the last few years cultural appropriation seems to have emerged as a hot, sexy, 'woke' topic, up there with 'activist models' and corporate feminism, enjoying features in glossy magazines that wouldn't have touched the topic – or indeed us – five years ago. So let's celebrate! A new day has dawned: our time has come. That shit sells – hell, we sell. Black people *sell*. Forgive my scepticism, but the commodification of black lives didn't work out too swell the first time round.

Until recently there was a robust critique of capitalism in black activism. The scholar Cedric Robinson describes the Black Radical

Tradition that emerged from a split in the black community. On one side, there were those with 'a liberal, bourgeois consciousness . . . packed with capitalist ambitions and individualist intuitions'. Their objective was 'essentially to gain access to the roles and rewards monopolized by whites'.[3] Yet on the other side 'there was a radical proletarian consciousness that sought to realize a higher moral standard than the ones embraced by whites and their black imitators.'[4] As George Lipsitz explains, this is the radical consciousness we witnessed when Du Bois condemned the 'dream of material prosperity' as America's emerging ethical and political goal. Du Bois felt that a people who had once been positioned as objects of commerce should have particular insight into the shortcomings of capitalism. He was concerned that the pursuit of commercial value would destroy the 'social reciprocity needed for the survival, humanity and democratic hopes of the vast majority of the black population'.[5]

Today, despite a landscape of increased rights, increased representation and greater personal freedoms (although with the global rise of the right from the US to Brazil and parts of Europe who knows what the immediate future holds), the infrastructure of authority has not changed much. Wealth and power are still concentrated in mostly white, mostly male hands. Where power resides in black hands, what really changes if they are the hands of the 'black imitators' identified by Robinson?

A company might be black-owned, but who designed the business model? A system might become inclusive, but what exactly are we being included in? Is it a world of our design? Or is it a world whose ethics, measurements of value, worth and success have been created in the image of and in service to (borrowing from Greg Tate) 'the same crafty devils that brought you the Middle Passage and the African Slave Trade'.[6]

The term 'cultural appropriation' is now part of the discourse. Liberals argue its finer points at dinner parties, it is debated in prime-time TV slots. Every couple of weeks there will be a high-profile accusation of cultural appropriation. This will most often be in relation to a white celebrity and a black hairstyle and will temporarily set the internet alight. Superficial discussions will follow, but nothing will be resolved; both sides will settle back down into their respective factions. Two weeks, perhaps a month later, the next story will blow up and same process will play out. Press repeat.

None of these 'conversations' changes the fact that, from Africa to Europe, South and North America, India and the Middle East, no matter where black people find themselves, they are generally structurally disadvantaged. This is the global legacy of colonialism and slavery, further perpetuated by the discriminatory practices and policies of neo-liberal market logic. In a world where being marked as 'black' is enough to get you killed, the appropriation of the cultural or physical signifiers of blackness – conveniently liberated from any of the costs associated with actually *being* black – adds unbearable insult to injury.

Stripped of gods, languages, institutions – even the culture around our hair isn't ours to keep. Sometimes it can feel as though black people are not allowed to keep anything (except seasoned food). Collagen and various other injectable substances have done wonders for the lips and posteriors of those not naturally endowed, but our hair is the one feature that remains hardest to imitate.

In the face of a centuries-long campaign about the ugliness of black hair, the message drilled into our heads is that it must be managed, hidden or disguised.

To this day, our children are told that their hair is not normal. Reading children's stories to my young son – often even those written by People of Colour – I find myself changing the hero's or protagonist's hair from 'straight' and 'silky' to 'thick' and 'curly' all the time. The publishers Usborne have a series of 'That's Not My . . .' books to introduce texture to infants. On the penultimate page of *That's Not My Fairy*, there is a picture of a brown child with frizzy, textured Afro hair. 'That's not my fairy, her hair is too frizzy,' the book declares. Don't panic, order is quickly restored once you turn to the next page, the home of 'the real fairy', the white, blonde, silky-haired child. 'That's My Fairy'. Phew! Get 'em young Usborne, get 'em young.

So it irks, to say the least, when members of groups who have historically benefited from black oppression (which they continue to perpetuate) are then prized for the appropriation of the hairstyles we remain marginalized for wearing.

I have neither the energy nor the inclination to react to the seemingly ceaseless instances of cultural appropriation. Don't @ me, bro. Challenging racism and inequality is about transforming the system that continues to perpetuate racism rather than responding to each demonstration of it. That said, those who dismiss these cases of CA with a flippant 'It ain't that deep,' or indeed, 'It's only hair,' are missing some fundamental truths.

For 500 years and counting, African cultural, physical and natural resources have been stolen in the service of European interests. That seems bad enough, but the culture of denial that obscures the reality is maddening. In many ways, the appropriation of black hairstyles behaves as a microcosm for the continued extraction of resources, both cultural and physical, from African peoples. It also reveals an awful lot about how race is constructed and the ways in which white supremacy is informed by complicated emotions relating to inferiority. How do we theorize the white desire to not only possess, *but to embody*, the same features black people are penalized for?

The cultural appropriation of black hairstyles by white celebrities shows no sign of slowing down. As I'm writing, at the dawn of 2018, Kim Kardashian is sporting some Fulani-inspired braids that she's accrediting to Bo 'cornrow appropriation queen' Derek, who copied the traditional African style in 1979 for her role in the movie *Ten*. The innovative hairstyle catapulted Derek from a bit-part player to iconic status while, forty years later, the same hairstyle worn by black women still results in suspensions and court cases. For Derek herself, none of this is open to debate. In *Cut* magazine she remarked that the controversy over Kylie Jenner's cornrows was 'stupid', and she noted that race never came up around discussions of her cornrows in *Ten*. 'It's a hairdo! That's all it is.' The mighty Bo has spoken.

A personal favourite of mine is from 2014 when the *Los Angeles Times*, without any trace of irony, announced that braids are more chic when worn by white people. The article in question showed an image of aristocratic actress and model Cara Delevingne, captioned by a quote from the well-regarded celebrity hair stylist Jon Reyman:

> Cornrows are moving away from urban, hip-hop, to more chic and edgy. There were spiral cornrows at Alexander McQueen, and I did fishtail cornrows woven with fabric. I have also been incorporating cornrows into center parts and side parts. Just one cornrow or a couple on the side is really cool [as opposed to a headful], but they have to be on the right person [lol, who on earth might Reyman be talking about?] with the right clothing. Obviously, McQueen is very gothic and strong, so that customer is looking for that Elizabethan or 'Game of Thrones' edginess.[7]

So, Mr Reyman, '*Game of Thrones* edginess'? No mention of *irun didi*, an African method of hairstyling so ancient that it can be observed on Stone Age walls? A TV programme that can construct a world where dragons and zombies are real but cannot stretch to one where black people are anything more than slaves. That is your reference point? OK.

THE QUEEN OF POP

We are spoilt for choice when it comes to examples, but let me focus on Madonna's 'Vogue'. It's thirty years old, but it's a goodie, not least because it shows how long this shit has been going on. The 'Queen of Pop' is still dining out on the merits of appropriated black creativity: her Aretha Franklin tribute at the 2018 MTV Video Music Awards was all about Madonna, and it's entirely apparent that, as she enters her sixtieth year, she remains entirely unrepentant. 'Vogue' is also an example that particularly grates on me because when I was little I adored Madonna. *Like A Virgin* was my first LP. I even had a replica of the outfit – complete with red tutu and black biker jacket – from *Who's That Girl*, the 1987 movie Madonna starred in. Let me tell you, at eight years old, this little black faux-punk cut quite a figure on the streets of Dublin 8.

But it's her 1990 hit 'Vogue' that remains a breathtaking gesture of erasure. Ciccone assertively chanted the names of iconic white celebrities over a central motif of Vogue and ballroom culture – queer, black, inner-city culture. It is about as far removed from straight, white suburban women like Madonna as you can get, but there you go, them's the breaks.

I was a child when I first heard this song. There was little to suggest its queer black origins. 'Vogue' was all about whiteness. 'Vogue' was all about Madonna. Like everything else around me, unless it fell into either of the clearly delineated tropes of blackness allowed to exist in the early 1990s – starving Africa (shout out to Geldof) or NWA-inspired fantasies of American gangbangers – then it wasn't black.

I assume the recognition of suppressed black brilliance was not at the forefront of the minds of Warner Brothers marketing team or any of the other brokers of popular culture. The depth of Madonna's personal delusion is evident in a 1990 break-up letter to a former lover:

> I'm being punished, and basically made to be quiet and sit in a corner, while other less interesting and exciting people are reaping the benefits *of the roads I've paved . . . Maybe this is what*

black people felt like when Elvis finally got huge. It's so un-
equivocally frustrating to read that Whitney Houston has the
music career I wish I had ... Not because I want to be these
women* because I'd rather die, but they're so horribly medi-
ocre, and they're always being held up as paragons of virtue or
some sort of measuring stick to humiliate me.[8] [my italics]

At the same time, Madonna is more than happy to position
herself front and centre of Vogue, a product of queer black innovation forged in the crucible of white supremacy.

The twisted power dynamics from which the products of black
genius emerge simultaneously marginalize black life and create
a commodity that Madonna, with the privilege of her racial position, is able to whitewash and capitalize on. Win!

Not content with the gift that keeps giving, Madonna manages
to somehow cast herself as a victim, while a black female artist
with the talent and soul of Whitney Houston becomes the perpe-
trator of an imagined crime against her.

In his 2017 biopic *Whitney: Can I Be Me*, British filmmaker
Nick Broomfield argues that, to achieve success in a racist America, Whitney, the beautiful black girl from the hood, had to be
sanitized and divorced from anything that could be interpreted as
a threatening manifestation of blackness. Whitney Houston was
reinvented; a bland, wholesome all-American girl next door, a
palatable pastiche of herself.

Critics of Madonna, on the other hand, point out that she was
potentially the far blander prospect who then reinvented herself as
the reverse, becoming an edgy punk, a high-school drop-out, with

---

* Madge has a pop at Sharon Stone, who generously replied that it was 'absurd'
that some of Madonna's private letters were being published and auctioned. Stone
continued that she refused to be pitted against Madonna through an 'invasion of
our personal journeys', a sentiment I strongly agree with; I think the attempt, pre-
sumed to be by an ex of Madonna, to monetize their private exchanges is a disgusting act. Nonetheless, now that the information is out, it does give us an insight into
her thoughts regarding the career and talent of Whitney Houston and is thus pertinent to a discussion of Madonna and cultural appropriation.

a persona largely cobbled together from characters to be found on the New York club scene.

During her lifetime, Whitney Houston was plagued by rumours that she was in a closeted lesbian relationship with her best friend and later creative director Robyn Crawford. In contrast, during the course of her career Madonna has stage-managed high-profile lesbian stunts with women ranging from Jenny Shimizu and Sandra Bernhard to Britney Spears, Miley Cyrus and Nikki Minaj – whoever happened to be media flavour of the month. While the suggestion of being a lesbian in the 1980s was anathema to the career of a black woman like Houston, the effect on Madonna's was the exact reverse. Broomfield makes the claim that Whitney's life of secrecy resulted in her eventual separation from Robyn. Accordingly, the rumours, the secrets and lies and eventual break-up in turn played a hugely significant role in her personal problems, which ended in tragedy on the night of 11 February 2012, when she was found dead in a bathtub in Las Vegas.

Madonna smashed it with the critically acclaimed 'Vogue'. Commercially, it remains one of her biggest hits, having topped the charts in over thirty countries, including Australia, Canada, Japan, the UK and the US. Shifting over 6 million copies, it was the world's bestselling single of 1990. The Rock and Roll Hall of Fame listed it as one of the '500 Songs that Shaped Rock and Roll'.

The spoken-word section of the song is particularly egregious, reproducing and carving out a special place for itself in the cultural appropriation hall of fame. Ms Ciccone does not see fit to list even one African-American performer in her roll call of virtuosos, while happily acknowledging Marlene Dietrich.

Who is included? Well we've got Greta Garbo, Marilyn Monroe, Marlene Dietrich and Joe DiMaggio. Madonna also sees fit to include both Marlon Brando and Jimmy Dean. Up next we have Grace Kelly and Jean Harlow, followed by Gene Kelly, Fred

Astaire and Ginger Rodgers. On and on it goes, this roll-call of whiteness, and while Madge is impressed by ladies who have attitude, seemingly this doesn't extend to a single black performer!

Madonna, with her androgynous dressing and badass boss-bitch vibe, is a direct performative descendant of Dietrich. As such, this is some seriously meta shit – an act of erasure with a fascinating historicity of which I suspect Madonna herself was not directly cognizant. Josephine 'The Black Venus' Baker was the originator of much of Dietrich's schtick, from her provocatively androgynous style of dress to *The Blonde Venus*, a film that even commentators at the time remarked had strong parallels with Baker's life.

Baker's opinion of Dietrich is well documented: 'That German cow has copied me my whole life. The only thing left for her to copy will be my funeral' (and indeed, both stars had extravagant French state-sponsored funerals).

A history of unparalleled theft is the real reason emotions run high when Susan throws her hair into the 'messy buns' 'invented in 2014 by white fashion designer Marc Jacobs'. It's the explanation of the anger when a white girl flexes some 'boxer braids' (ahem), another cornrowed style popularized by Kim K. And it's the reason why it is more than frustrating when Kylie Jenner is celebrated for her 'edgy dreadlock style' or feted for canerows, the same protective hairstyle that the American military forbade black women to wear until 2014. How can it be that an art that is by definition classical can be re-imagined as 'gangster' or 'urban' (we know what they really mean).

The practices around black hairstyling are, like our hair texture itself, dismissed as coarse then elevated to an entirely different status when copied or appropriated by white people. Just another example of the many ways black bodies are positioned as either lesser or threatening. This positioning in turn is used to justify the regulatory procedures enacted upon them.

In a 2011 court case, St Gregory's Catholic Science College in Harrow, London, defended its right to exclude a twelve-year-old boy for having cornrows. The headmaster, Andrew Prindiville, argued that the ban

> plays a critical role in ensuring that the culture associated with gangs of boys in particular – e.g. haircuts, bandanas, jewellery, hats and hoodies – has no place in our school. What I am saying is that if we were to permit the wearing [of] any particular non-traditional haircut, such as cornrows, this would lead to huge pressure to unravel the strict policy that we have adopted, and which is a vital part of our success in keeping out of our school influences which have no place there – gang culture and pop culture.[9]

'Gang culture and pop culture'? Hmmm, OK, this makes sense – if you are an unwitting racist (or perhaps even an openly explicit one), but I see it entirely differently. Let's consider European styles. Go back less than a hundred years, let alone two or three centuries, and they look *old*. They are historic relics of the past, impossibly dated. Surely it is testimony to the futurism inherent in African cultures that they allow something so ancient that it was present at the dawn of humanity to still be seen in the twenty-first century as the cutting edge of popular culture, as new and edgy?

Black people are penalized for their creative expression while the scale at which black creativity is repackaged in the modern world as white in origin is unprecedented. The historian Sally Sommer of Duke University, New York, explains that this is a process at the heart of American culture and identity. I would extend this (to varying degrees) to most of Western culture.

Sommer advances a controversial proposition. She makes the argument that in the US 'only political and economic power are held by white males . . . Everything else, all the popular entertainment, all major American culture is, to me, black.'[10] In short, the creative genius that has dominated the modern world throughout the twentieth and twenty-first centuries is . . . black!

With caustic humour, the African-American writer, musician and producer Greg Tate breaks it down:

> Our music, our fashion, our hairstyles, our dances, our ana-
> tomical traits, our bodies, our soul, continue to be considered
> ever ripe for the plucking and the biting, by the same crafty
> devils that brought you the Middle Passage and the African
> Slave Trade. What has always struck Black observers of this
> phenomenon isn't just the irony of White America [or the UK,
> Ireland, Japan; pick a country, any country: they all hate us,
> they all crave us] fiending for blackness, when it was once (not
> so long ago) debated whether Africans even had souls. It's also
> the way they have always tried to erase the black presence from
> whatever black thing they took a shine to. Jazz, blues, rock and
> roll, doo-wop, swing-dancing, cornrowing, anti-discrimination
> politics, you name it.[11]

Yet according to Madonna there's no difference between being black or white.

The same sleight of hand credits Dietrich with many of Baker's innovations, remembers Fred Astaire and Ginger Rogers as the world's greatest dancers and allows Madonna to further validate whitewashed fantasies as she excludes black performers from her fantasy version of Vogue. Fred Astaire is a household name. We are far less familiar with Astaire's heroes the Nicholas Brothers. The actor and dancer Gregory Hines said it would be impossible to cast a movie about their lives, as no two dancers exist who could come even close to reproducing their movements. Yet, despite their celebrity in the 1930s and '40s, the Nicholas Brothers are largely forgotten today. They 'did not make the transition on screen from dancers to romantic leads, as Fred Astaire had done the previous decade. Their skin colour was an obvious barrier, although Astaire himself would think nothing of blacking up his face to perform the

"Mr Bojangles" number in *Swing Time*.[12] Likewise, the late and revered (black) tap dancer Honi Coles, arguably a far superior dancer to Astaire, remains unknown to most.

Astaire is certainly worth further consideration when discussing the important distinction between appropriation and borrowing, the latter undoubtedly being the basis of evolving culture. The writer Itabari Njeri states that in one sense, like the nation, Astaire could, culturally, be called African-American. Sally Sommer says that she prefers to think of what Astaire does as imitation rather than appropriation. 'It's not venal, as with the record industry,' where there's a long history of appropriation. Elvis Presley was a blatant example of that: 'a white man who was promoted because he could copy the black style the nation's youth hungered for without the social inconvenience of black skin'.[13] But it can be a dangerous distinction, at the very least requiring the type of nuance rarely found in the online spaces where these conversations often play out, because deniers of appropriation love to talk about 'borrowing'.

Many of them don't even 'see race', and to such progressive visionaries there is of course nothing sinister at play. To claim otherwise is a facile argument made by those silly blacks who do not understand cultural exchange, and want to childishly hoard something they mistakenly believe to be their own.

Itabari Njeri expands upon the definition of the black creativity which is at the centre of most of American and, by extension, global culture: 'Tap dancing is what people think of when they consider the African-American influence on Astaire.' They forget that black culture greatly influenced ballroom dancing.[14] As with techno, house and rock music, black people have created or transformed many genres that don't fit narrow descriptions of what is allowed to be black.

'Ballroom dancing became a fad in the United States around World War I. And all those trots: fox, turkey, etc., were African-American dance forms introduced to Vernon and Irene Castle by black bandleader James Reese Europe. The Castles "refined" these dances and used them to launch an African-based dance craze early in the century that hasn't let up yet.'[15] I remember trying to convince a nice young middle-class white man I was working with that the 1950s swing class his girlfriend attended was a style of dance developed in the black American inner cities, and he just could not get his head around it. It simply did not compute.

It is under the weight of all of this that I recently became incensed by what might seem to some nothing more than an innocent fashion shoot. It was a beauty feature shot in Dublin. The models' hair had been done in facsimiles of black styles from canerows to immaculately gelled babyhair, all captioned with hash-tags such as 'tribal doll realness'. Immediately recognizable styles had been given invented names (of course), as though this was just a lil suttin' those creative geniuses on the shoot had quickly thrown together rather than the product of many years of black hairstyling culture, often in the face of violent oppression.

When I was growing up, the African aesthetics of babyhair – the neatness, precision and attention to detail – were a million miles from the tousled wisps that white girls carelessly flicked back and forth across their faces. Never mind the impossibility of finding edge-control products; the inherent blackness of the aesthetic meant that it was certainly one to be avoided at all costs. This is the context that creates the tension I feel when I see these hairstyles being celebrated on white women.

Yet the irony is that this type of policing or possessive ownership of cultural production is far, far from the logic according to which most African cultures operate.

AFROPOLITAN MODERNITY AND CULTURAL EXCHANGE

In a 2007 essay on Afropolitanism, the Cameroonian philosopher Achille Mbembe suggested that the enduring insights of Afropolitanism (a term that emerges from the words 'Africa' and 'cosmopolitanism') should be its promise of 'vacating the seduction of pernicious racialized thinking',[16] its recognition of African identities as fluid, and the notion that the African past is characterized by 'mixing, blending and superimposing'. In opposition to custom, Mbembe insists that the idea of 'tradition' never really existed and reminds us there is a pre-colonial African modernity that has not been taken into account in contemporary creativity.[17] Boom!

African cultures tend to be syncretic. While all cultures blend, borrow and adapt, generally it is those of the European tradition – the British are a key example – who are overly concerned with strict categorization and the illusion of maintaining a sense of cultural purity. Indeed, we see this attitude across the entire globe now, the result of nationalisms and rigid binary identities that did not exist in the pre-colonial African context.

In contrast to the myth of a fixed, unchanging traditional Africa, most African cultures were far more fluid and dynamic than their European counterparts. Let's take something mistakenly understood as a fixed and foundational concept – ethnic identity. Before the 1884 Scramble for Africa and the following European annexation of the continent, ethnic identity would have been constructed in a very different way from what we imagine today. In *The Invention of Tradition* Terence Ranger states that, 'far from there being a single "tribal" identity, most Africans moved in and out of multiple identities, defining themselves at one moment as subject to this chief, at another moment as a member of that cult, at another moment as part of this clan, and at yet another moment as an initiate in that professional guild.'[18]

As a result of this, belonging is understood less as 'a matter of restrictive labeling, and more of choosing between various semantic classifications dependent on the particular contexts and identities involved'.[19] These shifting and contingent relations certainly did not foster the type of environment that leads to a jealous policing of cultural production.

The spiritual traditions of African origin that are diffused throughout the Americas and are currently enjoying a popular resurgence were in many instances banned and often had to be practised furtively. Religions such as Candomblé in Brazil and Santeria in Cuba celebrated Yoruba *orisha* under the guise of worshipping Roman Catholic saints. These saints acted as a sort of cover for the African gods. African cultures were remarkably adept at fusing what they brought with them with whatever they were forced to encounter, and from that combination creating something entirely new. Look at the different forms of cultural production that develop wherever there is a significant population of African descent. The African-Caribbean population in the UK have been particularly innovative. Consider the musical forms that have emerged here: jungle, hardcore, garage, grime. These styles could only have been created through the unique cultural fusion that is Britain, moulded and shaped by its resident black populations.

In black cultures there often remains an indomitable spirit that, even when violently suppressed, cannot be quelled. In many ways this can be credited to the tendency to mix and chop, to forge together and to fuse. It is dynamic, constantly evolving, always imitated, never equalled, and often ridiculed before being slavishly reproduced.

Sadly, the rules of engagement have been changed. We are not operating on a level playing field. Despite the anger that is caused by cultural appropriation, Afro-diasporic black cultures generally have more of a tendency towards openness and inclusivity than Anglo-American cultures. So it's grossly unfair when we are silenced with the old 'No one owns culture' card when we call out cultural appropriation. Suddenly, non-black folk are there to remind us: 'Hey, it's all about borrowing and exchange, guys.'

Well, thanks for the reminder. This was the logic underpinning most African cultures, but then *someone* kinda changed the rules. That whole process of creating an entire global infrastructure where you owned everything, our culture as well as our bodies, well, that kinda had an impact and well, it kinda has consequences, you know.

This is precisely why cultural appropriation provokes sentiments it wouldn't otherwise. Operating under the new rules of engagement, it would be nonsensical for black folk to be a hundred per cent chill about seeing the spoils of what they have created out of what have often been – let's be real – pretty shitty circumstances, and just be like, 'Yeah go for it, fuck it up, make that money!'

It's only made worse by the fact that white artists are celebrated for pale imitations of black ingenuity while black people are penalized, or even criminalized, for doing the same things better. It's a bitter pill to swallow. No doubt the sight of me doffing my cap with a 'Yessir, massa, whatever you thinks is best,' would mortify liberal sensibilities today but, essentially, this is what is being asked of me when it is suggested that I suspend both my critical faculties and my knowledge of history to greenlight Madonna as the Queen of fucking Pop, the inventor of Vogue, or either Bo Derek or Kim Kardashian as the originator of cornrows. Girl Bye!

'GOOD HAIR'

My full and cool hair would work if I were interviewing to be a backup singer in a jazz band, but I need to look professional for this interview, and professional means straight is best, but if it's going to be curly then it has to be the white kind of curly, loose curls or, at worst, spiral curls, *but never kinky.*[20] [my italics]

How does cultural appropriation relate to the natural-hair world? Despite all the advances made in embracing our hair, somehow the natural-hair world seems to have become dominated by curly hair. While we need to familiarize ourselves with all types of textured hair, the curly ideal should not be privileged at the expense of kinky textured hair. Throughout the broad range of hair types that could be described as black hair, each of the textures indicates African ancestry. Nonetheless, different textures are ascribed different values. Hair that might be 'good' in one context may be highly discriminated against in another. In fact, hair texture as a metaphor for anti-blackness sets the scene for one of my favourite movies, *Pelo Malo* (*Bad Hair*). The protagonist is a little mixed-race boy whose white Venezuelan mother is obsessed with his sexuality and terrified that he might be gay. Whether or not he is, is never established; what is shown is the extent to which the little boy hates his hair. With its big, black, defined curls, many black people would deem his hair 'good hair', yet its texture nonetheless identifies him as of African descent, and with this comes stigma in anti-black Venezuelan society. Even though he and I have very different hair textures, he shares the same fixation that I once had with making it straight, and I find deep resonance between his pain and my own as a child.

When Brazilian actress Taís Araújo, who usually wore her hair straightened, revealed her natural hair on Facebook in 2016, the image unleashed a staggering racist backlash. Given the size of the black population in Brazil, Afro-textured hair should be unremarkable. Of the estimated 11.5 million Africans that survived the Middle Passage, only approximately 450,000 went to the US, but over 5 million were transported to Brazil. The percentage of the population with African ancestry stands at well over 50 per cent, with some estimates placing the figure as high as 92 per cent. Brazil has the second-largest black population in the world, behind only Nigeria. It also has the largest Nigerian population in the world outside of Nigeria, and the spiritual belief systems of the Yoruba remain central in the practice of Candomblé, the presence of which is felt throughout Brazil. Yet all of this is intentionally obscured by Brazil's representation of itself as a white country. Black women make up only 5 per cent of overall media representation. Taís Araújo, the highest-profile black actress in a country that likes to keep its black women invisible, is a rare

Taís Araújo.

exception. Her hair, however, is irrefutable proof that she is of African descent, and as such it was unthinkable that she would publicly expose it. While Araújo's hair texture might be perceived as 'good', the ideal to aspire to for many in the US or UK black- or natural-hair communities, it was evidently *not good enough* to protect her from the violent bile of racists. Comments such as 'Who posted the picture of this gorilla on Facebook?', 'Lend me your hair, I wash dishes' and 'I did not know that [the] zoo has a camera' leave us in no doubt of the prevailing attitude towards black hair. Araújo's skin colour, a light to medium brown, had not caused outrage, but when combined with her russet corkscrew curls it was too offensive. And the Brazilian public made their disgust known.

While it is important to remember that all black hair textures can be discriminated against, type-4 hair is the least visible in the natural-hair community and remains the most misunderstood by mainstream culture.

PAPER-BAG TESTS

We might baulk at the memory of paper-bag tests, but it was not so long ago that they were the criteria for entry into elite black sororities and fraternities. Membership was assessed on the basis of possessing a complexion that was no darker than that of a brown paper bag. (If you were light enough for blue veins to be visible, that was an added touch of sophistication.) One could argue that the same logic underpins the meet-ups of the most popular European and American 'curl activists'. I look at the images from some of today's natural-hair conventions and I am reminded that not as much has changed between 1919 and 2019 as we might want to imagine. However, because our language about race throws the emphasis onto skin colour rather than hair texture, it allows for a certain degree of slippage.

Big brands sponsor bloggers and vloggers with curly-textured hair to appeal to a broader, allegedly more palatable demographic of women. Their ethnicity spans from white to (the right kind of) mixed – mixed people with my hair texture emphatically do not fit the criteria or feature in these campaigns. We are no longer in some scary niche world of black experience. Instead we have travelled to the amorphous, racially ambiguous, multiraciality so beloved of advertisers.

I remain surprised at the lack of any sustained critical commentary regarding this troubling phenomenon, but I have spoken with many kinky-haired bloggers and influencers and they express frustration that they do not get the same opportunities as the 'good hair' girls.

Some of the international natural-hair tours of these curl influencers leave me speechless. Whatever the realities of colourism in the UK, in countries like South Africa, with its fraught racial history of apartheid, or parts of the Caribbean islands, where access to material privileges and political power was and often still is determined by proximity to whiteness, and where, in the absence of a significantly large white population, light-skinned people of African descent have often historically acted as de facto whites, enforcing a strict social demarcation between light and dark, it seems tone deaf, if not dangerous, to promote a mixed-race, curly-haired ideal as the epitome of black beauty and the standard for natural hair.

In the face of a five-century-long campaign about the ugliness and inadequacy of our hair, black women have collectively turned round and said, 'Nah.' We have shared our hair stories, our journeys through pain into acceptance and to pride. In doing so, we have built a powerful international community from Lisbon to London to LA. Yet this, much like everything we create, is now ripe for exploitation. Gradually, there is a shift in the boundaries of what constitutes natural hair and, the next thing you know, you are erased from your own story.

Marion Anderson and her New Orleans Sorors at the reception given after a recital in 1941.

SHEA MOISTURE CONTROVERSY

Whatever the politics of black women with a certain, acceptable hair texture becoming the representatives of natural hair, the company Shea Moisture took things one step further. I'm under no illusion that big brands and multinationals are altruistic or that they operate as some sort of benign force that wishes us well. But I was shocked by the 2017 Shea Moisture advertising campaign. After my disappointments with natural-hair brands like Mixed Chicks, which weren't designed with my type of hair in mind, Shea Moisture felt familiar and reliable. They were a company that had grown *with* the natural-hair movement, even entering into the literary sphere when they featured as producers of Ifemelu's favourite product in her fictionalized *Americanah* blog post 'A Michelle Obama Shout-out, plus Hair as Race Metaphor'.[21]

The most controversial advert features three white and one mixed-race woman with soft, long, curly hair. Black women were incensed. Calls to boycott it came thick and fast. It is bad enough that natural hair is now most commonly represented as curly hair, hair that is the result of mixed ancestry or simply the curly texture that many phenotypically white people naturally have, but Shea Moisture really put the boot in by featuring white blondes and redheads, framing their stories through the struggle and language of black women with kinky textures.

'Hair hate is real, guys.'

Said by the light-skinned girl with the long, softly tumbling curls. The marketable 'empowering' narrative remains. The language of struggle and the overcoming of adversity still define the conversation. These are our words all right, but not from our mouths.

'Everybody wants to sing my blues, nobody wants to live my blues.'

Once again there is that sense that we're not allowed to own anything. Even our experiences of our own hair are not our own. Extract our expressions of pain and anger, our redemptive efforts, then superimpose all that energy on to white women and golden-brown mixed-race girls with long, silky, princess curls (extra points if it's blonde; hazel eyes are a bonus, blue and you can just skip straight to the finish line). Meanwhile, hair that is my texture – type-4 hair that is kinky, hair that is typically West African hair, hair that only people of African descent have – is barely granted visibility and becomes an anomaly sidelined from its own story.

For Richelieu Dennis, the owner of Shea Moisture, business

and trade seem to be in the blood. His grandmother Sofi Tucker, famed for passing down her knowledge of haircare products to her entrepreneurial grandson, is allegedly a Sherbro Tucker.

The Sherbro Tuckers have a remarkable lineage. They are an Anglo-African clan whose origins date back to the 1600s and the arrival of some of the earliest European traders on the coast of West Africa.

In 1665 John Tucker, an English agent of the Gambia Adventurers (a trading company led by the Duke of York, later King James II), set off to make his fortune in Sierra Leone. He was accompanied by another Englishman, Zachary Rogers. Local customs in the region dictated that trading rights were dependent on marriage. Before long, the two Englishmen had married daughters of the Sherbro chief. These unions produced numerous children and both men went on to become the founding fathers of two powerful mixed-race Sierra Leone clans, the Tuckers and the Rogers.

Sherbro society was matrilineal, so the Tucker offspring could claim chieftaincy through their mother while exploiting the trading contacts and English connections of their father. Some of the family members were schooled in the UK, but they took care to maintain important positions within powerful local African institutions such as the Poro, the secret male society of the Mende.

The Sherbro Tuckers rapidly expanded their territories. They gained control over more land and leveraged their contacts, becoming powerful traders. It wasn't long before they became major players in the most lucrative business of all, the newly developing trade in slaves. These mixed-race African families, including the Tuckers, the Rogers and the Caulkers,* were integral to the

---

* The family of Thomas Caulker, born in Cornwall to Irish parents. Like John Tucker and Zachary Rogers, he married a Sherbro princess, known to the English as the Senora Doll.

development and maintenance of the southern Sierra Leone slave trade. They amassed great fortunes and positioned themselves favourably in the politics and government of Sierra Leone. Their descendants remain influential to this day.

Dennis's own business acumen is apparent. His company Sundial, which owns Shea Moisture, goes from strength to strength. In 2015, they secured investment from Bain Capital, and then from Unilever in 2017. Dennis also purchased *Essence* magazine at the end of that year, an incredibly savvy business move for a brand that sells to the black community.

The announcement of the relationship with Bain raised eyebrows. Mitt Romney, the Republican presidential candidate who ran against Barack Obama in 2012, had been the CEO of Bain for many years, and people were suspicious of the association. Many loyal Shea Moisture customers, mostly black women, thought the investment appeared ominous. Was this yet another example of a black-owned business getting bought out and subsequently shifting its focus from its core black customers to chase the perceived big bucks of the mainstream (white) general market?

Dennis was quick with reassurances: the customers – the 'community' – remained the company's most important priority. In fact, Shea Moisture's deep commitment to community was what had motivated the deal with Bain. Shea Moisture chose Bain because the equity firm is 'a partner that understood how important community is', one 'that's already invested in community' and is 'meaningfully engaging in social missions'.[22] Shea Moisture hadn't been 'bought out', they remained *black-owned*. Bain was only a minority investor. Yet Bain Capital operates a business model charged with conducting corporate raids that effectively destroy smaller companies' assets and jobs. Josh Kosman, author of *The Buyout of America*, argues that Romney made his fortune through private equity. He describes this as the process through which a company like Bain acquires cheap credit which it then uses to take over another company in a leveraged buyout. The leverage is used in reference to the fact that the company that has been bought is now responsible for paying for approximately 70 per cent of its own acquisition. Following the buyout, the private-equity chaps start with an aggressive austerity make-over, characterized by redundancies and the cutting of all conceivable costs. Ultimately, the lack of resources and investment and the burden of debt repayment mean that it is difficult for companies to remain competitive. Kosman points out that, of the 'twenty-five companies that private-equity firms bought in the 1980s that had borrowed more than $1bn in junk bonds, more then half went bankrupt'.[23] This type of leveraged buyout has contributed to the rapacious destruction of local industry (and subsequently the communities that depended on it) and the hollowing out of America's heartlands. It could be argued that these activities contributed to the type of poverty, hopelessness and despair that proved such fertile ground for the election of Donald Trump.

As Bain was investing in rather than buying out Shea Moisture, the relationship between the two was different, but nonetheless, given Shea Moisture's emphasis on empowering marginalized communities, they seem like unlikely bedfellows. Bain hardly seems like a partner 'already invested in community' which is 'meaningfully engaging in social missions' in the way Richelieu Dennis described.

In late 2015 Shea Moisture's black core consumers were worried that they would be sidelined following the involvement of Bain. Although Dennis assured them they would remain top priority, by mid-2017 we know what their commercials looked like. Dennis responded to these controversies by claiming that, without expanding, Shea Moisture would not be able to 'do the things that people love about Shea Moisture'; the 'community projects', the 'millions of dollars we invest in Ghana' would not be sustainable. By the end of 2017 Shea Moisture was coming under fire again. Unilever would acquire Sundial brands, which would operate as a standalone unit with Dennis continuing on as CEO. Hair bloggers, influencers and other black women were disappointed once more. Didn't Unilever sell skin-lightening products in the 'developing' world?

THE WHITE MAN'S BURDEN AND THE THREE C'S OF COLONIALISM: COMMERCE, CHRISTIANITY AND CIVILIZATION

Shea Moisture says that 'Through its Community Commerce purpose-driven business model, the company creates opportunities for sustainable social and economic empowerment throughout its supply chain, as well as communities in the United States and Africa.' It claims its 'focus [is] on entrepreneurship, women's empowerment, education and wellness' and that

- 10% of Shea Moisture Community Commerce sales go to women-led businesses, to support communities that supply ingredients for our products, or to support The Sofi Tucker Foundation

- This helps them to earn a better living and support their families, making a better life possible within their communities[24]

Shea Moisture is hardly the only company or institution to make such claims. As a narrative, 'female empowerment' is big business. The emphasis on commerce to liberate Africa has long-standing antecedents. The colonial concept of the white man's burden was based on the promotion of the three C's: commerce, Christianity and civilization. When it comes to commerce, the extent to which this continues to frame relationships between Africa and the West is a solemn reminder that that history is far from past. What we have today is the continuation of a system that began with colonialism, starting with the imposition of wage labour, the subsequent erosion of community, lineage and kinship and the creation of markets that Africans were disadvantaged in. The same forces that produced poverty in the first place are then presented as offering the solution, often encouraging collaboration with exploitative multinationals.

As the anthropologist Jason Hickel explains, 'The logic of "female empowerment" promoted by multinationals and international financial institutions is so seductive because it sits very comfortably in the context of the Western liberal values of individualism and the very "personal" brand of what "freedom" means.' Hickel suggests that the other reason 'female empowerment' enjoys such popularity is because the 'story is apolitical enough to be safe for corporations and international banks to promote without undermining their own interests, and compelling enough for them to use as a PR campaign that effectively disguises the extractive relationships they have with the global South'.[25]

Promoting donations to schools and assistance to small groups of women as solutions to poverty obscures the role that development institutions and multinationals play in the perpetuation of poverty and the underdevelopment of Africa. Prominent economists, such as the American professor of economics William Easterly, have highlighted the direct relationship between IMF structural adjustment loans and economic collapse in the developing world. International institutions tie aid to development assistance, ensuring that public funding is cut, that national industries go unfunded and undeveloped – not unlike the process through which companies become bankrupt following leveraged buyouts.

One consequence of this is a supply of underpaid labour and resources from these countries, particularly from the labour of those who are most vulnerable: women and children. It's a strategy that guarantees markets for Western products, as the local products – which remain underfunded – cannot compete with often heavily subsidized American or European versions.

Hickel argues that shifting the responsibility for escaping poverty to the power of female entrepreneurs obscures the role that multinationals and financial institutions have played in producing poverty.

> These approaches seek to empower women to participate in the market and thus lift themselves out of poverty, but they ignore the fact that this kind of self-help is impossible on a large scale without the market regulations and state subsidies that favour small enterprises, and without welfare arrangements to support people when they fail. Yet both these arrangements are being rolled back, through structural adjustment, by the same organisations that promote micro-credit.[26]

In spite of the destruction they cause, it's a double win for the companies, who then get to sell the story of female empowerment that makes for fantastic PR.

Multinational corporations are well aware that Africa, and the global South more generally, promise huge and as yet untapped markets of consumers. Since colonization, access to these markets has been the objective of Western interests in Africa. The pursuit of markets was indeed one of the significant factors in the abolition of the slave trade. This detail tends to be left out when Britain eulogizes its role in abolition.

It was only when I was much older that I understood that Oludah Equiano, my childhood hero, saw trade as a primary rationale for abolition:

> As the inhuman traffic of slavery is now taken into the consideration of the British legislature, I doubt not, if a system of commerce was established in Africa, the demand for manufactures would most rapidly augment, as the native inhabitants would insensibly adopt the British fashions, manners, customs, &c. In

proportion to the civilization, so will be the consumption of British manufactures . . .

Europe contains one hundred and twenty millions of inhabitants. Query. – How many millions doth Africa contain? Supposing the Africans, collectively and individually, to expend 5£ a head in raiment and furniture yearly when civilized, &c. an immensity beyond the reach of imagination . . .

Cotton and indigo grow spontaneously in most parts of Africa; a consideration this of no small consequence to the manufacturing towns of Great Britain. It opens a most immense, glorious, and happy prospect – the clothing, &c. of a continent ten thousand miles in circumference, and immensely rich in productions of every denomination in return for manufactures.[27]

Colonialism put in place an infrastructure of extraction that has only become more entrenched. Multinationals like Unilever target low-income and rural consumers. Shea Moisture states that 'Sundial's approach complements the Unilever Sustainable Living Plan (USLP).'[28] One of their aims is to improve the livelihoods of low-income farmers. But development experts like Bill Vorley insist that 'big brands like Unilever aren't the answer to helping Africa's farmers'. Rather than selling straight to multinationals, many smallholders would be much better off participating in their local informal economies, where their products can often fetch far higher prices than global commodity prices. International organizations pressure governments not to invest in their own economies. The subsequent absence of provision for schooling and healthcare means many of these households are also desperate for cash. It can be of much greater value to sell to traders for cash than to get caught up in the bureaucracy of 'contracts, membership of producer groups, delayed payments and strict compliance with standards for quality', yet, under pressure from donors and multinationals, officials in these countries often subject those who trade in the informal market to 'harassment and downright hostility' as they perceive this work as 'tax avoiding and anti-progress'.[29]

This is the part of the story that doesn't make it on to the press releases of our favourite brands.

Africa is the gift that keeps giving. African and Afro-diasporic cultures continue to be presented as lesser, as primitive and under-developed, while the systematic extraction of their resources – physical, cultural and material – continues on at a merry pace. This is the missing context in conversations about cultural appropria-tion. Stay woke.

6
Ancient Futures: Maths, Mapping, Braiding, Encoding

Everything you have been taught about Africa is a lie, a story designed to justify the continent's exploitation. African classical sophistication is not acknowledged. African culture and its descendants are not lauded – rather they are dismissed as barbaric at worst, or ghetto at best. Meanwhile, we are taught that certain European art forms, often far less ancient yet far more dated, are what constitute the canon. Traditional African hairstyles are subject to this treatment.

While each braided hairstyle is ephemeral, the enduring repetition and popularity of certain styles and methods suggests a relationship with the infinite. Since Aristotle, European mathematicians had disregarded the concept of infinity as basically too much of a head-fuck to contend with. Yet Africans have been casually repping it throughout their design culture for centuries.

The story of indigenous African technology and its spiritual and philosophical orientations is little known. Unpicking the braid reveals much more than we might ever imagine. To this day, there exists an agenda that perpetuates the idea that Africans could barely produce mud huts, let alone grasp technological innovation. Technology is not really a concept we associate with traditional Africa, and tech certainly isn't the first image conjured up when we speak of hairstyling.

Yet proof of advanced astronomy, mathematical plotting, indigenous calculation systems, geometry and scaling can be found throughout the continent. Africa is home to mathematical bodies of knowledge so vital they provide the bedrock of modern computing.

From sculpture, to architecture, spiritual belief and divination systems – and, perhaps even more surprisingly, hairstyles – maths is everywhere. Through African hairstyles we can observe beauty standards and aesthetics, spiritual devotion, values and ethics, and even, quite literally, maps from slavery to freedom.

When I was researching my PhD I spoke to many young men who shared memories of their schooldays. These included stories of being excluded from school activities because they wore their hair in what the schools deemed to be gang-affiliated styles. I have experienced this type of discrimination myself. There is a dramatic alteration in the way I am treated when my hair is cornrowed – *kolese*, in particular, seems to quicken white heart rates. When you've lived your life fixed under the gaze of whiteness, you become keenly sensitive to its attentions, to its shifts and sensibilities. The culture of denial, the incessant 'But surely not's, the repeated accusations that 'You're just imagining it', the 'But what about . . . ?'s ring frequently in your ears.

But it can be explicit, too, and for me, wearing cornrows seems to trigger racists. Rocking the rows, I might be trailed around shops, have accusations of shoplifting lobbed at me or indeed the word 'nigger' screamed at me from passing vehicles. All of these are relatively recent experiences, occurring over the last seven or eight years, provoked, it seems, by my hairstyle. More recently, things seem to have shifted a little and the adoption of these styles by fashion alongside the boom in braid bars, where white women pay inflated prices for simple black hairstyles given new names, appears to have reduced the vitriol provoked. Although, I imagine, were I dark-skinned or male it might be another story. Yet even to this day it's just as likely to present itself as a white associate expressing surprise that I can 'look thuggish' so easily. And not long ago a mixed-race acquaintance, socialized in a white environment, the type that just wants to 'fit in', expressed alarm when I said I was going to cornrow my child's hair. 'Oh, no, don't!' she cried. 'It's just so stereotypical.'

Yes, I suppose it is stereotypical, in that it is how black people style their hair. This response made me consider the ways in which blackness is always marked. Stereotypical things that some white people do – socializing with babies and small children in bars and pubs – are not universal cultural norms. Or the staunch refusal to adequately season chicken. But these things are not seen as representative of 'white' culture. They are not racialized; instead, they are understood as normal, the standard from which everybody else deviates.

The attitude expressed by my not-yet-woke buddy is common. I'm intimate with the attempt to avoid behaviours that will mark you out or signpost your blackness, even when the denial of them is suffocating. It is a tendency at the crux of the psychosis of assimilation. It's the same mentality that meant teenage Emma would have rather died than have gelled her babyhairs.

BLACK PEOPLE COUNT

I don't know what your memories of learning maths at school are but, for me, even thinking about it now leaves me sick with anxiety. Maths was not for me! Or so I believed. Early on, I had missed out on some fundamental building blocks, and without that foundation it was at first hard and then impossible to keep up. Yet when I think about maths now, its alchemic possibilities appear endless. Formulas to unlock the secrets of the universe. It is dizzying, exciting stuff. Sadly, this dormant interest was not piqued as a child. Boredom, frustration and a sense of my own inadequacy characterized my relationship to maths.

When it comes to maths, the African, Arab and Chinese mathematical systems are largely ignored and the origins are located with the Greeks. At the same time, other potent stereotypes of black people are advanced, and these have travelled far and wide. Even off out there in the far reaches of Europe, on a lil ole speck in the Atlantic Ocean, reductive imported ideas of blackness loomed large in the Irish imagination.

While Ireland itself has been a victim of colonialism, this is far from the entire story. Much less attention has been afforded to the multiple ways in which many Irish were complicit in the same processes that caused so much suffering to its own people.

The relationship between Ireland and the US is long-standing and complex. There is generally little awareness of the process through which the Irish and other European immigrants *became* white in the New World – at times an uneasy, but ultimately successful, journey of inclusion in the 'white race', with all its attendant material advantages. Nonetheless the active racism necessary to attain and maintain the whiteness of Irish-Americans did not foreclose the solidarity that emerged between Irish revolutionaries and Pan-Africanists, both seeking to liberate themselves from oppressive imperialist regimes.

It was with much excitement that I discovered that W. E. B. Du Bois held the famed Irish humanitarian and revolutionary Roger Casement in high esteem, and that for the decade after his execution for his involvement in the 1916 Easter Rising* both Casement himself and the Rising became potent symbols of anti-imperialist politics among black radicals in Harlem. Likewise Marcus Garvey, the Jamaican Pan-Africanist, added a green stripe to his Universal Negro Improvement Association uniform to represent solidarity with the Irish struggle for freedom, while writers of the Harlem Renaissance saw Irish nationalist writers like W. B. Yeats as inspiration when it came to producing liberatory poetic and literary work, concerned with the expression of subjugated national identities;

---

* During Easter Week April 1916 a group of Irish Republicans launched an armed insurrection against British rule. While the public were initially hostile towards the Rising, over the course of the week opinion shifted in support of the Republicans. While the Rising itself failed, it was part of the trajectory that saw Ireland achieve independence six years later in 1922. Most of the leaders of the Rising were arrested and executed following court-martial in Kilmainham Jail. One of those included a personal hero of mine, James Connolly. Connolly was so badly injured from the fighting that he was shot tied to a chair, an image that loomed large in my childhood imagination. Casement himself was arrested three days prior to the Rising. He was tried in London for high treason and hanged in Pentonville Prison on 3 August 1916.

pretty generous, given the historical treatment of black Americans by Irish Americans.*

Nonetheless, while the myth of Irish slaves has been readily advanced – often in pursuit of White Supremacist agendas and despite the fact that some Irish people were brutally exploited as indentured labourers in the early days of the colony of Barbados – the Irish were involved in the Atlantic slave economy in other ways too. The reality is that many Irish made their livings, and indeed some their fortunes, as sailors, merchants and plantation owners. But this story is far less familiar to us.

Despite these Atlantic-world connections, there has not been much of a visible black Irish population until very recently. However, seemingly no one was going to let the absence of actual black people get in the way of racist bants. One early source of this in Ireland was the American minstrel show.

Minstrels fulfilled an important role in American society. To some extent they sated white demand and desire for the consumption of black performance – while continuing the work of debasing black people as 'other', and positioning them as vastly inferior to white, a process that has been so central to the construction of white-American identity. To understand the extent to which the idea of black inferiority is encoded into the DNA of modernity, it is worth considering that the American minstrel show was that nation's first truly homegrown popular entertainment form.

While we might be aware of minstrelsy's popularity in the US, it comes as more of a surprise that it was highly regarded in Ireland too. The Irish historian Liam Hogan argues that:

> Blackface performers were immensely popular in Ireland . . .
> This famously raised the ire of Frederick Douglass during his

* In July 1863 riots broke out in lower Manhattan. In the largest racially motivated insurrection in US history (outside of the Civil War itself), working-class whites, mostly Irish immigrants, reacted against being drafted into the Civil War by attacking and lynching black people throughout the city. The violence precipitated the movement of large numbers of black people to Brooklyn.

sojourn in Ireland in 1845, when he noticed that an Irish actor was lampooning the Negro for money, remarking that he was 'sorry to find one of these apes of the Negro had been recently encouraged in Limerick'.[1]

On the other side of the Atlantic, the scholar Robert Nowatski claims that this 'in turn shaped how Irish-Americans saw themselves as they distanced themselves from African-Americans through denigration and differentiation'.[2]

In some ways things didn't seem to have changed all that much by the time I was growing up, well over one hundred years later. I was constantly confronted with one-dimensional caricatures of black people. I remember watching *Menace II Society*, and the lads I was watching it with struggled to get their heads around why I didn't sound like I was from South Central LA, even though they had known me for years and knew I was from around the corner to them. In school I was expected to have certain characteristics, whereas other abilities were very much not assumed. I was put on the basketball team (and swiftly removed because I was rubbish).

I was a good dancer – no surprises there – but the attention my dancing received eventually made me so self-conscious that I became awkward. 'Are you a singer?' was another frequent question; my response: 'No, why?' 'You just look like you would be.' I vowed never to sing.

It is important to challenge the idea that maths is the exclusive heritage of other races and that black people can only excel in the performing arts. While I heard nonsense phrases like, 'Show us your Michael Jackson!' far more times than I should have, there was never any expectation that I might have some inherent mathematical capabilities. No one assumed that counting and coding were embedded somewhere deep within my DNA in the way that my ability to entertain, or to use my body in an athletic way was supposed.

The story of indigenous African mathematical prowess isn't widely known. It doesn't fit the narrative of black primitivism. Yet maths is everywhere in Africa. Ron Eglash has done ground-breaking work on indigenous mathematical systems as well as the way they can be utilized to teach maths to American children, particularly those of African descent.

While the evidence of Africa's mathematical history is scattered, there's enough to suggest the existence of a lively and advanced mathematical culture existing across the entire continent. Observers from Claudia Zaslavsky to Ron Eglash have referenced age-grade systems as key institutions for social cohesion throughout traditional African societies, and as places where complex mathematical systems are part of everyday procedures: 'with an age-grade system . . . the little kids learn this one, and then the older kids learn this one, then the next age-grade initiation, you learn this one. And with each iteration of that algorithm, you learn the iterations of the myth. You learn the next level of knowledge . . .'[3]

The same exists in games:

> All over Africa, you see this board game. It's called Owari in Ghana . . . it's called Mancala here on the East Coast, Bao in Kenya, Sogo elsewhere. Well, you see self-organizing patterns that spontaneously occur in this board game. And the folks in Ghana knew about these self-organizing patterns and would use them strategically. So this is very conscious knowledge.[4]

Eglash argues that, while binary coding is recognized as the foundation of modern computing, its African origins have, in typical fashion, been almost entirely obscured: 'The most complex example of an algorithmic approach to fractals that I found was actually not in geometry, it was in a symbolic code, and this was Bamana sand divination.' He goes on to explain that this type of divination is popular throughout the continent, from east to west:

> often the symbols are very well preserved, so each of these symbols has four bits – it's a four-bit binary word – you draw these lines in the sand randomly, and then you count off, and if it's

an odd number, you put down one stroke, and if it's an even number, you put down two strokes. And they did this very rapidly . . . And it turns out it's a pseudo-random number generator using deterministic chaos. When you have a four-bit symbol, you then put it together with another one sideways. So even plus odd gives you odd. Odd plus even gives you odd. Even plus even gives you even. Odd plus odd gives you even. It's addition modulo 2, just like in the parity bit check on your computer. And then you take this symbol, and you put it back in so it's a self-generating diversity of symbols. They're truly using a kind of deterministic chaos in doing this.

Now, because it's a binary code, you can actually implement this in hardware – what a fantastic teaching tool that should be in African engineering schools . . . And the most interesting thing I found out about it was historical. In the 12th century, Hugo of Santalla brought it from Islamic mystics into Spain. And there it entered into the alchemy community as geomancy: divination through the earth.

Leibniz, the German mathematician, talked about geomancy in his dissertation called 'De Combinatoria'. And he said, 'Well, instead of using one stroke and two strokes, let's use a one and a zero, and we can count by powers of two.' Right? Ones and zeros, the binary code. George Boole took Leibniz's binary code and created Boolean algebra, and John von Neumann took Boolean algebra and created the digital computer. So all these little PDAs and laptops – every digital circuit in the world – started in Africa.[5]

Despite the origin of these systems in Africa, Ron made a pertinent point about this fact in a recent email exchange we had:

Ever since my TED talk, I have been getting a lot of questions about the use of binary codes in Africa and their significance in the history of Western computing. The temptation is to dive into the competition over 'who discovered it first'. But that kind of competition is a framework created for Intellectual Property rights, for the 'Solitary Genius' view of history.

The indigenous traditions that created braiding algorithms, binary divination codes, etc. were a lot better at sharing knowledge. That doesn't mean they lacked standards: you don't do complicated braiding until you study with a professional; you only learn divination coding by apprenticeship. But no one argues that they 'own' a braid pattern or divination code.

Reversal never works: 'We discovered it first' is not a rebuke of white supremacy, it is just adopting their tactics. That is what Audre Lorde meant when she said: 'the master's tools will never tear down the master's house'. [my italics]

In the same way we considered beauty in an earlier chapter, arguing that black is beautiful is not enough, reversal here is not enough either. Instead of reversal, or an attempt to assert one form of supremacy over another within the extant system, we should *refuse* the terms of engagement. This is our only real hope, the means through which we might actually tear down the master's house and create the type of society we might all truly find peace and contentment within.

When the master's tools are all we have access to, the task of uncovering what else exists becomes ever more urgent. Time and again Africa's mathematical past has been disregarded in the retelling of tales about the continent. The life of Muhammad Ibn Muhammad, a Fulani from what is now Nigeria who worked as a mathematician, astronomer, astrologer and mystic during the 1700s, is little known, but it gives the lie to the idea that Africans were sitting around waiting for the generous opportunities presented to them by slavery. Which is probably why you have never heard of him.

What's more, Ibn Muhammad wasn't an anomaly; he came from a region whose expertise in mathematics, astronomy and numerology was reputed far and wide. He moved to Cairo, where he formed part of an elite intercontinental team of scholars founded by the renowned Somali scholar Hasan al-Jabarti. While there he produced a work on magical squares entitled *Bahjat al-afaq wa-idah al-labs wa-l-ighlaq-fi 'ilm al-huruf wa-l-awaq* (*A Compilation on the Occult*).

Some of his writings remain: 'Do not give up, for that is ignorance and not according to the rules of this art'; 'Like the lover, you cannot hope to achieve success without infinite perseverance.'

In the diaspora, characters such as Thomas Fuller, nicknamed the Virginia Calculator, provide further evidence of a strong tradition of calculation among seventeenth-century Africans. Fuller, a 'prized asset' of his owners, astonished all who met him. He could accurately count the hairs in a cow's tail, or the number of grains in bushels of wheat or flax seed. He developed a method of calculating how far apart objects were, and of performing complex astronomy-related computations that today would be done by computers.

Modern-day mathematicians believe his skills were the product of his formative years spent in West Africa. Different sources suggest Fuller was born somewhere between present-day Liberia and Benin, while others believe it was Guinea or the Senegambia region. Eglash posits that he might have come from the geographic area where the Bassari people live. In Eglash's research into Bassari counting systems, he discovered that in pre-colonial times traditional forms of calculation were performed by specialists trained in the memorizing of sums. Whether it was Bassari or Benin, the point remains: he would have been in an environment with a strong tradition of mathematical calculation.

Sadly, we don't know Fuller's birth name. We do know, however, that in 1724, when he was about fourteen years of age, he was kidnapped and shipped to the US, to a life of enslavement. In order to maintain the status quo, the enslaved population was forbidden from reading and writing, a rule that was brutally enforced. Denied the opportunity to learn either skill, it is highly unlikely that Fuller's knowledge of numeration systems, number words, arithmetical operations, riddles and mathematical games could have been acquired on the lowly Cox Farm near Alexandria, Virginia. The owners of the farm, a white couple called Presley and Elizabeth Cox, were themselves illiterate.

Reports from incredulous contemporary European observers around that time support the idea that many of the inhabitants of West Africa possessed advanced mathematical abilities that allowed them to make impressive calculations on the spot. Despite his contempt for Africans, the French slaver John Bardot's account of the inhabitants of Fida (on the coast of Benin) in 1732 notes a mathematical ability at odds with his usual reports of barbarism: 'The Fidasians are so expert in keeping their accounts, that they easily reckon as exact, and as quick by memory, as we can do with pen and ink, though the sum amount to never so many thousands: which very much facilities the trade the Europeans have with them.'[6]

This 1786 passage from Thomas Clarkson about the purchase of African slaves is similarly descriptive:

> It is astonishing with what facility the African brokers reckon up the exchange of European goods for slaves. One of these brokers has ten slaves to sell, and for each of these he demands ten different articles. He reduces them immediately by the head to bars, coppers, ounces ... and immediately strikes the balance.
>
> The European, on the other hand, takes his pen, and with great deliberation, and with all the advantage of arithmetic and letters, begin to estimate also. He is so unfortunate, as to make a mistake: but he no sooner errs, than he is detected by this man of inferior capacity, whom he can neither deceive in the name or quality of his goods, nor in the balance of his account.[7]

I see echoes of this calculative ability in the use of binary code by the young London MC Ace Mally, who performs freestyle, mixing bits of both binary and Morse code into his bars:

Figure out who I am
But it's cool 'cause I'm a . . .
01000001
Ay, ay, ay
01001101*

No remorse; code
Dot-dot, don't give a . . . bout dot-dot-dash
4-1-dash-dash-dash.

Fuller explained his skill as coming from experiments he conducted around the Cox farm. He died there in 1790, at the age of eighty. His death was marked in a number of the local papers:

Died – Negro Tom, the famous African Calculator, aged 80 years. He was the property of Mrs. Elizabeth Cox of Alexandria. Tom was a very black man. He was brought to this country at the age of 14, and was sold as a slave . . .This man was a prodigy. Though he could never read or write, he had perfectly acquired the art of enumeration . . . He could multiply seven into itself, that product by seven, and the products, so produced, by seven, for seven times. He could give the number of months, days, weeks, hours, minutes, and seconds in any period of time that any person chose to mention, allowing in his calculation for all leap years that happened in the time; he would give the number of poles, yards, feet, inches, and barley-corns in any distance, say the diameter of the earth's orbit; and in every calculation he would produce the true answer in less time than ninety-nine men out of a hundred would produce with their pens. And, what was, perhaps, more extraordinary,

* This translates into his initials, A and M.

though interrupted in the progress of his calculation, and engaged in discourse necessary for him to begin again, but he would . . . cast up plots of land. He took great notice of the lines of land which he had seen surveyed. He drew just conclusions from facts; surprisingly so, for his opportunities.[8]

While researching Fuller, I came across a teaching resource used to introduce him to fourth and fifth graders. While clearly juvenile, the words of the poem struck a chord with me:

What an inspiration, someone to admire
To have such a talent and no way to acquire,
an education or a job or a life of his own
To think what he could do and what he must have known

He spent his life as a slave, I'm sure he wanted more
I owe it to him not to waste or to ignore
The chances that I'm given, opportunities galore
I can be anything if I let my mind soar.[9]

Thomas Fuller was a mathematical prodigy, demeaningly referred to as Negro Tom, condemned to the limited existence of an eighteenth-century rural Virginia field hand, the property of an illiterate, uneducated white couple.

There is little incentive to uncover and preserve historic black achievement, so it remains crucial that legacies such as Fuller's are recognized and his contributions remembered. Perhaps in this way we can, to some tiny extent, right these grave historical wrongs. A kind of historical Black Lives Matter, or Say Her Name.

The closing lines of Thomas Fuller's *Colombian Centennial* obituary are heartbreaking:

Had his opportunity been equal to those of thousands of his fellow-men . . . even a NEWTON himself, need not have been ashamed to acknowledge him a Brother in Science.

Who knows what groundbreaking discoveries Fuller would have made, what he might have invented? Instead he slaved away, a field hand imprisoned on a tiny farm in a racist backwater. The suppression of black genius has surely stunted society as a whole.

In the Western educational system maths is taught as something abstract, removed from everyday life. In contrast, African hairstyling culture is a place where maths is unconsciously applied in each step of the process. In 1998 the mathematician Gloria Ford Gilmer conducted research in braiding patterns in New York and Baltimore.[10] Gloria and her assistants interviewed both stylists and clients about tessellations in box braids, brick and triangle-like patterns, a method of dividing the hair that determines its movement. The stylists in Gilmer's study claim that they are not consciously mathematical, but the process of black hairstyling could not exist without multiple and complex calculations. Measuring the extensions necessary for uniform braids requires algebra, actual braiding itself uses geometry.

Impressed by the ability to create such immaculately uniform braided extensions or by the intricate designs and complex geometric shapes I have seen appearing on my own head, I have asked stylists how they do what they are doing with such astonishing precision. Not once has anybody specifically referenced mathematical calculation. Recently I posted a new style on Instagram. Shortly afterwards I received an email asking me about it. The request was from a white designer: 'I'm intrigued to know how the stylist divides the geometric sections with such straight parting lines between them? It's a real work of art! I'd have to do a scale drawing or make a template before starting anything that geometrically complex and precise.'

When I next saw her I asked my hairdresser how she had designed my previous style and, more generally, how she worked: 'I design it as I'm going along. I just know. You're the academic, you tell me how I know,' she quipped.

The type of knowledge she possesses might be understood as what the American artist and academic Nettrice Gaskins describes as belonging to 'embodied memory institutions' or 'technologies of the African past'. That this particular stylist is African-Caribbean demonstrates a connection that has been passed down over centuries, sustained across both oceans and time, a direct link back to a past that the European understanding of history describes as unrecoverable.

For Gaskins, cornrowing invokes other African practices that have survived the Middle Passage. She explains that braiding functions as another example of the 'weaving or interweaving of cultures, identities, images, fabric and sound'[11] that are not only a defining characteristic of African diasporic culture but operate as part of the pool of cultural resources. These constitute part of what sustained the descendants of those stolen Africans through the long dark centuries of exile in the West.

Although most commonly discussed in terms of music, Gaskins observes the same process in cornrowing hair. In fact, much of African cultural production, as well as that of its American descendants, is polyrhythmic. The 'music theorist Adam Rudolph describes the weaving of threads or "thematic fibers" in repeated patterns of rhythmic regularity and irregularity as polyrhythm'.[12] If an algorithm is the process of following a set of rules to complete a procedure, it is not too much of a stretch to describe braiding as algorithmic. Thus Gaskins builds the case for cornrowing to be described as a technology:

> Cornrows are created through braiding the hair very close to the scalp, using an underhand, upward motion to produce a continuous, raised row. Cornrows are often formed in simple, straight lines (rows), but they can also be formed in complicated geometric or curvilinear designs. In mathematical terms, the braiding of hair shows the formal possibilities of geometric variation. Hair braiding demonstrates an inclination for interrupting the expected line; braids are composed through juxtapositions of sharply differing units and abrupt shifts of form. Certain

patterns are amenable or open to algorithmic modeling – but 'amenable' need not connote the simple – a square is easier to simulate and repeat but the process of braiding, knitting or weaving these shapes into designs is more about complexity arising from simplicity. In other words, it is not the braid itself but the act of interweaving shapes that form the intricate patterns that unify the design. In mathematics and computing the algorithm is a step-by-step procedure for calculations. Algorithmic art is often referred to as computer generated art. However, traditional hair braiders do not use computers to make their calculation . . . Hair braiding is a technology.[13]

FRACTALS

'Rather than imposing an alien analysis from afar, [we should attempt to] allow the rich complexity of African culture, in all its global diversity, to enter into dialogue with nonlinear dynamics, complexity theory, and other mathematical and computational frameworks in which fractals occupy a central role'[14]

Fractals are the shape of the universe, patterns that repeat themselves at many scales. In addition to our organs, fractal shapes make up the world around us: trees, rivers, coastlines, mountains, clouds, seashells, hurricanes are all fractal in design. Our lungs, our circulatory system, even our brain, all are fractal structures. We are fractal. But although we are made of fractals, most of us never think about them.

The Fractal Foundation defines these little badboys as 'infinitely complex patterns that remain the same regardless of scale, created by repeating a simple process over and over in an ongoing feedback loop'.[15] Fractals are found throughout indigenous African design yet were only 'discovered' by Europeans in 1975, when a Polish mathematician, Benoit Mandelbrot, invented the word.

Fractal braiding.

Mandelbrot used the term to describe a large class of objects not immediately similar but sharing an internal and an external logic. In 1877 the German mathematician George Cantor had reignited the infinity debate in Western mathematics. Cantor drew a line and erased the middle third. He then took the two resulting lines and repeated the same recursive process. One line became two, and then four, and so on. This process can be carried out an infinite number of times. An infinite number of lines can be generated and each of these infinite lines would have an infinite number of points along it. Cantor's work proved that the algebraic numbers are countable and that transcendental numbers are uncountable. This seemingly mundane fact is now standard in the mathematics curriculum, but at that time it was akin to heresy. The problem? Cantor had created (a deceptively simple) method for demonstrating the mind-blowing complexity of infinity. To represent infinity was seen as a direct challenge to God's omnipotence and beyond the limits of social acceptability.

Cantor was defamed. Leopold Kronecker, a prominent mathematician and head of the mathematics department at the University of Berlin, said his ideas were a 'grave disease', infecting the discipline of mathematics. Kronecker accused Cantor of being a 'scientific charlatan', a 'renegade' (is that so bad?) and, most extraordinarily, a 'corrupter of youth'. The combined effect of all this and the realization that you could create a set whose number of elements were larger than infinity proved too much for Cantor to cope with. He had a breakdown and was swiftly dispatched to a sanatorium.

However, the idea didn't entirely disappear with Cantor. In 1904 the Swedish mathematician Helge von Koch experimented with the incendiary concept, daredevil that he was! The difference now was that instead of subtracting lines he added them together. As Ron Eglash explains, the result was a shape, or shapes, that shares the property of self-similarity: the part looks like the whole. It's the same pattern on many different scales. Once more these new structures were looked upon with mistrust, dismissed as pathological and pretty much consigned to the dustbin of mathematical history, until Mandelbrot in 1975. Or so the official history goes . . .

The ancient Greeks found infinity so potentially destabilizing that Aristotle redefined it. Infinity was to be understood as a limit one could tend towards but which must not be considered a legitimate object of inquiry in itself. Until the disruptive Cantor came along, this set the tone for the attitude of European mathematicians.

Yet in Africa a very different fractal landscape was unfolding. Eglash's research reveals that the designs of African villages, which European colonial observers considered disorganized and thus primitive, were in fact anything but. It 'never occurred to them that Africans might have been using a form of mathematics that they hadn't even discovered yet'.[16] Rather than the mud huts of African primitivism, Eglash discovers buildings not only constructed in ways that repeat patterns from the natural world but whose design

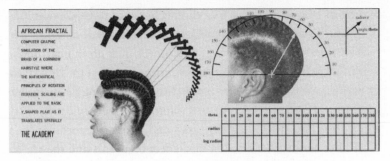

Fractal geometry in *African Fractals: Modern Computing and Indigenous Design* by Ron Eglash. It demonstrates the scaling in the cornrow style known in Yoruba as *ipako elede*.

demonstrates the mathematical and philosophical concept of infinity: 'Recursive models: buildings within buildings, the same shape but decreasing in scale, down to minute models of spirit villages. And housed within those spirit villages are more spirit villages, which contain tinier spirit villages,'[17] ad infinitum!

Eglash discovers that fractal technology is evident across the continent, from sculpture to Yoruba *idire* cloth design or the *kente* cloth of Ghana, and that it is often at its most developed in the divination knowledge systems. Accordingly, the most complex example of an algorithmic approach to fractals that he finds is not in geometry but, as we saw, the symbolic code of Bamana sand divination. And, he explains, the symbols of the same divination system are found all over Africa, from the east to west coast. But what is of most interest for us is the frequency with which this evidence of fractals and concepts of infinity appears in traditional African hairstyles. In stark contrast to themes of criminality or lack of class, African cornrow styles showcase the mathematical concepts that are a part of everyday life across the continent.

Eglash describes the way in which even the humble *ipako elade* reveals the use of mathematical calculation. *Ipako elade* demonstrates conformal mapping, where the pattern is fitted along the contours of an already existing structure.[18] Although adaptive scaling of this nature has less mathematical sophistication than some of the other braided styles, or the deterministic chaos of the Bambara divination system created from a binary code, it is important to include it nonetheless. By adapting the scale of a pattern to fit various forms, a number of aesthetic and practical effects can be achieved and, in the case of escaping slavery, it's a practical application that might just save your life.

While conformal mapping exists where a pattern follows the contours of a pre-existing object, Eglash cautions against interpreting this as the work of artisans who are strongly guided by concrete forms. To describe it in that way has echoes of the racist colonial discourse which purported that Africans lacked the intellectual capabilities of abstract thought. On the contrary, Eglash argues that 'Adaptive scaling can also be seen in more abstract examples: global transformations in which space itself is distorted. This is a common operation in Western geometry, the most frequent example being a mapping between the plane and a sphere.'[19] And we need look no further than the classic Yoruba hairstyle *koroba* ('bucket') to see a plane design mapped on to a spherical surface.

Braiding is an embodied display of what the photographer Bill Gaskins calls 'ancestral recall'. It operates as a bridge spanning spaces between the past, present and future. Braiding is a tangible material thread connecting people separated by thousands of miles and hundreds of thousands of years.

Almost 10,000 miles away from Yorubaland there is a Colombian town named San Basilio de Palenque. Founded some time in the dawn of the sixteenth century, the epic history of the Palenque is little known to the wider world. One of numerous palenques that once existed, San Basilio is the only one that remains today. It has a population of approximately 3,500 people and has been recognized since 2005 by UNESCO as a Masterpiece of the Oral and Intangible Heritage of Humanity. A style very similar to the Yoruba *koroba* can be found in the Palenque too, although the

Colombian version goes by another name. According to folklore, *la totuma* is inspired by an organic vase like a calabash used by the indigenous people to drink water. Given *koroba* and *la totuma*'s roles as representing vessels that collect water, the historical meaning behind *la totuma* makes perfect sense. The inhabitants of the Palenque describe it as a hairstyle that reflected their experiences in the 'continent that made us cry'. *La totuma* is a container for tears.

Palenque hairstyles are rich with meaning, and some of them have been no less than lifesaving. The founder of San Basilio de Palenque was a man named Benkos Biohó. He was a member of the royal family who ruled the islands off the coast of what is today Guinea-Bissau. In the 1590s Biohó was captured by a Portuguese slave trader before being 'resold' numerous times throughout the 1590s.

Biohó was emphatically not about that life.

An early attempt at escape was cut short, but by 1599 our intrepid hero had escaped again, making his way into the marshy wetlands south-east of Cartagena in what is now Colombia. There, along with ten others, Biohó founded the Palenque – the first independent settlement in the entirety of the Americas. Even more remarkable is the fact that not only was it a free settlement, it was free and black, having been founded and entirely populated by Africans. Biohó's army came to dominate all of the surrounding Montes de María region, and the extensive intelligence network he created helped thousands of enslaved people escape and find refuge in the Palenque.

One of the most remarkable tools of this intelligence network was the use of hairbraiding. Hair was utilized as a form of mapping that would be unintelligible to the Spanish. Braided maps worked as a type of underground railway, but the emphasis was on hiding in plain sight. Women would encode important messages into their hair patterns; it was a means of communication for the enslaved, enabling them to share plans and eventually make their way to liberation and freedom in the Palenque. For example, the hairstyle 'The Mother' is described as an 'unequivocal sign that everything was planned'; 'The women elaborated the hairstyle as a form of signal . . . So that the escape could happen in blocks of four slaves.'[20]

As a strategy, it was effective. The sheer volume of escapees to the Palenque presented a serious risk to Spanish rule. Moreover, Biohó used the title King of Arcabuco, posing a significant challenge to Spanish claims of authority, as well as to the myth of African inferiority on which the entire colonial enterprise was based. The impudence of a former slave, who had rejected that reality and reinstated himself to his rightful position as king, could not be tolerated.

In 1605, desperate to prevent the loss of more slaves but unable to defeat the maroons, the Spanish offered a peace treaty. They promised to recognize the autonomy of the Palenque on the conditions that they stopped assisting escapees and they ceased referring to Biohó as king.

The treaty was finalized in 1612. By 1619, the Spanish had reneged on it. They captured Biohó and he was hanged, drawn and quartered two years later, on 16 March. The Spanish may have destroyed the body of its founder but they couldn't kill his spirit of defiance, which remained strong in the Palenque, and the town flourished.

Throughout the Palenque's history, hair braiding has remained an activity at the heart of its existence. A local poem, 'Looking Back', describes a hairstyle that bears much similarity to the Yoruba *kolese*:

Palanque is a community woven with the hair of its women.
It is very blessed both today
and blessed also in its history.
We can see those paths which inspired freedom,
but today they urge us 'Don't look back.'
Let the hairstyle be that of 'Enough: No more'
As a way to progress
A way to move forward
Because history
makes you cry . . .[21]

While the Palenque could be described as an African community in Colombia, assertions such as this must always be made with caution. In the perennially wise words of Jamaican-British cultural theorist Stuart Hall, we should remember that cultural identities, like everything that is historical, undergo constant transformation: 'Far from being eternally fixed in some essentialized past, they are subject to the continuous "play" of history, culture and power.'[22]

African cultures are characterized not by some spurious belief in unchanging tradition but rather by their dynamism and adaptability. Dr David Hughes at Kent State University in Ohio refers to the crucial 'tradition of innovation' that characterizes African tradition. Louis Gates Jnr identifies an African theme of 'repetition with revision'.[23] Rather than slavish attention to reproducing the past, it is an unparalleled ability to utilize existing cultural resources in order to birth new life from old that defines African cultures and their descendants.

A Cameroonian style similar to *el caracol*, 'the snail'.

As the earth turns around the sun
We turn around the world.
With the snail hairstyle
When we saw the snail
Sadness overcame us
As the boat gave many turns and enslavement never ended.[24]

Eglash tells of confrontations he has had with other Western scholars who insist Africans could not have true fractal geometry because they lack the advanced mathematical concept of infinity. Contesting this, he argues that there exist culturally specific representations of infinity from across the continent and that these demonstrate 'a strong engagement with the same concepts that coupled infinity and fractals in contemporary Western mathematics'.[25]

He explains that the most common African visualizations of infinity are snail shells. For the ancient Greeks, infinity was anathema, a nightmare of infinite regression, associated with troubling paradox and pathology. However, within African intellectual traditions, the infinite typically has a positive association. In the case of the snail, it is seen to invoke prosperity without end. It seems no little coincidence to discover that 'the snail' is a popular hairstyle in the Palenque. Through it we see the repurposing of an African symbol of enduring prosperity, where a centuries-long enslavement subverts the natural order of an African worldview.

For the intergenerationally enslaved, slavery must have seemed a never-ending hell. But the snail, like so many of these hairstyles, was far more enduring than any of these empires and, unlike slavery, the snail survived, and is today much admired. I am reminded once more of a sensibility which informs much of African and Afro-diasporic thought, an ancestral impulse that seeks its fulfilment in achieving a state of being where 'it be better in my mouth / Than in the mouth of my ancestors' or, perhaps, in less esoteric terms, as the T-shirt says: 'I am my ancestor's wildest dreams!'

THE BEGINNING AND THE END

European history interrupted African development. Whatever markers we use – time, resources, food even – Africa was, comparatively, a place of abundance until Europeans arrived. Since that time the continent has been materially impoverished. The best solutions offered today seem to be entirely dependent on economic systems that require inequality and exploitation in order to function.

As the 21st-century Scramble for Africa rages on, the obsession with Africa's resources overlooks the continent's most valuable ones. Wole Soyinka suggests that this as yet untapped resource is the essence of African spirituality. Some might refer to it as *uBuntu*, a philosophical concept from southern Africa, 'the belief in a universal bond of sharing that connects all humanity'. It has different names throughout the continent, but it's a concept recognizable across indigenous African culture. Kofi Owusu-Daaku describes growing up in the rural Ashanti heartlands of Ghana where the Akan word *nnoboa* emphasized the importance of cooperation for better communal living. Among the Mande, *mogoya* is the ideal of personhood, a concept that emphasizes caring for others. And in the Bamanan worldview, an individual human being is not necessarily a person; to achieve full personhood requires cooperation with others in the community.[26]

Professor Musa Dube of Duke University explains that if *uBuntu* were practised, ethnic discrimination, patriarchy and the marginalization of people on the basis of class, sexuality or race would be rendered meaningless. As Dube states, 'our failure to affirm and welcome the other only speaks of our failure to be human.'[27]

Soyinka urges Africans to reconsider the value systems others taught us were worthless, encouraging 'a quarrying inwards, before reaching outwards'. It is here that we might find the 'key to the "Renaissance" that is so tantalizingly projected on a receding horizon'.[28]

Races of people cannot be conveniently divided along lines that decree one as good, the other as bad. However, self-organizing systems can be either destructive or complementary to more equal systems for organizing society. Over the last 500 years, as Europe expanded and conquered the rest of the world, it imposed an operating system that encouraged individualism, the rapacious exploitation of resources and the hoarding and accumulation of wealth. The invention of race and its offspring, racism, remained central to its operating logic. Today, as in the past, its agents are not all white. Many black and brown imitators are active participants, freely operating for personal gain, within a model of extraction and exploitation that was once imposed. This has been, to date, the enduring victory of colonialism.

Yet if we observe indigenous cultures from a more decolonized perspective, it becomes apparent in everything from divination, to architectural design, to the patterns of our braids, that there exist 'self-organizing properties in African cultures, indigenous African methods for doing self-organization, these are robust algorithms. These are ways of doing self-organization – of doing entrepreneurship – that are gentle, that are egalitarian.'[29]

The master's tools will never dismantle the master's house. If we could stop trying to reproduce African versions of Western norms doomed to fail at best, destroy the earth at worst, if we could attune our senses to listen to the subaltern speak, we might, just might, like our ancestors finding their way to Palenque, discover the modern-day pathways to the freedom that we seek.

Notes

1. IT'S ONLY HAIR

1. Wole Soyinka, *Of Africa* (Yale University Press, 2012), p. 26.
2. Dr C. E. Lysaght, excerpt from a report on industrial schools and reformatories submitted to the Irish Minister for Education, 1966.
3. Frantz Fanon, *Black Skin, White Masks* (Pluto Press, 1986), p. 112.
4. Joseph Arthur, Comte de Gobineau, *Essay on the Inequality of the Human Races*, (1853–5).
5. J. C. Nott and George R. Gliddon, *Types of Mankind: Or, Ethnological Researches, Based Upon the Ancient Monuments, Paintings, Sculptures, and Crania of Races* . . . (Lippincott, Grambo and Co., 1854), p. 75.
6. Quoted in Adam Dewbury, 'The American School and Scientific Racism in Early American Anthropology', in *Histories of Anthropology Annual*, vol. 3 (University of Nebraska Press), p. 142.
7. Orlando Patterson, *Slavery and Social Death* (Harvard University Press, 1982), p. 61.
8. Michael Eric Dyson, *Holla If You Hear Me: Searching for Tupac Shakur* (Basic Civitas Books, 2001), p. 52.
9. Ayana D. Byrd and Lori L. Tharps, *Hair Story: Untangling the Roots of Black Hair in America* (St Martin's Griffin, 2001), p. 17.
10. 'Iman Opens Up about Deeply Upsetting Career Moment', *Huffington Post*, 9 September 2015.
11. Ginetta E. B. Candelario, 'Hair Race-ing: Dominican Beauty Culture and Identity Production', *Meridians*, vol. 1, no. 1 (Autumn, 2000), p. 148.
12. Elizabeth Pears, 'Colourism: Why Even Black People Have a Problem with Dark Skin', *New Statesman*, 15 October 2013.
13. See The Natural Haven website: http://www.thenaturalhavenbloom.com/2011/10/does-shiny-hair-healthy-hair.html#comment-form.
14. Susan Bordo, 'Cassie's Hair', in Stacy Alaimo and Susan Hekman (eds.), *Material Feminisms* (Indiana University Press, 2008).

15. Ibid.
16. Benjamin Oyetade, 'Body Beautification', in N. S. Lawal et al. (eds.), *Understanding Yoruba Life and Culture* (Africa World Press, 2004), p. 389.
17. Tom Burrell, *Brainwashed: Challenging the Myth of Black Inferiority*, (Smiley Books, 2010), p. 78.
18. Kobena Mercer, 'Black Hair/Style Politics', *New Formations*, 3 (1987), p. 33–54.
19. John Thornton, *Africa and Africans in the Making of the Atlantic World, 1400–1800* (Cambridge Univerity Press, 1998), p. 230.
20. Jonathan Adams and Thomas McShane, *The Myth of Wild Africa: Conservation without Illusion* (University of California Press, 1997).
21. Sylvia Ardyn Boone, *Radiance from the Waters: Ideals of Feminine Beauty in Mende Art* (Yale University Press, 1996), p. 186.
22. Shane White and Graham White, 'Slave Hair and African American Culture in the Eighteenth and Nineteenth Centuries', *Journal of Southern History*, vol. 61, no. 1 (February 1995), p. 72.
23. Boone, *Radiance from the Waters*, p. 192.
24. Karin Barber, *I Could Speak until Tomorrow: Oriki, Women, and the Past in a Yoruba Town* (Edinburgh University Press, 1991), p. 2.
25. Ibid., p. 27.
26. Elizabeth Grosz, *The Nick of Time: Politics, Evolution, and the Untimely* (Duke University Press, 2004), p. 116.
27. Ulli Beier, cited in Barber, *I Could Speak until Tomorrow*, p. 34.
28. Ibid.
29. Ibid., p. 14.

2. AIN'T GOT THE TIME

1. Shane White and Graham White, 'Slave Hair and African American Culture in the Eighteenth and Nineteenth Centuries', *Journal of Southern History*, vol. 61, no. 1 (February 1995), p. 72.
2. Ibid.
3. Benjamin Oyetade, 'Body Beautification', in N. S. Lawal et al. (eds.), *Understanding Yoruba Life and Culture* (Africa World Press, 2004), p. 92.
4. Gordon Innes, *A Mende–English Dictionary* (Cambridge University Press, 1969), p. 62, cited in Boone, *Radiance from the Waters*, p. 184.
5. Boone, *Radiance from the Waters*, p. 98.
6. Innes, *A Mende–English Dictionary*, p. 60, cited in Boone, *Radiance from the Waters*, p. 186.

7. Jesse McCarthy, 'The Low End Theory: Fred Moten's Subversive Black-studies Scholarship', *Harvard Magazine*, January–February 2018.

8. Angeline Morrison, 'Irish and White-ish:Mixed "Race" Identity and the Scopic Regime of Whiteness', *Women's Studies International Forum*, vol. 27, no. 4 (October–November 2004), pp. 385–96.

9. Audre Lorde, 'Scratching the Surface: Some Notes on Barriers to Women and Loving', collected in *Sister Outsider* (Penguin Books, 2019), p. 38.

10. Sylvia Ardyn Boone, *Radiance from the Waters: Ideals of Feminine Beauty in Mende Art* (Yale University Press, 1990), p. 189.

11. Audre Lorde, 'Eye to Eye: Black Women, Hatred, and Anger', collected in *Sister Outsider*, p. 171.

12. White and White, 'Slave Hair and African American Culture', p. 69.

13. Ibid.

14. Ibid., p. 70.

15. David Doris, *Vigilant Things: On Thieves, Yoruba Anti-Aesthetics, and the Strange Fates of Ordinary Objects in Nigeria* (University of Washington Press, 2011), p. 268.

16. Ibid., p. 269.

17. Susan Bordo, 'Cassie's Hair', in Stacy Alaimo and Susan Hekman (eds.), *Material Feminisms* (Indiana University Press, 2008).

18. Olfert Dapper, *Description of Africa* (1668).

19. Fred Pearce, 'African Queen', *New Scientist*, no. 2203 (11 September 1999).

20. See Mawuna Koutonin, 'Benin City, the Mighty Medieval Capital Now Lost without Trace', *Guardian*, 18 March 2016 (https://www.theguardian.com/cities/2016/mar/18/story-of-cities-5-benin-city-edo-nigeria-mighty-medieval-capital-lost-without-trace).

21. Quoted in Koutonin, 'Benin City'.

22. *A New General Collection of Voyages and Travels: Consisting of the Most Esteemed Relations which Have Been Hitherto Published in Any Language, Comprehending Everything Remarkable in Its Kind in Europe, Asia, Africa, and America* (2 vols., known as the Astley Collection, 1743–5), vol. I, p. 582.

23. Ibid., vol. II, p. 214.

24. Ibid., p. 63.

25. Ibid., p. 271.

26. John Thornton, *Africa and Africans in the Making of the Atlantic World, 1400–1680* (Cambridge University Press, 1992), p. 230.

27. Ibid.

28. John S. Mbiti, *African Religions and Philosophy* (Heinemann, 1970).
29. Clarence R. Robbins, *Chemical and Physical Behavior of Human Hair* (5th edn, Springer, 2012), p. 181.
30. *Missionary Chronicle*, January 1826, pp. 37, 38.
31. *A New General Collection of Voyages and Travels*, vol. II, p. 319.
32. A. G. Adebayo, 'Money, Credit, and Banking in Precolonial Africa: The Yoruba Experience', *Anthropos*, 89 (1994), p. 398.
33. Walter Rodney, *How Europe Underdeveloped Africa* (Pambazuka Press, 2012), p. 227.
34. Oyèrónké Oyěwùmí, *The Invention of Women: Making an African Sense of Western Gender Discourses* (University of Minnesota Press, 1997), p. 150.
35. Ibid., p. 151.
36. Ibid., pp. 151–2.
37. Ibid., p. 152.
38. Quoted in Frank Herreman and Roy Sieber (eds.), *Hair in African Art and Culture* (Prestel, 2000), p. 26.
39. See Dustie Spencer, 'The Subaltern Kashmiri: Exploring Alternative Approaches in the Analysis of Secession', *Hydra*, vol. 1, no. 1 (2013).
40. Ron Eglash, 'An Introduction to Generative Justice', *Revista Teknokultura*, vol. 13, no. 2 (2016), p. 373.
41. See http://www.divinechocolate.com/us/about-us/divine-story.
42. Wole Soyinka, *Of Africa* (Yale University Press, 2012), p. 19.
43. Robert S. Smith, *Kingdoms of the Yoruba* (University of Wisconsin Press,1988), p. 20.
44. Henry Clapperton, *Journal of Second Expedition into the Interior of Africa, from the Bight of Benin to Soccatoo* (John Murray, 1829), p. 39.
45. Stefano Harney and Fred Moten, *The Undercommons: Fugitive Planning and Black Study* (Minor Compositions, 2013), p. 12.

3. SHHHH . . . JUST RELAX

1. Willie M. Coleman, 'Among the Things That Use to Be', in Barbara Smith (ed.), *Home Girls: A Black Feminist Anthology* (Kitchen Table, 1983), p. 213.
2. Kim Smith, 'Strands of the Sixties: A Cultural Analysis of the Design and Consumption of the New London West End Hair Salons *c.* 1954–1975', doctoral thesis (2014), p. 218.
3. Ibid., p. 338.

4. Ibid., p. 220.
5. Rob Baker, 'Winifred Atwell: The Amazing Honky Tonk Woman', https://flashbak.com/winifred-atwell-the-amazing-honky-tonk-woman-374573/.
6. Smith, 'Strands of the Sixties', p. 224.
7. Ibid., p. 222.
8. Susan Bordo, 'Cassie's Hair', in Stacy Alaimo and Susan Hekman (eds.), *Material Feminisms* (Indiana University Press, 2008), p. 403.
9. Ayana D. Byrd and Lori L. Tharps, *Hair Story: Untangling the Roots of Black Hair in America* (St Martin's Griffin, 2001), p. 19.
10. Shane White and Graham White, 'Slave Hair and African American Culture in the Eighteenth and Nineteenth Centuries', *Journal of Southern History*, vol. 61, no. 1 (Febuary 1995), pp. 55–6.
11. Kobena Mercer, 'Black Hair/Style Politics', *New Formations*, no. 3 (1987), p. 41.
12. W. E. B. Du Bois, *The Souls of Black Folk* (Dover Publications, 1903), pp. 2–3.
13. Jill Nelson, 'Good Hair Day', *New York Review of Books*, 5 December 2002.
14. A'lelia Bundles, *On Her Own Ground: The Life and Times of Madam C. J. Walker* (Scribner, 2001), p. 139.
15. Ibid., p. 140.
16. Ibid.
17. Ibid.
18. Quoted in the 1976–81 Black Women Oral History Project (BWOHP).
19. Gary B. Nash, *Red, White, and Black: The Peoples of Early North America* (Prentice-Hall, 1974), pp. 289–90.
20. Levi Coffin, *Reminiscences* (Western Tract Society, 1876), p. 566.
21. J. C. Furnas, *Goodbye to Uncle Tom* (Apollo, 1956), p. 142.
22. White and White, *Slave Hair and African American Culture*, p. 68.
23. White and White, *Slave Hair and African American Culture*, p. 68.
24. Ibid., pp. 68–9.
25. Bundles, *On Her Own Ground*, p. 66.
26. Quoted in Nelson, 'Good Hair Day'.
27. All quotations in the next few pages are from BWOHP unless otherwise attributed.
28. Victoria W. Wolcott, *Remaking Respectability: African American Women in Interwar Detroit* (University of North Carolina Press, 2001).

29. Blain Roberts, *Pageants, Parlors, and Pretty Women: Race and Beauty in the Twentieth-Century South* (University of South Carolina Press, 2014), p. 264.

30. Stokely Carmichael and Charles Hamilton, *Black Power: The Politics of Liberation in America* (Random House, 1967), pp. 37, 40–41.

31. Blain Roberts, *Pageants, Parlors, and Pretty Women: Race and Beauty in the Twentieth-Century South* (University of South Carolina Press, 2014), p. 266.

32. Paul Gilroy, *Postcolonial Melancholia* (Columbia University Press, 2005), p. 17.

33. Chimamanda Ngozi Adichie, *Americanah* (Knopf, 2013), p. 204.

34. Susan Bordo, 'Postmodern Subjects, Postmodern Bodies', *Feminist Studies*, vol. 18, no. 1 (1992), p. 159.

35. Robin D. G. Kelley, 'What is Racial Capitalism and Why Does It Matter?' https://www.youtube.com/watch?v=--gim7W_JQQ.

36. Angela Y. Davis, 'Afro Images: Politics, Fashion, and Nostalgia', *Critical Inquiry*, vol. 21, no. 1 (1994), pp. 37–45.

37. Mercer, 'Black Hair/Style Politics', p. 255.

38. Ibid., p. 256.

39. Cited in Byrd and Tharps, *Hair Story*, p. 116.

40. 'A Conversation with Zazie Beetz on *Atlanta*, Hair Touching and the Nuance of the "Angry Black Woman"', https://themuse.jezebel.com/a-conversation-with-zazie-beetz-on-atlanta-hair-touchi-1787399543

4. HOW CAN HE LOVE HIMSELF AND HATE YOUR HAIR?

1. Eldridge Cleaver, *Soul on Ice* (Ramparts Press, 1968), p. 107.

2. Toni Morrison, *Song of Solomon* (Knopf, 1977), p. 315.

3. Chimamanda Ngozi Adichie, *Americanah* (Knopf, 2013), pp. 210–11.

4. John Berger, *Ways of Seeing* (BBC/Penguin Books, 1972), p. 52.

5. Ibid., p. 63.

6. Ibid., p. 47.

7. Patricia Hill Collins, *Black Feminist Thought: Knowledge, Consciousness, and the Politics of Empowerment* (2nd edn, Routledge, 2000), pp. 89–90.

8. Berger, *Ways of Seeing*, p. 47.

9. Kathy Davis, 'Surgical Passing: Or Why Michael Jackson's Nose Makes "Us" Uneasy', *Feminist Theory*, vol. 4, no. 1 (2003), p. 79.

10. Susannah Walker, *Style and Status: Selling Beauty to African American Women, 1920–1975* (University Press of Kentucky, 2007), p. 47.
11. Berger, *Ways of Seeing*, p. 134.
12. Walker, *Style and Status*, p. 47.
13. Ibid.
14. *The Autobiography of Malcolm X* (Grove Press, 1965), p. 138.
15. Personal communication.
16. Babatunde Lawal, 'Orilonise: The Hermeneutics of the Head and Hairstyles among the Yoruba', in Frank Herreman (ed.), *Hair in African Art and Culture* (Prestel, 2000), p. 97.
17. Samuel Johnson, *The History of the Yorubas: From the Earliest Times to the Beginning of the Protectorate* (Routledge, 1921), p. 62.
18. Lawal, 'Orilonise', p. 104.
19. Shane White and Graham White, 'Slave Hair and African American Culture in the Eighteenth and Nineteenth Centuries', *Journal of Southern History*, vol. 61, no. 1 (Febuary 1995), p. 49.
20. Ibid., pp. 50–51.
21. Ibid., p. 58.
22. Ibid.
23. Oyèrónké Oyěwùmí, *The Invention of Women: Making an African Sense of Western Gender Discourses* (University of Minnesota Press, 1997), p. 2.
24. Ibid., pp. 2–3.
25. Kwame Anthony Appiah, 'An Aesthetics for Adornment in some African Cultures', in the catalogue of the exhibition *Beauty by Design: The Aesthetics of African Adornment* (African-American Institute, 1984), p. 19.
26. Benjamin Oyetade, 'Body Beautification', in N. S. Lawal et al. (eds.), *Understanding Yoruba Life and Culture* (Africa World Press, 2004), p. 92.
27. *Imagine: Toni Morrison Remembers*, BBC documentary (2015).
28. Kobena Mercer, 'Black Hair/Style Politics', *New Formations*, no. 3 (1987), p. 41.
29. Naomi Wolf, *The Beauty Myth: How Images of Beauty are Used against Women* (Chatto & Windus, 1990), p. 187.
30. Shaun Dreisbach, 'Fifty States of Women', *Glamour*, 1 August 2017, https://www.glamour.com/story/50-states-of-women.
31. Quoted in Walker, *Style and Status*, p. 81.
32. Stefano Harney and Fred Moten, *The Undercommons: Fugitive Planning and Black Study* (Minor Compositions, 2013), p. 12.

5. EVERYBODY WANTS TO SING MY BLUES, NOBODY WANTS TO LIVE MY BLUES

1. Langton Hughes, 'Note on Commercial Theatre', collected in *The Norton Anthology of American Literature* (shorter 7th edn, W. W. Norton, 2008).
2. Alain Locke, as quoted, for example, in the outro to a version of the song 'Strange Fruit' by Sounds of Blackness, on their album *Africa to America*.
3. Cedric Robinson, *Black Movements in America* (Routledge, 1997), p. 96.
4. Ibid.
5. George Lipsitz, 'What is this Black in the Black Radical Tradition?', in Gaye Theresa Johnson and Alex Lubin (eds.), *Futures of Black Radicalism* (Verso, 2017), p. 111.
6. Greg Tate, 'Introduction', in Greg Tate (ed.), *Everything But the Burden: What White People are Taking from Black Culture* (Broadway, 2003), p. 2.
7. Ingrid Schmidt, 'Head-Turning Hair Fashions for Fall: Bangs, Rows and Tails', *Los Angeles Times*, 20 September 2014.
8. See https://www.huffingtonpost.co.uk/entry/madonna-letter-sharon-stone-whitney-houston_uk_5968987ae4b017418626a26b.
9. Hannah Pool, 'Cornrows? Non-traditional? What Rubbish', *Guardian*, 17 June 2011.
10. Quoted in Itabari Njeri, 'Trickle-Down Culture: Sharing, Sampling, Scanning, Recycling', *Los Angeles Times*, 28 August 1994, at articles.latimes.com/1994-08-28/magazine/tm-31971_1_popular-culture/5.
11. Tate, 'Introduction', p. 2.
12. Judith Mackrell, 'Mean Feet: the Tap-dancing Duo Who were Fred Astaire's Heroes', *Guardian*, 6 October 2016.
13. Njeri, 'Trickle-Down Culture'.
14. Ibid.
15. Ibid.
16. Emma Dabiri, 'Why I'm not an Afropolitan', https://africasacountry.com/2014/01/why-im-not-an-afropolitan/.
17. Achille Mbembe, 'Afropolitanism', in *Africa Remix: Contemporary Art of a Continent*, ed. Simon Njami (Jacana Media, 2007).
18. Terence Ranger, 'The Invention of Tradition in Colonial Africa', in Eric Hobsbawm and Terence Ranger (eds.), *The Invention of Tradition* (Cambridge University Press, 1983), p. 248.

19. D. C. Conrad and B. E. Frank (eds.), *Status and Identity in West Africa: Nyamakalaw of Mande* (Indiana University Press, 1995, pp. 11–12.
20. Chimamanda Ngozi Adichie, *Americanah* (Knopf, 2013), p. 204.
21. Ibid., p. 297.
22. Michelle Breyer, 'The Truth about the SheaMoisture + Bain Capital Partnership', at https://www.naturallycurly.com/curlreading/learn/the-truth-about-the-sheamoisture-bain-capital-partnership-hi.
23. Josh Kosman, 'Why Private Equity Firms Like Bain Really Are the Worst of Capitalism', *Rolling Stone*, 23 May 2012.
24. https://www.sheamoisture.com/?SID=9eltir2ghkq4r2009cjmjo1iio.
25. Jason Hickel, 'The "Girl Effect": Liberalism, Empowerment and the Contradictions of Development', *Third World Quarterly*, vol. 35, no. 8 (2012).
26. Ibid.
27. Olaudah Equiano, *The Interesting Narrative of the Life of Olaudah Equiano* (1837).
28. 'Unilever to acquire Sundial Brands' (press release), https://www.unilever.com/news/press-releases/2017/unilever-to-acquire-sundial-brands.html.
29. Bill Vorley, 'Big Brands Like Unilever aren't the Answer to Helping Africa's Farmers', *Guardian*, 31 August 2016, https://www.theguard ian.com/sustainable-business/2016/aug/31/unilever-africa-farmers-inclusive-business-agrifood-development.

6. ANCIENT FUTURES

1. Liam Hogan, 'Frederick Douglass and His Journey from Slavery to Limerick', *Old Limerick Journal*, No. 49 (2015), pp. 21–6.
2. Robert Nowatski, 'Paddy Jumps Jim Crow: Irish-Americans and Blackface Minstrelsy', *Éire-Ireland*, vol. 41, nos. 3 and 4 (January 2007), pp. 162–84.
3. Ron Eglash, *African Fractals: Modern Computing and Indigenous Design* (Rutgers University Press, 1999).
4. Ron Eglash, 'The Fractals at the Heart of African Design', TED Talk, 2007.
5. Ibid.
6. John Bardot, *A Description of the Coasts of North and South-Guinea* (1732).
7. Thomas Clarkson, *An Essay on the Slavery and Commerce of the Human Species* (J. Phillips, 1786).

8. *Columbian Centennial*, no. 707 (29 December 1790), p. 123, col. 32.
9. See https://www.emich.edu/ugrronlinecourse/docs/URRQualityLessonsCTfuller.pdf.
10. Gloria Gilmer, *Mathematical Patterns in African American Hairstyles*, http://www.math.buffalo.edu/mad/special/gilmer-gloria_HAIRSTYLES.html.
11. Nettrice Gaskins, 'Hair Braiding is Technology' (2014), https://www.recessart.org/nettrice-gaskins-critical-writing/.
12. Ibid.
13. Ibid.
14. Ron Eglash and Audrey Bennett, 'Fractals in Global Africa', *Critical Interventions*, vol. 6, no. 1 (2014).
15. The Fractal Foundation, https://fractalfoundation.org/.
16. Eglash, 'The Fractals at the Heart of African Design'.
17. Ibid.
18. Eglash, *African Fractals*, p. 81.
19. Ibid, p. 83.
20. Ereillis Navarro Cáceres, *Origen y Resistencia de los Peinados Afrodescendientes como Estrategia Pedagógica* (n.p., n.d.).
21. Ibid.
22. Stuart Hall, 'Cultural Identity and Diaspora', in Patrick Williams and Laura Chrisman (eds.), *Colonial Discourse and Post-colonial Theory* (Harvester Wheatsheaf, 1994), p. 225.
23. See Eglash, *African Fractals*, p. 219.
24. Eglash, *African Fractals*, p. 148.
25. Personal communication.
26. Cáceres, *Origen y Resistencia de los Peinados Afrodescendientes*.
27. Personal communication.
28. Wole Soyinka, *Of Africa* (Yale University Press, 2012), p. 20.
29. Eglash, 'The Fractals at the Heart of African Design'.

Picture Credits

p. 7 Photographs: Twitter

p. 13 University College London, Galton Collection

p. 81 Photograph: Len Garrison. Reprodued by kind permission of Black Cultural Archives

p. 98 Cartoon, 'Don't Cut Too Near the Bone!', by A Burman, 1963. (Published in the *Hairdressers' Journal*)

p. 109 Reproduced by kind permission of the Freeman Institute, Black History Collection

p. 121 Reproduced by kind permission of the Freeman Institute, Black History Collection

p. 143 Photographs by Bill Gaskins. Reproduced by kind permission of Bill Gaskins

p. 147 Reproduced by kind permission of Michael McMillan

p. 167 From Esi *Sagay, African Hairstyles: Styles of Yesterday and Today* (Heinemann, 1983)

pp. 168, 169, 170, 231 From Roy Sieber and Frank Herreman, *Hair in African Art and Culture* (Museum of African Art, NY/ Prestel, 2000)

p. 199 Reproduced by kind permission of the Amistad Research Centre, Tulane University, New Orleans

p. 227 From Ron Eglash, *African Fractals: Modern Computing and Indigenous Design* (Rutgers University Press, 1999)

Acknowledgements

With special thanks to Remi, Ian, Jhon Salgado, Matthew, Sheila, Leslieanne, Funmi and Akin Oyetade for the various things you provided, from inspiration to support, resources, images, translations and hairstyles. Much love.